TERRIFIC

GARDEN

TONICS!

www.jerrybaker.com

Other Jerry Baker Good Gardening Series books:

Jerry Baker's Year-Round Bloomers

Jerry Baker's Giant Book of Garden Solutions

Jerry Baker's Flower Garden Problem Solver

Jerry Baker's Perfect Perennials!

Jerry Baker's Backyard Problem Solver

Jerry Baker's Green Grass Magic

Jerry Baker's Terrific Tomatoes, Sensational Spuds, and Mouth-Watering Melons

Jerry Baker's Great Green Book of Garden Secrets

Jerry Baker's Old-Time Gardening Wisdom

Jerry Baker's Good Health Series books:

Jerry Baker's Anti-Pain Plan

Jerry Baker's Homemade Health

*Jerry Baker's Oddball Ointments, Powerful Potions
& Fabulous Folk Remedies*

Jerry Baker's Kitchen Counter Cures

Jerry Baker's Herbal Pharmacy

Jerry Baker's Good Home Series books:

Jerry Baker's Supermarket Super Products!

Jerry Baker's It Pays to Be Cheap!

Jerry Baker's Eureka! 1001 Old-Time Secrets and New-Fangled Solutions

To order any of the above, or for more information
on Jerry Baker's *amazing* home, health, and
garden tips, tricks, and tonics, please write to:

Jerry Baker, P.O. Box 1001
Wixom, MI 48393

Or, visit Jerry Baker on the World Wide Web at:

www.jerrybaker.com

TERRIFIC

345 Do-It-Yourself, Fix 'Em Formulas for

GARDEN

Maintaining a Lush Lawn & Gorgeous Garden

TONICS!

By Jerry Baker,
America's Master Gardener®

Published by American Master Products, Inc.

Copyright © 2004 by Jerry Baker

Published by American Master Products, Inc. / Jerry Baker
Executive Editor: Kim Adam Gasior
Managing Editor: Cheryl Winters-Tetreau
Copy Editor: Nanette Bendyna
Interior Design and Layout: Nancy Biltcliff
Cover Design: Kitty Pierce Mace
Indexer: Nan Badgett
Some images in this book were sourced from Clipart.com.

Publisher's Cataloging-in-Publication

Baker, Jerry.
    Jerry Baker's terrific garden tonics! : 345
do-it-yourself fix-em formulas for maintaining a lush
lawn & gorgeous garden / author, Jerry Baker.
    p. cm. – (The good gardening series)
    Includes index.

    ISBN 0-922433-56-9

    Gardening.   I. Title. II. Title: Terrific
garden tonics!

SB453.B31745 2004   635
                QBI03-200940

Printed in the United States of America
4 6 8 10 9 7 5 3 hardcover

CONTENTS

Introduction...xi

Chapter 1: Lovely Lawns...1

Chapter 2: Terrific Trees & Shrubs...56

Chapter 3: Fabulous Flowers...98

Chapter 4: **Ravishing Roses...162**

Chapter 5: A Bounty of Bulbs...193

Chapter 6: Divine Vines & Groundcovers...212

Chapter 8: Happy Houseplants...309

Bonus Section: Tonics for the Gardener...336

Index...350

INTRODUCTION

NO DOUBT ABOUT IT—there's nothing I love better than putterin' around in my yard. Whether I'm mowing the lawn, admiring my flower-filled gardens, or harvesting home-grown veggies at the peak of perfection, I'm happy as a clam. But I have to tell you: What really gets my gray matter goin' is figuring out how to face those little challenges that Ma Nature offers up from time to time. Rather than spend my hard-earned dough on pricey, store-bought chemicals, I like to make do with everyday items I can find right around my house. A dash of this and a splash of that, and before you know it, I've got myself a fabulous formula that'll do the job. Whether it's a matter of sending pests packing, fending off dastardly diseases, or keeping critters at bay—you name the problem, and I've got a terrific tonic that's guaranteed to do the trick!

Of course, great gardening isn't just about stopping bad things from happening. It's also about growing the lushest lawn, the best-tasting veggies, and the brightest blooms on the block.

Over the years, I've come up with all kinds of mixers, fixers, and elixirs to get my yard and garden off to a great start at planting time, and keep them growin' like gangbusters all season long. Now, by popular demand, I've gathered all my best time-tested tonics and put them in one handy-dandy place for you!

TERRIFIC TONICS: THE WHYS AND WHEREFORES

My tonics may work like magic, but there's really nothing mysterious about them; they're based on good, old-fashioned grow-how. You may be asking yourself, "How can common household products like baking soda and mouthwash possibly help my plants grow bigger, bloom better, and stay healthier?" Well, when you mix 'em and use 'em according to my directions, these excellent elixirs really do work—guaranteed! And every single one of my ingredients is in there for a darn good reason. Here's the lowdown on the major ingredients in my timely tonics and the role that each one plays in keeping your yard in tip-top shape.

AMMONIA is a readily available source of nitrogen that'll help encourage leafy plant growth. The ammonia you buy at the grocery store is a solution of ammonium hydroxide. It's a clear liquid with a very penetrating odor. Watch out—this is very potent stuff! To avoid burning your plants, never apply it right out of the bottle; always dilute it as specified in my tonic recipes. Ammonia can burn you, too, so always wear gloves when you work with it, and don't get it anywhere near your eyes. And never, ever combine it with vinegar or bleach (or products containing either one). The resulting chemical reaction releases toxic fumes.

ANTISEPTIC MOUTHWASH does the same thing in your garden that it does in your mouth. Yep, it actually destroys those nasty germs that cause big-time trouble if you don't get after them. Don't waste your money buying fancy flavored mouthwash for your tonics, though. The plain stuff works just fine, and your plants won't mind having "medicine breath"!

BABY SHAMPOO and **DISHWASHING LIQUID** help to soften the soil and remove dust, dirt, and pollution from leaves, so important plant functions like photosynthesis can take place more easily. These simple

GRANDMA PUTT'S POINTERS ☞ Next time you brew a pot of coffee, consider these five, not-so-common ways Grandma Putt liked to use the leftovers around her yard and garden:

1. Control red spider mites by spraying plants with a weak solution of brewed coffee diluted with water.

2. Combine coffee grounds with dead leaves or straw to create a mulch (don't use coffee grounds alone; they tend to cake together).

3. Mix tiny seeds with dried grounds to keep the seeds from clumping, and to make them easier to handle.

4. Place coffee grounds in planting holes to boost the growth of various acid-loving plants like blueberries, gardenias, and evergreens.

5. Sprinkle grounds around your carrot patch to repel root maggots.

soaps make other sprays stick to leaves better, too. And bugs hate the taste (especially of the lemon-scented types), so they head for the hills in a hurry! Just make sure you never substitute detergent for these soaps, and, in particular, don't use antibacterial detergent, because it can damage your plants.

BEER serves as an enzyme activator to help release the nutrients that are locked in the soil. It also wakes up and energizes organic activity. Foreign or domestic, stale or freshly opened—whatever you have on hand will work just fine.

COLA helps feed the good bacteria that keep your soil in great condition. Just be sure you stick with the real thing—bacteria need real sugar, not the artificial sweeteners used in diet drinks.

GREAT IDEA!

Garlic's good for more than spaghetti sauce!

It's also the prime ingredient in a powerful concentrate that can solve big-time bug problems. Simply mince one whole bulb of garlic and combine it with 1 cup of vegetable oil in a glass jar with a tight lid. Put the mixture in the refrigerator to steep for a day or two, then test it for "doneness." If your eyes don't water when you open the lid, add another half-bulb of minced garlic, and wait another day. Strain out the solids, and pour the oil into a fresh jar. Keep it in the fridge until you're ready to use it. Dilute as indicated in any recipe that calls for garlic oil.

CORN SYRUP and **MOLASSES** stimulate chlorophyll production in plants, and they help to feed the good soil bacteria, too. (I'll bet you didn't know that your garden has a sweet tooth, did you?)

EPSOM SALTS are a super source of magnesium, which helps deepen flower colors and thicken petals. Magnesium also improves the root structure—and that means strong, healthy plants that are your first line of defense against pests, diseases, and even nasty weather.

GARLIC is great in the kitchen, but it's even better in your garden! Its powerful aroma sends pests scurryin', and it even acts like an antibiotic that can help sickly plants get growing on the right root again.

TEA contains tannic acid, which helps plants digest their food faster and more easily. As I always say—a well-fed plant is a happy, healthy plant!

TOBACCO is pretty nasty stuff, no matter how you look at it. It poisons bugs when they ingest it, or when they simply come into contact with it. The same thing happens to some of the germs that cause plant diseases.

URINE from any source (your choice) has a powerful—and frightening—smell that will send all kinds of critters, from deer to gophers, galloping off to find friendlier territory.

GRANDMA PUTT'S POINTERS ☞ When garden pests were a problem for Grandma Putt, the first thing she'd do is snitch a bit of Grandpa's tobacco and brew up a batch of tobacco tea. To try it for yourself, place half a handful of chewing tobacco in an old nylon stocking. Fill a clean milk jug (or similar container) with a gallon of very hot water, then soak the tobacco-filled stocking in the hot water until the mixture turns dark brown. Label the container, then use the tobacco tea whenever one of my tonics calls for it.

WHISKEY, whether it's bourbon, Scotch, or the plain old rot-gut variety, acts as a mild disinfectant to keep bugs and thugs away. It helps provide some nutrients, too.

BE A MASTER MIXOLOGIST

No matter whether you're using a homemade remedy or a store-bought chemical—when it comes to mixing it up, safety is the name of the game. Even though most of my tonic ingredients are safe and natural, some can cause your eyes or skin to be irritated, especially if you have allergies. So mix them carefully (wearing rubber gloves is a good idea) in a well-ventilated area.

Set aside a special set of measuring cups and spoons just for the tonics, and label them clearly so you never use them for measuring other things, like food. And you certainly wouldn't want any of these mixes to be mistaken for something that someone could eat or drink, so be sure to label each tonic clearly, and keep all products safely stored out of the reach of children and pets.

If you want to reuse containers, stick to the same or similar products. You don't want to use an herbicide container for mixing fertilizer, for example, because you just might end up spraying a little leftover herbicide on your prize-winnng flowers. And that would be tragic!

ASK JERRY

Q *If my plants are looking a little sickly, can I apply more fertilizer than usual to help them out?*

A When it comes to plant food, more is <u>not</u> better! Always mix and apply my tonics at the recommended rate, and if you use commercial plant food, be sure you apply it exactly per the directions on the label.

SAFETY FIRST!

When applying any tonic or other material to your yard or garden, always think safety first! Just follow these simple steps:

◆**Step 1:** Before using any sprayer, read all of the directions on the sprayer jar.

◆**Step 2:** Before applying any material with the sprayer, "test drive" it using plain water. This will let you see exactly how it works and what it will do.

◆**Step 3:** Dress sensibly. Don't wear shorts or a bathing suit when spraying! Do wear gloves (plastic throwaways will do) and a hat if you're spraying at or above eye level. Also, wear sun or safety glasses when spraying, and place a bandanna over your mouth, since an unexpected breeze can blow the spray back into your face.

◆**Step 4:** Measure the proper amount of tonic or material, then always apply it according to the directions.

◆**Step 5:** To minimize drifting of spray to non-target areas, spray only on a nice, calm day. Never spray any tonic or material on a windy day.

◆**Step 6:** For maximum effectiveness—not to mention less wear and tear on you—spray in the cool of the day (the morning or evening).

◆**Step 7:** When you are finished, dispose of unused tonics or other materials properly; don't just pour them down your drain.

◆**Step 8:** Thoroughly clean your sprayer with a mild solution of soap and water after each use, then let it drain and dry before putting it away.

◆**Step 9:** Always store all gardening materials out of the reach of children and pets, preferably in a locked cabinet.

◆**Step 10:** Always keep materials in their original containers, and never remove the label. Also, never mix 'n' match different gardening materials.

◆**Step 11:** Always dispose of partially filled or empty containers properly (as recommended on the label). Do not burn them!

◆**Step 12:** Always read all of the directions on labels, stickers, and packages—and I mean ALL of them! Don't take anything for granted, and don't take any shortcuts. Read the entire label before you take the cap off, then mix only at the recommended rate or less, never more.

REMEMBER: IT'S ALWAYS BETTER TO BE SAFE, THAN SORRY!

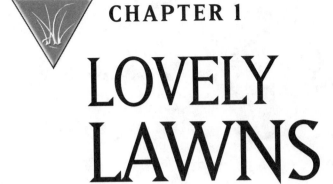

CHAPTER 1

LOVELY LAWNS

AS MY GRANDMA PUTT always said, you never get a second chance to make a first impression, and that's especially true when it comes to your lawn. After all, it's the first thing folks see when they drive up to your house. A lush, green lawn makes the world's best backdrop for trees, shrubs, and flowers and sets your house off to a T, making it look like a million bucks. Plus, a healthy lawn helps create a healthy environment, and that's good for everyone. Growing picture-perfect turf is easier than you might think—just try my world-famous tonics for green grass success!

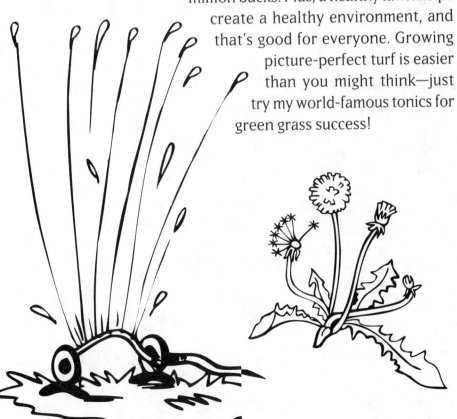

AROUND the YEAR

What's the secret to growing gorgeous green grass? It's knowing what to do and when to do it! Follow my step-by-step turf-care program for the best-looking lawn around.

 ## Spring

◆ Step 1: Start the season off right by bathing your whole yard with my Rise-'n'-Shine Clean-Up Tonic (see **page 42**):

1 cup of Murphy's Oil Soap®
1 cup of tobacco tea*
1 cup of antiseptic mouthwash
¼ cup of Tabasco® sauce
Warm water

Mix the Murphy's Oil Soap, tobacco tea, mouthwash, and Tabasco sauce in a 20 gallon hose-end sprayer, filling the balance of the jar with warm water. Apply to your lawn and everything in your yard to the point of run-off.

To make tobacco tea, place half a handful of chewing tobacco in an old nylon stocking and soak it in a gallon of hot water until the mixture is dark brown.

◆ Step 2: As your grass starts waking up from its winter nap, apply my Spring Wake-Up Tonic (see **page 45**):

50 lbs. of pelletized gypsum
50 lbs. of pelletized lime
5 lbs. of bonemeal
2 lbs. of Epsom salts

Mix these ingredients in a wheelbarrow, and apply with a broadcast spreader no more than two weeks before doing Step 4.

◆ Step 3: Immediately follow Step 2 with a good, healthy dose of my Turf Builder Tonic (see **page 52**):

1 cup of baby shampoo
1 cup of ammonia
1 cup of regular cola (not diet)
4 tbsp. of instant tea granules

Mix these ingredients in a 20 gallon hose-end sprayer, and apply to the point of run-off. This tonic will get your grass off to a great start!

◆ Step 4: Within two weeks of applying the Spring Wake-Up Tonic and Turf Builder Tonic, feed your lawn with a mix of 3 lbs. of Epsom salts per bag of premium dry lawn food (enough for

2,500 sq. ft.). Apply at half of the recommended rate on the package label, going first north to south, then east to west.

◆ **Step 5:** Within two days of completing Step 4, energize your lawn by liberally applying my Lawn Snack Tonic (see **page 34**):

1 can of beer
1 cup of dishwashing liquid
Ammonia

Mix the beer and dishwashing liquid in a 20 gallon hose-end sprayer, filling the balance of the jar with ammonia. Overspray your lawn to the point of run-off. The best time to apply this tonic is early in the morning, or any time before noon.

◆ **Step 6:** One week later, apply the other half of the Step 4 Epsom salts/fertilizer mix in the same way.

◆ **Step 7:** Head off weed problems with my Weed Killer Prep Tonic (see **page 53**):

1 cup of dishwashing liquid
1 cup of ammonia
4 tbsp. of instant tea granules
Warm water

Mix the dishwashing liquid, ammonia, and tea in a 20 gallon hose-end sprayer, filling the balance of the jar with warm water. Apply to the point of run-off, then spread or spray on a preemergent weed control to kill annual weeds like crabgrass before they sprout.

◆ **Step 8:** As soon as the weather warms up, look for new mole tunnels in your lawn. Treat any tunnels and holes that you find with my Mole Chaser Tonic (see **page 37**):

2 tbsp. of Tabasco® sauce
1 tbsp. of dishwashing liquid
1 tsp. of chili powder
1 qt. of water

Mix these ingredients in a bucket, then pour a little of the tonic every 5 feet or so in the mole runways to make the moles run away!

◆ **Step 9:** After your initial spring feeding, fertilize your lawn every three weeks, in the morning, for the rest of the growing season with my All-Season Green-Up Tonic (see **page 8**):

1 can of beer
1 cup of ammonia
1/2 cup of dishwashing liquid
1/2 cup of liquid lawn food
1/2 cup of molasses or clear corn syrup

Mix these ingredients in a large bucket, pour into a 20 gallon hose-end sprayer, and spray everything in sight—not just your lawn, but also your trees, shrubs, flowers, and even vegetables.

✦ Summer

◆ Step 10: Proper watering is a must for a healthy lawn! Always water your lawn before noon to minimize evaporation. And then follow up with my Summer Soother Tonic (see **page 48**):

2 cups of weak tea water*
1 cup of baby shampoo
1 cup of hydrogen peroxide

Mix these ingredients in a 20 gallon hose-end sprayer, and give everything in sight a good soaking.

Soak a used tea bag and 1 teaspoon of dishwashing liquid in a gallon of warm water until the mix is light brown.

◆ Step 11: Make your time in the yard more enjoyable by getting rid of mosquitoes with regular applications of my Buzz Buster Lemonade (see **page 14**):

1 cup of lemon-scented ammonia
1 cup of lemon-scented dishwashing
    liquid
Warm water

Pour the ammonia and dishwashing liquid into a 20 gallon  hose-end sprayer, filling the balance of the jar with warm water. In the early morning or late evening, thoroughly soak any places around your yard where mosquitoes tend to gather. Repeat this process three times each week, and it will keep the little buzzers away.

◆ Step 12: If drought threatens, keep your lawn strong and healthy with my Drought Buster Brew (see **page 19**):

1 can of beer
1 cup of Thatch Buster™
1/2 cup of liquid lawn food
1/2 cup of baby shampoo

Mix these ingredients in a 20 gallon hose-end sprayer, and apply to the point of run-off early in the morning.

✦ Fall

◆ Step 13: To prepare your lawn for the cool weather that's around the corner, use my Fall Clean-Up Tonic (see **page 22**):

1 cup of baby shampoo
1 cup of antiseptic mouthwash
1 cup of tobacco tea*
1 cup of chamomile tea
Warm water

Mix the shampoo, mouthwash, and teas in a bucket, then add 2 cups of the mix to a 20 gallon hose-end sprayer, filling the balance of the jar with warm water. Spray your lawn when the temperature is above 50°F.

To make tobacco tea, place half a handful of chewing tobacco in an old nylon stocking and soak it in a gallon of hot water until the mixture is dark brown.

◆ **Step 14:** As a final fall feeding, treat your turf to a taste of my Fall Lawn Food Mix (see **page 23**):

3 lbs. of Epsom salts
1 cup of dry laundry soap
1 bag of dry lawn food (enough for
    2,500 sq. ft.)

Mix these ingredients together, and apply at half of the recommended rate with a broadcast spreader.

◆ **Step 15:** Within two days of completing Step 14, overspray your lawn with my Lawn Snack Tonic (see Step 5).

◆ **Step 16:** Finish up the feeding with my Last Supper Tonic (see **page 32**):

$^1/_2$ **can of beer**
$^1/_2$ **cup of apple juice**
$^1/_2$ **cup of Gatorade®**
$^1/_2$ **cup of urine**
$^1/_2$ **cup of fish emulsion**
$^1/_2$ **cup of ammonia**
$^1/_2$ **cup of regular cola (not diet)**
$^1/_2$ **cup of baby shampoo**

Mix these ingredients in a large bucket, pour into a 20 gallon hose-end sprayer, and apply to the point of run-off.

◆ **Step 17:** Zap nasty lawn bugs by applying a dose of my Cutworm Chaser Tonic (see **page 17**):

1 cup of Murphy's Oil Soap®
1 cup of tobacco tea*
1 cup of antiseptic mouthwash
Warm water

Mix the Murphy's Oil Soap, tobacco tea, and mouthwash in a 20 gallon hose-end sprayer, filling the balance of the jar with warm water. Saturate your lawn, then follow up with an application of a pyrethrum-based insecticide.

To make tobacco tea, place half a handful of chewing tobacco in an old nylon stocking and soak it in a gallon of hot water until the mixture is dark brown.

◆ **Step 18:** To keep the grassy areas around your walks and driveways in good shape during the winter, first sprinkle the areas with gypsum, then apply my Winter Walkway Protection Tonic (see **page 54**):

1 cup of dishwashing liquid
$^1/_2$ **cup of ammonia**
$^1/_2$ **cup of beer**

Mix these ingredients in a 20 gallon hose-end sprayer, and apply over the gypsum to the point of run-off.

Don't spend your hard-earned dough buying bagged mulch for your gardens! Grass clippings make a magnificent mulch for everything in your yard. So rake 'em up and spread 'em around the base of trees, shrubs, flowers, and even vegetables for a little "mulch magic."

All-Purpose Yard Fertilizer

Your lawn will let you know when it's hungry. As the soil warms up in the spring, plant roots stretch out farther in the soil, seeking food. When they can't find enough, their growth is stunted and the plants start to show signs of starvation. If your green lawn becomes spotty or lighter in color, pay attention—it's begging for food! Give it a hearty meal of my All-Purpose Yard Fertilizer, and watch it grow.

INGREDIENTS:

1 can of beer
1 can of regular cola (not diet)
1 cup of apple juice
1 cup of lemon-scented dishwashing liquid
1 cup of ammonia
1 cup of all-purpose plant food

INSTRUCTIONS: Mix these ingredients in a large bucket, then pour 1 quart of the mix into a 20 gallon hose-end sprayer. Apply to everything in your yard to the point of run-off every three weeks during the growing season, and you'll see fantastic growing results!

◆ BREAKFAST, ANYONE?

As a rule of "green thumb," always apply lawn fertilizer (either liquid or dry) early in the morning, before noon. This allows your grass to digest the food right away, before the hot afternoon sun can burn it and give it an upset tummy.

◆ ...OR MAYBE A LATE LUNCH?

For best results, apply weed or disease controls on a bright, sunny afternoon. They'll get to work solving your lawn problems right away!

GRANDMA PUTT'S POINTERS ☞

Want to grow the toe-ticklin'est turf on the block? Then do what Grandma Putt did, and aerate your lawn after you water it or after a heavy rain—the soil will be much easier to penetrate when it's moist.

All-Season Clean-Up Tonic

This is the one tonic that you absolutely need to use religiously throughout the growing season. The shampoo cleans the plants and helps the other ingredients stick better; the mouthwash kills bad bacteria and discourages insects; and the tobacco tea contains nicotine, which does a double whammy on those pesky pests.

INSTRUCTIONS: Mix these ingredients in a 20 gallon hose-end sprayer, and give everything in your yard a good shower every two weeks in the early evening throughout the growing season. You'll have the healthiest yard in town—guaranteed!

INGREDIENTS:

1 cup of baby shampoo
1 cup of antiseptic mouthwash
1 cup of tobacco tea*

To make tobacco tea, place half a handful of chewing tobacco in an old nylon stocking and soak it in a gallon of hot water until the mixture is dark brown.

◆ THUMBS UP FOR NEMATODES

You may know of nematodes as garden pests, but in truth, not all nematodes are troublemakers. In fact, these microscopic worms feed on some of the most common and destructive lawn pests, including cutworms, Japanese beetles, and sod webworms. Buy them from garden product suppliers and apply them to your lawn with a 20 gallon hose-end sprayer. They really work wonders!

ASK JERRY

Q *My bluegrass lawn looks great in summer, but in early spring, I see a lot of gray patches that I think are caused by snow mold. Got any suggestions?*

A Rake up the moldy patches as soon as you can in spring. Given good care and feeding, those spots should fill in nicely by early summer. The fungus that causes snow mold isn't active in warm weather, so there's no point in treating your lawn with fungicide.

All-Season Green-Up Tonic

Once you've gotten your grass off to a super start with a good spring feeding, it's time to begin your lawn's regular light meals that will carry it through the rest of the growing season. The best meal for my money is my All-Season Green-Up Tonic. Nobody likes to eat big, heavy meals when the weather warms up, and the same goes for your grass, too. That's why this tonic works great year-round, and best during the warm summer months.

INGREDIENTS:

1 can of beer
1 cup of ammonia
$\frac{1}{2}$ cup of dishwashing liquid
$\frac{1}{2}$ cup of liquid lawn food
$\frac{1}{2}$ cup of molasses or clear corn syrup

INSTRUCTIONS: Mix these ingredients in a large bucket, pour into a 20 gallon hose-end sprayer, and spray everything in sight—not just your lawn, but also your trees, shrubs, flowers, and even vegetables. Apply this tonic every three weeks right up through the first hard frost, and I can guarantee you that your lawn will come through the hot summer months with flying colors!

◆ WIPE OUT WEEDS

A thick, healthy lawn actually keeps weeds out—there is simply no room for them to "muscle in." So if you want to avoid using weed killers on your lawn, feed it regularly, dethatch often, and dig out what few weeds you do have. You can also spot-kill weeds with my Wild Weed Wipeout Tonic (see **page 308**).

TERRIFIC TIME⌛SAVERS

Fill a hand-held sprayer with your favorite broadleaf weed killer and water, and take it with you every time you go out to mow your lawn. If you spot any weeds, zap them with the spray right on the spot. Before you know it, your weed problem will be history!

Anti-Summer Patch Elixir

Hot, humid weather is hard on people and plants, but it's perfect for a host of funky fungi that just live to lunch on your lawn. One of the worst is a condition called summer patch. It looks just like it sounds: small, scattered, wilted patches of turf that turn tan in color. If you see any signs of it appearing in your lawn, give this tonic a try.

INSTRUCTIONS: Mix these ingredients in a large bucket, and pour into a 20 gallon hose-end sprayer. Apply this elixir to the point of run-off at the first sign of trouble and then every three weeks thereafter, and it will keep summer patch, dollar spot, and other fungal diseases from developing in your lawn.

To make tobacco tea, place half a handful of chewing tobacco in an old nylon stocking and soak it in a gallon of hot water until the mixture is dark brown.

INGREDIENTS:

1 cup of dishwashing liquid
1 cup of antiseptic mouthwash
1 cup of tobacco tea*
1 cup of ammonia
3 tbsp. of saltpeter

◆ CHANGE YOUR SHOES, PLEASE!

Don't wear your golf shoes or aerating lawn sandals on other folks' lawns, because you could bring their lawn problems back to your own piece of paradise. And if possible, avoid loaning out your yard tools for the very same reason.

GREAT IDEA!

Dull mower blades make jagged cuts that leave your grass at risk for developing diseases or being damaged by the hot sun.

To ensure clean cuts that'll heal quickly and prevent problems, sharpen your rotary-mower blades every four to six weeks during the mowing season.

Aphid-Away Spray

Aphids, also known in some parts as greenbugs and plant lice, are tiny bugs with pear-shaped bodies no bigger than $1/16$ of an inch long. If you spot them troubling your turf (see below for symptoms), give my Aphid-Away Spray a try.

INSTRUCTIONS: Put all of these ingredients into a blender, and blend on high. Let the mixture sit overnight, and then strain through a coffee filter. Pour the liquid into a hand-held sprayer, and apply liberally at the first sign of aphid trouble to send these little suckers scurryin'!

INGREDIENTS:

1 small onion, chopped finely

2 medium cloves of garlic, chopped finely

1 tbsp. of baby shampoo

2 cups of water

◆ GET A FIX ON APHIDS

Aphids are small in size, but these pests can do *big* damage as they suck the life out of your grass! Their feeding causes the blades to turn yellow, then orange, and finally, dead brown. Aphids especially like to attack northern lawns, and specifically, shady places during the heat of summer. A few aphids are not a problem, but if they multiply to the point of damaging your lawn, douse them with Aphid-Away Spray (above), Plant Shampoo™, insecticidal soap, or—for major infestations—my Squeaky Clean Tonic (see **page 46**).

Why spend time or money on aphid controls, when Mother Nature can do the work for you? Lacewings and lady beetles are your ideal natural allies in the fight against aphids; neither harms your lawn or shoos away good lawn critters. To attract more of these great guys to your yard, plant ornamental grasses, sunflowers, and prairie wildflowers, such as black-eyed Susans (*Rudbeckia*) and purple coneflowers (*Echinacea*).

Awesome Aeration Tonic

Shoes, paws, and mowers—oh my! With all this weight coming down from above, it's no wonder that the soil underneath your lawn sometimes becomes compacted and hard. Fortunately, you can slow down soil compaction and improve spray penetration by dosing your lawn regularly with this terrific tonic.

INGREDIENTS:

1 cup of dishwashing liquid
1 cup of beer
Warm water

INSTRUCTIONS: Mix the dishwashing liquid and beer in a 20 gallon hose-end sprayer, filling the balance of the jar with warm water. Apply to your turf once a month to the point of run-off. Believe you me, you'll be amazed at how much healthier your lawn will look thanks to this one simple step.

◆ SPIKE IT!

With a little help from you, your lawn won't ever get seriously compacted. Basically, aeration punctures holes in the invisible surface tension barrier at the soil line to allow food, water, oxygen, and my terrific tonics to get down to the grass roots. Golf spikes are the simplest form of aerators—that's why I'm always reminding you to wear them when you mow! Aerating lawn sandals are also helpful, or you can always rent a power aerator.

GREAT IDEA!

So, just how airy is your soil?

Here's a simple test that'll answer that question in a flash: Just poke a large screwdriver or a sturdy stake into the ground. If it goes in easily, the soil is not compacted. But if it only goes in with difficulty, that's a clear signal that your soil is compressed and needs some breathing room in a hurry. So grab your golf shoes and get out there!

Blight-Buster Lawn Tonic

Are you seeing spots—in your lawn, that is? If you notice brown circles with spots of green grass in the middle, pythium blight might be your problem. Summertime is when this blight typically comes to light. To fight it, apply this tonic at the first sign of trouble.

INSTRUCTIONS: Mix these ingredients in a 20 gallon hose-end sprayer. Apply this tonic early in the morning to the point of run-off to restore the green and get your turf back on track.

INGREDIENTS:

1 cup of baby shampoo
1 cup of antiseptic mouthwash
1 cup of tobacco tea*
$\frac{1}{2}$ cup of ammonia
8 tbsp. of rose/vegetable dust
3 tbsp. of saltpeter

To make tobacco tea, place half a handful of chewing tobacco in an old nylon stocking and soak it in a gallon of hot water until the mixture is dark brown.

◆ FIGHT FUNGI WITHOUT FUNGICIDES

Looking for an all-natural way to stop funky fungi before they start ruining your lawn? Treat your turf to a light coating (about $\frac{1}{3}$ of an inch deep) of screened compost each spring, or douse it regularly with my Compost Tea (see **page 120**). Why compost? Because it's loaded with microorganisms that nurture plants while putting them on high alert to defend themselves against the bad guys. And that's not such a bad thing, now is it?

TERRIFIC TIME✕SAVERS

To prevent diseases in the first place, make sure your lawn has good drainage to keep water from building up (especially when those heavy summer showers strike). If drainage problems are too much for you to fix on your own, call a lawn professional to help out. A little bit of effort now will save you years of aggravation in the future!

Brown Patch Brew

Brown patch ranks high on my Lawn Enemy Top 10 List. Be on the lookout for irregular, brownish patches of turf, with a grayish color on the grass at the outer edge of the brown patch. You may also notice filmy, white tufts covering the grass during the morning dew. Fight back with this fantastic fix-it formula.

INSTRUCTIONS: Mix these ingredients together in a large bucket, then apply with a hand-held sprayer by lightly spraying the turf. DO NOT drench or apply to the point of run-off. Repeat in two to three weeks, if necessary. If brown patch persists even with treatment, follow up with a fungicide applied over your entire lawn. You want to knock down this disease before it spreads everywhere.

INGREDIENTS:
1 tbsp. of baking soda
1 tbsp. of instant tea granules
1 tbsp. of all-season horticultural oil or dormant oil
1 gal. of warm water

◆ A SPRITZ IN TIME SAVES...YOUR LAWN!

This pesky fungus-among-us usually kills the blades of grass, but not the roots, hanging out right on the soil surface. It'll spread on grass clippings, mowing equipment, and even on your shoes, so don't take any chances—treat problem patches right away to stop them from spreading throughout your turf.

GREAT IDEA!

Brown patch does the most damage during warm, wet weather, especially if you've gone overboard and fertilized your lawn with too much nitrogen.

So go easy on the feeding. Follow the application directions on the lawn fertilizer bag, and don't be tempted to add a little more for good measure. Remember, a little is good, but more is not necessarily better!

Buzz Buster Lemonade

Who wants to spend their evenings swatting at mosquitoes, when they should be relaxing in their favorite patio chair? Keep these little bloodsuckers away from you on warm summer nights with this lemony elixir.

INSTRUCTIONS: Pour the ammonia and dishwashing liquid into a 20 gallon hose-end sprayer, filling the balance of the jar with warm water. In the early morning or late evening, thoroughly soak any places around your yard where mosquitoes tend to gather. Repeat this process three times each week, and it will keep the little buzzers away. This tonic also works nicely for the rest of the yard, too.

INGREDIENTS:

1 cup of lemon-scented ammonia
1 cup of lemon-scented dishwashing liquid
Warm water

◆ BUZZ OFF, SUCKERS!

Mosquitoes like to set up housekeeping in areas of stagnant water, like puddles. Getting to work improving any drainage troubles will go a *long* way toward eliminating mosquitoes in your yard. They also like to hunker down in pets' water dishes, birdbaths, and shallow wading pools. Be sure to change pet water daily, refill birdbaths every few days, and empty the wading pool at the end of the day and turn it upside down.

ASK JERRY

Q *If mosquitoes can breed in any standing water, does that mean they might be in my water garden, too?*

A You bet! I suggest adding some fish to your water garden to gobble up the mosquito larvae before they turn into biting adults. You can also purchase mosquito dunks—tablets that contain the natural insecticide Bti (*Bacillus thuringiensis israelensis*), which kills the young mosquitoes in the water.

Chinch Bug Tonic

As far as your lawn is concerned, a chinch bug is the equivalent of a vampire. It sucks the nourishing juice from grass blades, causing them to wither and die. What's left are scattered patches of yellowish or brownish dead spots that make your lawn look lousy. Fortunately, this brew is a "cinch" to make, and it does a super job of controlling these bugs, too!

INSTRUCTIONS: Mix these ingredients in a 20 gallon hose-end sprayer, and then saturate your lawn with the mixture. For a real "kick," use Murphy's Oil Soap® in place of the dishwashing liquid. Your chinch bug woes will be a thing of the past!

> **INGREDIENTS:**
> 1 cup of dishwashing liquid
> 3 cups of warm water

◆ FUNGUS AMONG US

Believe it or not, some fungi can actually be *good* for your lawn! You see, lawn scientists have cultivated many varieties of "endophytic grasses," which have itty-bitty fungi (the endophytes) growing inside their leaf blades. These fungi are poisonous to chinch bugs as well as to many other lawn pests, including armyworms, billbugs, sod webworms, and a whole slew of others. These grasses send a clear message: *No bad bugs welcome here!* So if you're having pest problems—or if you want to avoid them in the first place—take my advice, and look for endophyte-enhanced grass varieties the next time you shop for grass seed.

GREAT IDEA!

Stopping thatch buildup can help prevent chinch bug problems, because these pests seem to thrive in poorly maintained lawns.

Once you've cleared your lawn of thatch, reseed the bald spots with endophytic grass varieties such as Chewings fescue, 'Tribute' tall fescue, and 'Palmer II' perennial ryegrass, which chinch bugs won't eat.

Crabgrass Control Energizer Elixir

One of the fastest-growing weeds on the planet, annual crabgrass is larger and coarser than any lawn grass, so it can really spoil the looks of an otherwise lovely lawn. The best way to control crabgrass is to prevent the seeds from sprouting in the spring. Before you apply any pre-emergent crabgrass control, I want you to wash down your turf with this energizing crabgrass control elixir.

INGREDIENTS:

1 cup of baby shampoo
1 cup of hydrogen peroxide
2 tbsp. of instant tea granules

INSTRUCTIONS: Mix these ingredients in a 20 gallon hose-end sprayer, and saturate the turf to the point of run-off. This potent potion will jump-start the crabgrass control into action and stop this wicked weed from showing its ugly head in your beautiful lawn! (Share this recipe with your neighbors, too.)

◆ RED ALERT!

I mark all parts of my weed sprayer—both head and jar—with a dab of red nail polish. That way, I know it's been contaminated with chemicals and I won't use it for anything else in the yard. I also keep a red or orange golf ball in the sprayer jar as an extra reminder. The ball doubles as an agitator to keep the solution mixed up and flowing freely.

GRANDMA PUTT'S POINTERS ☞ Check with your local Cooperative Extension Service to get the best dates for applying a pre-emergent crabgrass control. Or do what Grandma Putt did, and simply wait until the forsythias and dogwoods start blooming—they're Mother Nature's sure sign that soil temperatures are almost warm enough for crabgrass seeds to sprout.

Cutworm Chaser Tonic

If you've spotted circular or irregularly shaped dead patches in your lawn, cutworms might be the culprits. These fat, brownish black, striped caterpillars particularly love to munch on new lawns in all but the very coldest climates. So if you suspect trouble in your turf, head it off next spring by giving your lawn a good soaking this fall with my Cutworm Chaser Tonic.

INGREDIENTS:

1 cup of Murphy's Oil Soap®
1 cup of tobacco tea*
1 cup of antiseptic mouthwash
Warm water

INSTRUCTIONS: Mix the Murphy's Oil Soap, tobacco tea, and mouthwash in a 20 gallon hose-end sprayer, filling the balance of the jar with warm water. Saturate your lawn (and gardens, too), then follow it up with an application of a pyrethrum-based insecticide for total control.

To make tobacco tea, place half a handful of chewing tobacco in an old nylon stocking and soak it in a gallon of hot water until the mixture is dark brown.

◆ WATCH OUT FOR WEBWORMS, TOO

Of course, cutworms aren't the only caterpillars that can trouble your turf. Sod webworms are grayish or tan, black-spotted caterpillars that thrive in heavily thatched or dry areas of the lawn, where they create small, irregular dead patches of grass that slowly get larger and larger. Control these bad boys with Btk (*Bacillus thuringiensis kurstaki*), beneficial nematodes, or my All-Season Clean-Up Tonic (see **page 7**).

GREAT IDEA!

Are flocks of birds constantly feeding on your lawn?

Then it's time to check for caterpillars in your turf. Birds just can't resist these tasty treats!

Doggy Damage Repair Tonic

To fix those ugly brown or yellow spots in your lawn caused by dog droppings, remove the dead or dying grass in the affected area. Over-spray the turf with 1 cup of baby shampoo per 20 gallons of water, and then apply gypsum at the recommended rate. Wait a week, then mix up a batch of my repair tonic to turn it green again...fast!

INSTRUCTIONS: Mix these ingredients in a 20 gallon hose-end sprayer, and overspray your turf every other week. To prevent future problems, take a stroll over your lawn with a pooper-scooper every day or so, and dispose of the droppings before they can damage your grass. (For ways to keep dogs off your lawn, see **page 24**.)

INGREDIENTS:

1 can of beer
1 cup of ammonia
1 can of regular cola (not diet)

◆ THE SCOOP ON POOP

Doggy-doo-doo damage won't permanently ruin your lawn, but it's still important to keep things cleaned up on a regular basis. You see, besides the smell and unpleasant sight, fecal matter often contains microscopic parasites that can be harmful to people if their hands or feet touch contaminated soil. So remove dog waste as soon as possible; don't let it linger for somebody to step in!

TERRIFIC TIME⌛SAVERS

Want to know the quickest way to prevent dog-urine damage to your lawn? Keep a hose handy! Water down your dog's favorite spots immediately after the deed is done to dilute the urine, and chances are, you'll never have to worry about fixing bare spots later on.

Drought Buster Brew

When lawn grasses are getting plenty of moisture, they usually pop right back up after being trampled on. But if they're water-starved, they just don't have the strength to recover. Your lawn should sail through the hot weather with flying colors, if you overspray it once a week with this timely tonic.

INGREDIENTS:

1 can of beer
1 cup of Thatch Buster™
½ cup of liquid lawn food
½ cup of baby shampoo

INSTRUCTIONS: Mix these ingredients in a 20 gallon hose-end sprayer, and apply to the point of run-off in the early-morning hours to minimize evaporation and give the grass plants ample time to digest it.

◆ WATCH YOUR STEP

Keep off the grass! Turf will naturally go dormant during periods of drought, but will readily revive when water becomes available. Just be sure to keep people and pets off the lawn until it recovers. Otherwise, it'll be *hasta la vista,* baby!

◆ SUNSCREEN FOR YOUR TURF

One of the best ways to protect your grass from drought is by applying an anti-transpirant product, like Weatherproof™, which keeps the combination of hot sun and little rain from damaging your plants. It locks moisture in, while locking out the harmful effects of the weather and pollution. Just apply it any time *before* the really hot weather gets your lawn feeling down.

GRANDMA PUTT'S POINTERS 👉 When the almanac predicted a dry summer ahead, Grandma would get ready in late spring by spreading a ½-inch-deep layer of screened compost over her lawn. This good stuff acts just like mulch does in the flower garden, holding in moisture and keeping the soil cool for good root growth.

Drought Recovery Tonic

Summer dry spells can really do a number on your lawn, so plan on giving it a little TLC to help it recover. Once a drought is over in the fall, apply a dry, organic fertilizer at half of the recommended rate, adding 1 pound of sugar and 1 pound of Epsom salts per bag (enough for 2,500 sq. ft.). Then overspray the turf with this tonic.

INSTRUCTIONS: Mix these ingredients in a 20 gallon hose-end sprayer, and saturate the turf to the point of run-off every two weeks until the grass returns to normal. And remember that every time you water, the moisture needs to reach a good 6 to 8 inches below the surface. This deep watering will encourage strong, deep grass roots that will be able to stand up to periodic droughts.

INGREDIENTS:

1 can of regular cola (not diet)
1 cup of baby shampoo
1 cup of ammonia

◆ DON'T BE A WATER HOG!

It may surprise you to learn the healthiest lawns are those that are watered infrequently, *not* every day. At first blush, this doesn't seem to make much sense. But actually, lawns need only about 1 inch of water per week, which is enough moisture to reach deep into the soil where the root systems can drink it up. Grass plants aren't fussy about where the water comes from—rainfall, sprinklers, or a combination of the two!

ASK JERRY

Q *I've heard that it's not a good idea to fertilize my lawn during dry spells. Why is that?*

A The reason is simple: Going cold turkey off of fertilizer will slow down your lawn's growth, and when it's growing slower, the grass doesn't need so much water.

Fairy Ring Fighter Tonic

If you notice mushrooms running rings around your yard, you've got a fungus called fairy ring. Folklore says that these circles come from elves, leprechauns, and fairies dancing and prancing on the lawn at night. But in reality, they're simply the result of a foul fungus that depletes the soil of nutrients, turning rings of turf pale green. Get rid of the mushrooms as soon as you spot them, then puncture the turf with your golf shoes or aerating lawn sandals. Sprinkle 1 cup of dry laundry soap over the area, then give your lawn a fighting chance with this magical mix.

INGREDIENTS:

1 cup of baby shampoo
1 cup of antiseptic mouthwash
1 cup of ammonia

INSTRUCTIONS: Mix these ingredients in a 20 gallon hose-end sprayer, and overspray the problem area to the point of run-off. Want to prevent future problems? Make sure your lawn has adequate nitrogen to keep it lush and fairy ring free!

◆ TAKE FAIRY RINGS IN HAND

When it's time to clean up fairy rings, I want you to collect the mushrooms by hand, rather than running over them with your lawn mower. Why? Because the mature mushrooms produce spores that start off the next generation! So put them in the garbage as soon as you gather them, then set the next crop back with my Fairy Ring Fighter Tonic (above).

TERRIFIC TIME✕SAVERS

Tired of struggling with screwing your watering hose onto and off of the outdoor faucet every time you want to use your hose-end sprayer? Then go to the hardware store, and buy a two-headed faucet adapter for each and every outside water hookup. Attach the hose to one of the heads, and leave the other one open for when you need the water faucet to fill up a bucket. Talk about saving time!

Fall Clean-Up Tonic

If you've follow my time-tested regimen for putting your lawn to bed in the fall, you'll be able to rest easy all winter long knowing that your turf is snoozing away happily under its snowy blanket. First off, apply this fall tonic to fend off snow mold, fungus, and any other wintertime nasties.

INSTRUCTIONS: Mix the shampoo, mouthwash, tobacco tea, and chamomile tea in a bucket, then add 2 cups of the mixture to a 20 gallon hose-end sprayer, filling the balance of the jar with warm water. Overspray your turf when the temperature is above 50°F. Follow up with your regular fall lawn feeding and a dose of my Last Supper Tonic (see **page 32**) to put your turf to bed.

*To make tobacco tea, place half a handful of chewing tobacco in an old nylon stocking and soak it in a gallon of hot water until the mixture is dark brown.

> **INGREDIENTS:**
>
> 1 cup of baby shampoo
> 1 cup of antiseptic mouthwash
> 1 cup of tobacco tea*
> 1 cup of chamomile tea
> Warm water

◆ AUTUMN IS FOR OVERSEEDING

As the growing season winds down, it's the ideal time to buck up cool-season lawns with a fresh supply of seed. About six weeks before the first frost is expected, reseed with Kentucky bluegrass, perennial ryegrass, or tall fescue. This'll give the grass time to germinate and grow strong enough to survive freezing winter temperatures.

GREAT IDEA!

Time to reseed your lawn, and you've got no spreader?

No need to fret—just punch holes in the bottom of a coffee can. Then pour your grass seed inside, put on the plastic lid, and walk all over your yard, shaking the can as you go!

Fall Lawn Food Mix

Come fall, your flower and vegetable gardens are slowing down, but your grass is gearing up for another burst of growth. So give it a taste of this fortified lawn food, and be prepared for a great-looking lawn that'll sail right through the worst winter can throw at it!

INSTRUCTIONS: Mix these ingredients together, and apply at half of the recommended rate with a broadcast spreader. Within two days, overspray this dry feeding with my Lawn Snack Tonic (see **page 34**) to energize the fertilizer and wash it down into the soil, where the hungry grass roots can gobble it up.

> ### INGREDIENTS:
>
> 3 lbs. of Epsom salts
> 1 cup of dry laundry soap
> 1 bag of dry lawn food
>   (enough for 2,500 sq. ft.)

◆ KEEP CALM, PLEASE!

For obvious reasons, broadcast spreaders work best on calm, windless days. After all, you want the treatment to reach your lawn, not the stars! So hold off fertilizing on those days when you feel like you're walking down the wild streets of the Windy City!

As another growing season comes to an end, it's time to prepare your lawn for its long winter nap. Fall is a crucial time to feed your lawn, but don't waste your money on a fast-acting fertilizer, because it'll wash away long before your grass can use it up. Instead, look for an organic or "winterizer" fertilizer that has a balance of nitrogen and phosphorus (in other words, a high middle number—at least as high as the first one in the fertilizer analysis). For best results, use that type of fertilizer as the "dry lawn food" in my Fall Lawn Food Mix (above).

Go Home, Dogs! Tonic

Dogs may be man's best friend, but they certainly aren't a lawn's best pal. When dogs gotta go, they seek relief outdoors—and when they do their business on your turf, you've got a problem. Fortunately, this simple solution can help keep cruisin' canines at bay.

INGREDIENTS:
2-3 cloves of garlic
3-4 hot peppers
2-3 drops of dishwashing liquid
2 gal. of water

INSTRUCTIONS: Purée the garlic and peppers in a blender, then mix them with the dishwashing liquid and water. Dribble the elixir around the edges of your lawn, driveway, and sidewalks. Repeat frequently, especially after each rain.

◆ FENDING OFF FIDO

Let's say you've managed to train your dog on the dos and don'ts of doggy doo-doo. But what about those neighborhood dogs? Try any or all of these homemade repellents:

- ◆ Spread mothballs, dried blood, or oil of mustard in areas that are favorite doggy haunts.

- ◆ Sprinkle cayenne pepper or mothball flakes in and around prime urination areas.

- ◆ If all else fails, consider pricier alternatives: Install a fence or electronic repeller, or plant a hedge of thorny shrubs.

✳ IDEA!

Like people, dogs are sensitive to the capsaicin in hot peppers.

So make a habit of sprinkling my Go Home, Dogs! Tonic (above)—or even just straight chili powder—on newly seeded soil. Fido will associate bare ground with a burning nose and won't even try to dig where you've planted—whether the pepper is there or not!

Good-Bye, Gophers! Tonic

Are gophers tearing up your turf? These little rascals are active at all times of the day, so it'll be hit or miss trying to catch them in the act. But when you spot 'em, mix up a batch of this tonic.

INSTRUCTIONS: Mix these ingredients in a 20 gallon hose-end sprayer, and saturate the turf to the point of run-off. This simple solution should encourage those gosh-darn gophers to move on and leave your lawn alone.

INGREDIENTS:
1 cup of dishwashing liquid
1 cup of castor oil
2 tbsp. of alum (dissolved in hot water)

◆ THESE SOLUTIONS STINK!

Looking for more ways to persuade gophers to go away? Place fish heads, human or dog hair, bleach, mothballs, used cat litter, or dry ice in their tunnels. Or, block all exits except the main tunnel entrance; then stick in a hose, turn it on, and flood them out!

◆ GO FOR A GOPHER FENCE

It's a big job to tackle, but if you live where gophers are causing problems everywhere, your best option is to defend your territory with a secure gopher fence. Most of the structure goes underground, because that's where gophers travel. Bury a length of chicken wire or hardware cloth 18 inches below the surface, leaving 6 to 12 inches rising above ground level.

GRANDMA PUTT'S POINTERS ☞ If you see evidence of gophers (or moles) excavating in your yard, gum 'em up with this great trick I learned from Grandma Putt: Insert sticks of unwrapped Juicy Fruit gum (don't ask me why, but only this brand will do), slit lengthwise, into the gopher or mole runs. The critters will eat the gum, but cannot digest it, and they will die within a few weeks.

Grandma Putt's Homemade Organic Fertilizer

Back in the good old days, folks couldn't just drop in at their local garden center to pick up a bag of fertilizer for their lawn. Instead, they had to make do with materials they could find around home or get from their local mill. Here's a recipe that my Grandma Putt came up with to keep her lawn looking great—and it still works wonders today!

INGREDIENTS:

5 parts seaweed meal
3 parts granite dust
1 part dehydrated manure
1 part bonemeal

INSTRUCTIONS: Thoroughly mix these ingredients in a large wheelbarrow. Apply it evenly over your turf with a broadcast spreader, then stand back and watch the remarkable results!

◆ THE LOWDOWN ON LAWN FOOD

Fertilizers are classified by how they are made—either organic or synthetic. I like to go with organic fertilizers whenever possible. They are made of 100 percent manure, fish emulsion, or other high-quality natural ingredients (and no chemicals!) that provide plenty of digestible nitrogen, the all-important nutrient for great green grass. They won't burn plants *and* they provide long-lasting nutrients for your lawn to grow on.

ORGANIC FERTILIZER

✳ IDEA!

GREAT

Can't find ingredients for the fertilizer recipe above?

Then try mine! Just mix 2 parts alfalfa meal with 1 part bonemeal and 1 part wood ashes. Apply this mix at a rate of 25 pounds per 1,000 sq. ft. of lawn area last thing in the fall, and next spring, watch for the greenest grass you've ever seen!

Grass Clipping Compost Starter

Every time you add a batch of grass clippings to your compost pile, spray the pile with this mixture. Every once in a while, toss the pile with a garden fork, just like it's a big salad, to mix in lots of air and speed up the composting process.

INSTRUCTIONS: Mix these ingredients in a 20 gallon hose-end sprayer, and soak each new layer of grass clippings with this tonic. This will help the clippings break down more quickly, so you'll have usable compost in just a few weeks, instead of months!

INGREDIENTS:

1 can of regular cola (not diet)
$1/2$ cup of ammonia
$1/2$ cup of liquid lawn food
$1/2$ cup of dishwashing liquid

◆ GO FOR THE GOLD

The discarded grass clippings you've been adding to the compost pile in your backyard can be called into active duty once they've broken down and become compost: This "black gold" is great for your lawn! Compost fortifies the soil, helps slow water evaporation, cools down soil temperatures, and suffocates weed seeds. Use it for patching bare spots, or even as a yearly topdressing. For new lawns, work compost into the soil prior to seeding or sodding.

Have more grass clippings than you know what to do with? Well, never fear: They make a marvelous—and *free*—mulch for trees, shrubs, flowers, and vegetables, too! Just make sure you never use contaminated clippings in your gardens. If you've applied a chemical control to your lawn, wait at least a month after each application before using any grass clippings as mulch, or tossing them onto your compost pile.

Grass Clipping Dissolving Tonic

If you don't pick up your grass clippings after mowing, treat your lawn to an inexpensive "facial" to help it breathe better. Spray it with my Grass Clipping Dissolving Tonic at least twice a year to help the clippings break down more quickly and give your lawn a chance to breathe better, too!

INSTRUCTIONS: Mix these ingredients in a bucket, and pour them into a 20 gallon hose-end sprayer. Apply to the point of run-off. This'll really help speed up the decomposition process for any clippings that are left on your lawn, and will help minimize thatch buildup as well.

INGREDIENTS:
1 can of beer
1 can of regular cola (not diet)
1 cup of ammonia
1 cup of dishwashing liquid

◆ SAVE WORK—AND MONEY, TOO

By leaving clippings on your freshly mowed lawn, you can actually cut the amount of fertilizer you need by up to 25 percent! Yes, 25 percent! That's because the nutrients in the clippings break down and become organic material for your grass plants to feed on.

ASK JERRY

Q *I've just bought my first house, which means I've also gotten my first lawn to mow. I'm okay on the mowing part, but is there a "best" way to rake up the clippings?*

A You bet! My secret is to rake a newly mown lawn in the opposite direction of the way the grass blades are leaning. It makes them stand up straighter and easier to cut the next time you mow. No time to rake? Then spray the lawn with the above tonic right after you mow, and the clippings will be gone in no time!

Grass Seed Starter Tonic

Ready to start a new lawn from seed? Time your sow-to-grow day just before the grass type's season kicks in to its fastest growth spurt. For warm-season grasses—Bermuda grass, carpet grass, and Bahia grass—the season to sow is late spring, when the temperatures are consistently about 75° to 80°F during the day. In cool-season-grass country—home of Kentucky bluegrass, perennial ryegrass, creeping fescue, and the like—sow seeds during the late summer or early fall. In ANY area, the secret to getting grass seed off to a great start is giving it a good soaking with this tonic. It'll guarantee almost 100 percent germination every time!

INSTRUCTIONS: Mix these ingredients in a large container, drop in your grass seed, and put the whole shebang in the refrigerator. After 48 hours, take the seed outside and spread it out on a smooth, flat surface, such as a clean-swept area of your driveway. Once the seeds are dry, it's time to sow.

INGREDIENTS:

¼ cup of baby shampoo
1 tbsp. of Epsom salts
1 gal. of weak tea water*

Soak a used tea bag and 1 teaspoon of dishwashing liquid in a gallon of warm water until the mix is light brown.

◆ THE LAST STRAW

Applying a thin layer of straw mulch over newly seeded lawn areas will provide consistent moisture and cool temperatures during the growing period, speeding up sprouting and promoting quick cover. Hose the straw down with water to help settle it and keep it from blowing away before your grass germinates.

MAKING CENTS

When you're buying grass seed, keep in mind that the cheapest seed may be no bargain in the long run. High-quality grass seed is the foundation of a great-looking lawn, and it will prove to be one of the best long-term investments you'll ever make.

Hopper Repeller Tonic

Leafhoppers can really do a number on a lawn, causing the grass to turn white, yellow, and finally brown as they suck out the juice. At the first sign of damage, treat your lawn with my Hopper Repeller Tonic to send these suckers hoppin' down the trail—and AWAY from your turf.

INSTRUCTIONS: Mix these ingredients in a 20 gallon hose-end sprayer, and apply to your lawn to the point of run-off at the first sign of yellowing, white-spotted grass blades. Then say so long to those pesky leafhoppers!

INGREDIENTS:

1 cup of Murphy's Oil Soap®
1 cup of tobacco tea*

To make tobacco tea, place half a handful of chewing tobacco in an old nylon stocking and soak it in a gallon of hot water until the mixture is dark brown.

◆ KNOW THINE ENEMY

Not sure if leafhoppers are troubling your turf? Look closely, and you'll see small, white spots on individual blades of grass. These pests can also cause turf to become thin and stunted. Adult hoppers are yellow, brown, or green, wedge-shaped insects up to $\frac{1}{4}$ inch long; young ones are wingless and hide in a white, frothy spittle that clings to stems and leaf blades. Leafhoppers of any age can be found anywhere attacking any type of grass, so it pays to be prepared with my Hopper Repeller Tonic (above).

GREAT IDEA!

Want to help your grass beat the heat?

When the weather is hot and dry, it's best to raise your mower blade a notch and cut your grass high and often. Tall grass withstands drought better, because the blades shade the soil—and less stress on your grass means fewer pest problems, too!

Kick-in-the-Grass Tonic

If your lawn needs some minor repairs, the ideal time to make them is when the soil and weather are most cooperative, which is usually in spring. Once you've leveled out the high spots and filled in the dips, give the whole area a good soaking with my Kick-in-the-Grass Tonic to help get your turf back in tip-top condition.

INSTRUCTIONS: Mix these ingredients in a large bucket, and then pour the mixture into a 20 gallon hose-end sprayer. Apply liberally to the point of run-off; wait two weeks, then apply again. And be sure to tread lightly around the mended areas until the grass is up and growing. Pretty soon, you won't even be able to tell where the bad spots were, because your whole lawn will look great!

INGREDIENTS:

1 can of beer
1 cup of antiseptic mouthwash
1 cup of dishwashing liquid
1 cup of ammonia
$\frac{1}{2}$ cup of Epsom salts

◆ HIT THE RIGHT HEIGHT

Careless summer mowing can be just as bad as anything Ol' Man Winter throws at your lawn. Before you start mowing each spring—and a few times during the summer, too—check the height of your mower blade. A too-close-to-the-turf setting can scalp a lawn quickly, leaving bald spots all over your yard. A properly set blade will cut off only the top third of the grass blades at any one time. And that light trim will keep your lawn looking lush.

TERRIFIC TIME⌛SAVERS

Fed up with struggling to mow around big tree roots in your lawn? Your best bet is to replace the grass under your trees with groundcovers, or simply put down a wide circle of bark mulch. It'll be better for your trees and save you loads of mowing time, too!

Last Supper Tonic

Within a week or so of applying my Fall Clean-Up Tonic (see **page 22**), feed your lawn with my Fall Lawn Food Mix (see **page 23**), then my Lawn Snack Tonic (see **page 34**). Finish up by treating your lawn to what I somewhat irreverently like to call my Last Supper Tonic.

INSTRUCTIONS: Mix these ingredients in a large bucket, pour into a 20 gallon hose-end sprayer, and apply to your lawn to the point of run-off. This tonic softens up the dry fertilizer mix, so that the nutrients can be easily digested by your lawn all winter long.

INGREDIENTS:

$\frac{1}{2}$ **can of beer**
$\frac{1}{2}$ **cup of apple juice**
$\frac{1}{2}$ **cup of Gatorade®**
$\frac{1}{2}$ **cup of urine**
$\frac{1}{2}$ **cup of fish emulsion**
$\frac{1}{2}$ **cup of ammonia**
$\frac{1}{2}$ **cup of regular cola (not diet)**
$\frac{1}{2}$ **cup of baby shampoo**

◆ DON'T LEAVE THOSE LEAVES!

Never let fallen leaves blanket your lawn through the cold winter months. Rake them up and add them to your compost pile before the first snowflakes fly. (Mowing over them several times first will help speed up the decomposition process.) This simple step will help your lawn hibernate in a healthy way!

MAKING CENTS

If you have a large lawn, you already know that using a rake to clean up fall leaves is a lost cause. Instead, consider investing in a lawn sweeper. Save some money by renting instead of buying, or share the tool with your neighbors and divide the cost up among the group. Set up a schedule for its use so everyone gets a fair turn, and pretty soon, you'll have the best-looking neighborhood in town!

Lawn Freshener Tonic

Not sure if it's time to water your lawn? Strap on your aerating lawn sandals or golf shoes, and take a stroll around your yard. If the grass doesn't spring back from your footsteps, it's definitely thirsty. Give it a good, long drink with my Lawn Freshener Tonic to help it recover and get back to health.

INSTRUCTIONS: Mix these ingredients in a 20 gallon hose-end sprayer, and apply to the point of run-off. You'll be amazed to see how quickly this simple solution can bring even the most tired-looking lawn back to life!

INGREDIENTS:

1 can of beer
1 cup of baby shampoo
$\frac{1}{2}$ cup of ammonia
$\frac{1}{2}$ cup of weak tea water*

Soak a used tea bag and 1 teaspoon of dishwashing liquid in a gallon of warm water until the mix is light brown.

◆ WISE WATERING 101

The secret to successful lawn watering is actually no secret at all: Water *deeply*, not *often!* Light daily sprinkles encourage grass roots to stay up close to the surface, so if you miss a day or two, your turf will suffer badly. Instead, water slowly and deeply to moisten the top 6 to 8 inches below the surface, then don't water again until the top 2 inches are dry. This thorough watering encourages roots to go down deep, and deep roots help the plants survive better in times of drought.

ASK JERRY

Q *I just got a new water softener, and I've heard that the salt in softened water is harmful to grass. Is this true?*

A Yes, it's true. Too much salt can make a lawn go belly up. Fortunately, the answer to your problem is simple: Just make sure your outdoor faucets are not connected to the water-softener system. (Besides saving your grass, you'll save money on water-softener salt!)

Lawn Snack Tonic

Ready to have better-looking turf than you've ever imagined? Start with my Spring Wake-Up Tonic (see **page 45**), follow it up with my Turf Builder Tonic (see **page 52**), then apply a good feeding of dry lawn fertilizer fortified with Epsom salts. Now, within two days of putting down the dry fertilizer/Epsom salts main meal, it's time to energize that meal with this snack tonic.

INSTRUCTIONS: Mix the beer and dishwashing liquid in a 20 gallon hose-end sprayer, filling the balance of the jar with ammonia. Overspray your lawn to the point of run-off. The best time to apply this mix is early in the morning, any time before noon. It'll get your lawn up and growing like gangbusters in both spring and fall, when you need rapid root action and thatch breakdown.

INGREDIENTS:

1 can of beer
1 cup of dishwashing liquid
Ammonia

◆ TESTING, TESTING

Even a healthy-looking lawn can benefit from regular checkups. Just as you and I make a habit of seeing our doctors for annual physicals, you need to take on the role of "lawn doctor" and make a house call to your turf. To do so, make it a habit to test your soil's pH at least every three to five years.

MAKING CENTS

When it's time to test your soil's pH, save a few bucks by testing your soil yourself. Use a do-it-yourself kit, available from garden centers and supply catalogs. These kits are not as accurate as professional lab tests, of course, but they're ideal if you don't suspect a major problem with your soil. They'll give you a pretty good idea of the pH and, sometimes, the N-P-K (nitrogen, phosphorus, potassium) levels.

Lawn Starter Tonic

Putting in a new lawn? Start the process by collecting some soil samples, and send them off to a testing lab to check the pH and fertility levels. While you're waiting for the results, loosen the soil with a rotary tiller, and rake the whole area to break up any big clods of dirt. Then apply the appropriate starter fertilizer, organic matter, and pH adjusters as recommended by the test results.

Three weeks after the first tilling, till and rake again to aerate the soil and remove any weeds. Finish up by overspraying the soil with this prep tonic, and you'll be all set to sow.

INGREDIENTS:

1 cup of fish emulsion
$\frac{1}{2}$ cup of ammonia
$\frac{1}{2}$ cup of baby shampoo
$\frac{1}{4}$ cup of clear corn syrup

INSTRUCTIONS: Mix these ingredients in a 20 gallon hose-end sprayer, and saturate the soil. Wait several days before you sow the seed. After planting, spray the area lightly with water three or four times a day. Pretty soon, you'll be rollin' in the green—grass, that is!

◆ MIX IT UP

My best advice for starting a new lawn? In a word—*diversify!* Instead of sowing just one kind of grass seed, use two or three different varieties. Just as it does in nature, diversity will help your lawn stand up against pests, diseases, drought, and whatever else the cold cruel world decides to dish out!

ASK JERRY

Q *How old does a new lawn have to be before I can use weed-and-feed on it?*

A My advice is to have your lawn undergo at least three mowings and one good, normal feeding before you use a commercial weed-and-feed product on it.

Magical Mildew Remover

When powdery mildew gets a foothold in your yard, you know it. First, tiny patches of white to light gray fungus show up on leaves; pretty soon, these patches get bigger and look powdery all over. Left untreated, the affected turf will turn yellow and then brown before dying. So at the first sign of trouble, treat your lawn with this magical potion.

INSTRUCTIONS: Mix the shampoo, hydrogen peroxide, and tea in a 20 gallon hose-end sprayer, filling the balance of the jar with water. Every week to 10 days, spray the affected areas, and pretty soon, your lawn will be back in the thick of things again!

> ### INGREDIENTS:
> 1 cup of baby shampoo
> 1 cup of hydrogen peroxide
> 4 tbsp. of instant tea granules
> Water

◆ A SURE CURE FOR MILDEW

If you have so much shade that powdery mildew keeps coming back, consider growing a moss lawn instead. Now, I know that some folks think of moss as an eyesore, but in the right place, it can be a disease-free replacement for unhealthy grass. And it's green all year long, too!

To get moss growing, you'll need to sour the soil a bit to bring the pH to a level of 5.5 or so. Don't fret, this isn't hard to do. Simply add sulfur or aluminum sulfate at the rate recommended on the package, which will kill the grass and encourage moss to grow.

GREAT ✳ IDEA!

Powdery mildew is a real problem in shady and protected areas—like on the north and east sides of your house or garage.

Give mildew the heave-ho by letting the sun shine in. How? By pruning or removing shrubs and trees that shade or border turf areas.

Mole Chaser Tonic

People often confuse moles with gophers, but they are totally different critters. Moles are smaller, with pointed snouts and large, clawed front paws that are well-suited for intense digging. You rarely see them, but you'll know they are there when you see the raised ridges in your lawn around their burrows, as well as the mounds of dirt they push out as they dig their tunnels. To send these critters on their way, try this potent tonic.

INGREDIENTS:
2 tbsp. of Tabasco® sauce
1 tbsp. of dishwashing liquid
1 tsp. of chili powder
1 qt. of water

INSTRUCTIONS: Mix these ingredients in a bucket, then pour a little of the tonic every 5 feet or so in the runways to make the moles run away!

◆ MOLE CONTROLS

Looking for more ways to convince pesky moles to move on? Place any of these in their tunnels:

- ◆ A mix of human hair and mothball crystals.

- ◆ Pieces of rose stem or other thorny stems.

- ◆ Castor beans or cotton balls soaked in castor oil.

ASK JERRY

Q *One neighbor tells me that moles will ruin my lawn, while another claims that moles are good for getting rid of grubs. Who's telling the truth?*

A Both sides are right! Moles love to eat underground insects, grubs, and worms and can burrow up to 200 feet in a single night in search of their favorite foods. But in the process, these energetic earth movers leave raised ridges in the lawn around their burrows, as well as piles of dirt in their "doorways." And that's definitely bad for the looks of your lawn.

Moss Buster Brew

I get loads of questions from folks asking how to get rid of moss in their lawn. They say they kill the moss and plant grass over the bare spots, but more often than not, the grass fails to grow and the moss returns. Why? The answer is simple: Moss thrives in acidic soil, while grass prefers neutral to slightly alkaline soil. So if you kill the moss, but don't change the soil's pH, the grass won't grow and the moss will return.

To get rid of moss once and for all, you have to make the soil a place where grass likes to grow. My brew is just what the doctor ordered! This powerful stuff will get moss and mold out of your lawn in a hurry.

INGREDIENTS:

1 cup of antiseptic mouthwash
1 cup of chamomile tea
1 cup of Murphy's Oil Soap®

INSTRUCTIONS: Mix these ingredients in a 20 gallon hose-end sprayer, and apply to your lawn to the point of run-off every two weeks until the moss and mold are history.

◆ No Mo' Moss

Once you've killed the moss in your lawn, it's time to get grass growing again before pesky weeds can move in. Rake away the dead moss and have the soil tested to determine its pH. Then add ground limestone according to the test recommendations. Finally, re-seed with the grass variety of your choice.

TERRIFIC TIME⊠SAVERS

Instead of fighting the moss, why not enjoy it? Create a moss garden by placing some rocks or driftwood around the moss to define the area. (Just avoid limestone rocks because they are alkaline, and moss prefers acidic conditions.) As the moss fills in, this little garden may become your favorite place in the entire yard!

Plug Perker-Upper Tonic

For quick and complete repair for patchy lawns, don't overlook two powerful allies: sprigs and plugs. In the turf world, a "sprig" refers to a piece of specialized stem—a stolon or rhizome—that has nodes (joints) that are able to take root and create new grass plants. "Plugs" are tiny squares or circles of turf made up of established plants and a couple of inches of soil.

Whether you opt for sprigs or plugs, you need to keep them moist and in the shade until you're ready to plant them. And keep them cool by mist-spraying them occasionally with this perk-up tonic.

INGREDIENTS:
1/4 cup of dishwashing liquid
1/4 cup of ammonia
1 gal. of weak tea water*

INSTRUCTIONS: Mix these ingredients together, then spray it on your grass sprigs and plugs to keep them as fresh as a daisy until you're ready to plant. When you're done planting, sprinkle any leftover tonic on the newly planted sprigs or plugs to give them a boost.

Soak a used tea bag and 1 teaspoon of dishwashing liquid in a gallon of warm water until the mix is light brown.

◆ TLC FOR NEW TURF

Keep a newly plugged lawn moist, but not soaked, until the roots settle and new top growth starts filling in. Overwatering causes disease and poor growth—and you don't want that! As your new lawn starts to grow, reduce the *frequency* of watering, but increase the *amount* of water. In four to six weeks, your new lawn should be ready for a regular watering program.

MAKING CENTS

Here's a real money-saver: Instead of going out and buying a bunch of plugs to fix bare spots in your lawn, purchase a single piece of sod instead. Then pull or cut it apart into individual plugs to patch the holes in your turf.

Pollution Solution Tonic

Dust, dirt, and pollution can accumulate like crazy over the winter, causing your lawn to look like a heck of a wreck. But don't worry, 'cause relief is at hand: As early as possible in the spring, give your lawn a big helping of my Pollution Solution Tonic.

INSTRUCTIONS: Mix these ingredients together and spread over 2,500 sq. ft. of lawn area. Then, wait at least two weeks before applying any fertilizer to the area to give the mix a chance to go to work. Pretty soon, your lawn will be clean, green, and growin' like you've never seen!

> ### INGREDIENTS:
> 50 lbs. of pelletized lime
> 50 lbs. of pelletized gypsum
> 5 lbs. of Epsom salts

◆ KEEP GAS OFF THE GRASS

Sure, we all know that you should *never* add gasoline to your mower when it's parked on the lawn. But if you take the risk and end up spilling gas on your grass, drench the soil with soapy water (½ cup of dishwashing liquid per gallon of water). Let it soak in for a few minutes, then grab your hose, and give the area a good dousing of water. If stubborn brown spots develop, cut out the dead grass and soil to a depth of at least 5 inches. Fill with new soil and then reseed the area.

GREAT IDEA!

Even great-looking grass can be considered a weed, if it's growing where you don't want it to.

So, if you have to cut unwelcome sod out of garden beds, use a dull, old, and very sturdy carving knife, slicing it as you go. Then use the cut-up pieces of sod to fix up bare spots in your lawn.

Postplanting Plug Mix

To perk up a sorry-looking lawn with plugs of new grass, first prep the soil as you would for seeding or sodding (see my Lawn Starter Tonic on **page 35**). Then set out the plugs in a checkerboard pattern, spacing them 4 to 6 inches apart, and water them in thoroughly. On the day you plant the plugs, skip forward on your calendar, and put a big red "X" on the date that's five weeks later. That's the optimal time to apply my Postplanting Plug Mix.

INGREDIENTS:

3 lbs. of Epsom salts
1 bag of dry lawn food
　　(enough for 2,500 sq. ft.)

INSTRUCTIONS: Apply this mix at half of the recommended rate with a broadcast spreader, being sure to evenly cover the whole lawn area. In no time, those plugs will grow together to form a great-looking lawn that'll be the envy of your neighbors!

◆ MOWER MORATORIUM

After all of your hard work getting your new lawn going, you need to mow that new patch of grass very carefully. Wait for at least three, and preferably six weeks after planting to allow the roots to get a good grip. The first few times you mow, be sure to set the mower deck higher than normal, so that you don't buzz-cut the new grass to death.

GRANDMA PUTT'S POINTERS ☞

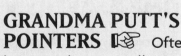

Often, the surest way to get rid of lawn weeds—especially in a new lawn—is the old-fashioned way: by hand-to-hand combat. To make the job a snap, remember what Grandma Putt always used to say: "The early gardener gets the weeds!" It's far easier to weed early in the morning, when the ground is still moist, than it is later in the day, after things dry out.

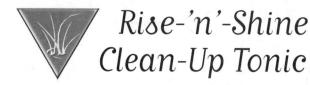

Rise-'n'-Shine Clean-Up Tonic

No matter what you do, you may occasionally notice discolored spots in and around your lawn. Take action to stop bad bugs from getting the upper hand. First thing in spring, I want you to spray down everything in your yard with this clean-up tonic.

INSTRUCTIONS: Mix the Murphy's Oil Soap, tobacco tea, mouthwash, and Tabasco sauce in a 20 gallon hose-end sprayer, filling the balance of the jar with warm water. Apply to everything in your yard to the point of run-off to nail any wayward bugs and thugs that were overwintering in your lawn.

INGREDIENTS:

1 cup of Murphy's Oil Soap®
1 cup of tobacco tea*
1 cup of antiseptic mouthwash
$1/4$ cup of Tabasco® sauce
Warm water

To make tobacco tea, place half a handful of chewing tobacco in an old nylon stocking and soak it in a gallon of hot water until the mixture is dark brown.

◆ GOT GRUBS?

The best time to go gunning for lawn-chomping grubs is early spring or late summer. Let them have it with one of my favorite biological controls: milky spore. Or, release a horde of beneficial nematodes to get rid of greedy grubs!

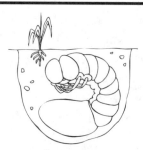

TERRIFIC TIME⌛SAVERS

If the same bad bugs pay a visit to your lawn year after year, chances are pretty good that you've got the wrong type of grass for your soil and climate conditions. (For example, Japanese beetles prefer Kentucky bluegrass, ryegrasses, and fine fescues.) Instead of struggling to beat the bugs every year, simply replace your lawn with a higher-quality grass that's strong enough to withstand the pesky pests.

Slug-Out-Slugs Spray

Sure, slugs can be a major pain in your flower and vegetable gardens, but they can also do a lot of damage to your lawn. These slimy slitherers love to feed on tender new shoots, and they can munch down a growing grass plant in no time flat. When the crowns of chomped plants grow again, the new blades often have ragged-edged holes all over them. To stop slugs in their tracks, take care of them with a blast of this anti-slug spray.

> **INGREDIENTS:**
>
> 1 ½ cups of ammonia
> 1 tbsp. of Murphy's Oil Soap®
> 1 ½ cups of water

INSTRUCTIONS: Mix these ingredients in a hand-held sprayer, and shake well. Overspray any areas where you see signs of slug activity, and shut down the "all you can eat" line for these bad boys!

◆ TRICK 'EM WITH TRAPS

Fortunately, slugs aren't real smart, and there are lots of options for controlling them. Try iron phosphate baits (they're much safer for pets and wildlife than other baits), or trap them in shallow pans of beer or fruit juice—but don't go broke; use the cheapest beer you can find.

For slugs that are too small to lure into traps, use my Slug-Out-Slugs Spray (above) once a week until these slimy pests are history.

GRANDMA PUTT'S POINTERS ☞ Grandma Putt knew that slugs like to spend the day in cool, moist places, so she'd leave hollowed-out citrus rinds or cabbage leaves around the slimers' favorite stomping grounds. Every morning, we'd pick up the traps, pluck out any captives, and drown them in a pail of salty water. It's a surefire way to slay slugs in a flash.

Spot Seed Tonic

Anywhere grass grows, bare spots usually appear at least once a season. The culprit can be anything or anyone: the kids, the dog, or even you, if you set your mower blade too close to the ground. Diseases, weeds, and bugs can do the dirty deed, too—and so can Mother Nature with her unwelcome droughts, heavy rains, bitter cold, and sweltering heat. Lucky for us, it's no big deal to fix these trouble spots. Start by cleaning up the dead grass and debris, then loosen the soil a bit with a rake or hoe. Scatter grass seed over the area, press it into the soil with the back of your lawn rake, and then overspray with my Spot Seed Tonic.

INGREDIENTS:

1 cup of beer
1 cup of baby shampoo
4 tbsp. of instant tea granules

INSTRUCTIONS: Mix these ingredients in a 20 gallon hose-end sprayer, and lightly apply the tonic to the newly seeded area. Keep the area moist until the new seedlings are strong and thriving, and those ugly bare spots will soon be a memory.

◆ HOW GREEN IS MY GRASS

When you plant grass seed in bare spots, be sure to select a variety that matches the green hue and leaf width of the other grass in your lawn. The last thing you want is the new stuff sticking out like a sore thumb!

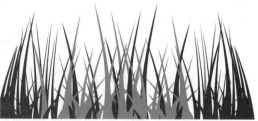

TERRIFIC TIME✖SAVERS

If you're continually trying to fix worn areas in your lawn, it's probably time to change your strategy. Instead of laboring to grow grass in high-traffic areas, why not install bricks or paving blocks, or make a simple path of gravel, coarse bark chips, or pine needles? Trust me—you'll save yourself a lot of time *and* aggravation in the long run!

Spring Wake-Up Tonic

Springtime is the right time to get your lawn off on the right foot, er, root. And there's no better way to do it than to apply this wake-up tonic as early as possible.

INGREDIENTS:

50 lbs. of pelletized gypsum
50 lbs. of pelletized lime
5 lbs. of bonemeal
2 lbs. of Epsom salts

INSTRUCTIONS: Mix these ingredients in a wheelbarrow, and apply to your lawn with a broadcast spreader no more than two weeks before fertilizing. This will help aerate the lawn, while giving it something to munch on until you start your regular feeding program.

◆ TO AER IS DIVINE

Spring is also a super time to aerate your lawn. For best results, aerate the morning after you water the grass, or else after a heavy rain—the soil will be easier to penetrate then.

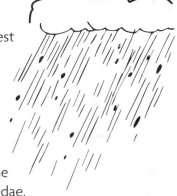

After you've poked holes in the soil, put some sifted peat moss, dried manure, or compost in a broadcast spreader, and apply a layer about ¼ inch thick to the whole area. Your lawn will love it—it's the lawn food equivalent to apple pie or a hot fudge sundae.

GRANDMA PUTT'S POINTERS ☞ Most folks dread dandelions popping up in their lawn, so who knew that these bad boys can actually be good for you? Grandma Putt, that's who! To cure whatever ails you—or to keep anything away that might—do what she did: Put 2 teaspoons of fresh dandelion roots and leaves in ½ cup of spring water. Bring the water to a boil, then remove the pan from the heat, and let the mix steep for 15 minutes. Drink half a cup of the tea up to three times a day.

Squeaky Clean Tonic

When you catch pest problems early, a mild tonic will usually clean things up lickety-split. If not, then it's time to pull out the big guns with a more-potent version of my All-Season Clean-Up Tonic (see **page 7**), like this one.

INSTRUCTIONS: Mix these ingredients in a bucket, then pour into a 20 gallon hose-end sprayer, and apply to the point of run-off. No matter what bad guys are buggin' your plants, this potent brew will stop 'em dead in their tracks!

INGREDIENTS:

1 cup of antiseptic mouthwash
1 cup of tobacco tea*
1 cup of chamomile tea
1 cup of urine
1/2 cup of Murphy's Oil Soap®
1/2 cup of lemon-scented dishwashing liquid

To make tobacco tea, place half a handful of chewing tobacco in an old nylon stocking and soak it in a gallon of hot water until the mixture is dark brown.

◆ AN OUNCE OF PREVENTION

Often, all that's needed to keep bad bugs from destroying your lawn is to change how you *care* for it. Merely adjusting the amount of water or fertilizer you give to your lawn can send some pests packing. (Chinch bugs, for instance, love to munch on underwatered lawns, while the tender shoots of overfertilized grass invite lots of insect pests.) Setting your mower blade slightly higher and keeping your lawn clear of thatch are also top-notch bug-off tactics.

ASK JERRY

Q *Okay—you've sold me on the idea of dethatching to keep pests and diseases at bay. But what I need to know is, when's the best time to do it?*

A Fall is prime time for getting rid of thatch. That's when vigorously growing grass plants will quickly fill in any bare spots left before weeds can invade your turf.

Stress Reliever Tonic

For those of you who live in the Sunbelt states, wintertime is feeding time for your lawn. First, apply any premium dry lawn food at half of the recommended rate, adding 1 pound of Epsom salts to each 25 pounds of lawn food. Then follow it up with this Stress Reliever Tonic to keep your lawn relaxed during the winter months.

INSTRUCTIONS: Mix these ingredients in a 20 gallon hose-end sprayer, and apply once a month to the point of run-off.

INGREDIENTS:

1 cup of baby shampoo
1 cup of antiseptic mouthwash
1 cup of tobacco tea*
¾ cup of weak tea water†
¼ cup of ammonia

*To make tobacco tea, place half a handful of chewing tobacco in an old nylon stocking and soak it in a gallon of hot water until the mixture is dark brown.

†Soak a used tea bag and 1 teaspoon of dishwashing liquid in a gallon of warm water until the mix is light brown.

◆ GREEN GRASS FOR WINTER

While cool-season grasses stay nice and green through winter weather, the warm-season types that make up southern lawns turn brown soon after the first frost. If that doesn't appeal to you, try this trick: Overseed your warm-season turfgrass in October with annual ryegrass. This cold-hardy grass will establish itself quickly, stay green all winter, then die away just as your warm-season lawn is greening up again in spring.

Contrary to popular belief, lime is not a lawn food! It is a soil amendment that changes the acidity of the soil. So save your pennies and please don't use it to feed your lawn. Use it only after a soil test indicates that your soil is acidic (sour).

Summer Soother Tonic

If you're like me and you enjoy watering your yard by hand from time to time, then why not kill two birds with one stone? Water AND soothe your plants at the same time with this nice relaxing shower.

INSTRUCTIONS: Mix these ingredients in a 20 gallon hose-end sprayer, and give everything in sight a good soaking. Your yard will thank you for it!

INGREDIENTS:

2 cups of weak tea water*
1 cup of baby shampoo
1 cup of hydrogen peroxide

Soak a used tea bag and 1 teaspoon of dishwashing liquid in a gallon of warm water until the mix is light brown.

◆ THAT SINKING FEELING

Sidewalks, driveways, patios, and walls are notorious for being summer "heat sinks": areas that collect sunlight and radiate heat back to nearby lawn areas. A great way to keep your grass from being barbecued is to create buffer gardens between the hot surface and your lawn. Fill these strips with flowers and herbs that can really take the heat—like lavender, verbenas, and lantana—and you've got yourself a solution that's pretty, as well as practical.

◆ HOLD OFF ON FEEDING, PLEASE

To be on the safe side, avoid fertilizing your turf during hot weather, especially if it's dry. Stressed-out grasses are much more prone to fertilizer burn during the "dog days."

MAKING CENTS

Who needs to pay a hefty membership fee, when you have the best gym in the world in your own backyard? Believe it or not, cutting grass with a push-type rotary mower burns about 400 calories per hour. That's a better workout than trimming hedges, raking leaves, stacking firewood, or even washing and waxing your car!

Terrific Turf Tonic

Keep your lawn looking its best by washing it down once a month with this tonic after you mow. This gentle, but effective elixir will help the grass plants recover faster from the shock of mowing.

INSTRUCTIONS: Mix these ingredients in a 20 gallon hose-end sprayer, filling the balance of the jar with warm water. Then apply it to your lawn to the point of run-off to soothe mowing stress and keep it growin' strong.

Soak a used tea bag and 1 teaspoon of dishwashing liquid in a gallon of warm water until the mix is light brown.

◆ AVOID A SHOWDOWN AT HIGH NOON

Whatever you do, don't get near your mower between noon and 3:00 P.M. if you can help it. That's when the sun is at its fiercest. Grass clipped during these hours is helpless against the blazing heat and drying power of direct sunlight and may get burned. Instead, schedule your mowing for either late afternoon or early evening; it's better for you and your lawn.

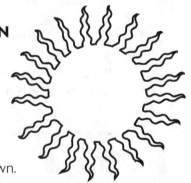

ASK JERRY

Q *Can you give me some idea of how often I should mow my lawn to keep it looking its best?*

A Schedule your mowing days by your lawn's needs, not by the calendar. During peak growth times (late spring and early fall), you may have to mow twice a week. During the summer, when growth slows down, you may need to cut your grass only twice a month. That's a good rule of thumb—for the North, anyway. For you folks living in the Sunbelt states, weekly cuts may be necessary all year-round.

Thatch Control Tonic

Thatch can disfigure and cripple a lawn in no time if you don't identify it and take steps to control it before it gets out of hand. So, what exactly IS thatch? It consists of a spongy, tight mass of undecomposed organic matter—leaves and grass roots, stems, stolons, and rhizomes—that lodges itself in your lawn. (Contrary to what you may have heard, thatch is NOT fresh grass clippings lying on your lawn.) Thatch crowds your grass plants, blocks water and nutrients from reaching grass roots, and makes mowing a hassle because the wheels sink into the soft material. Blast it out of your turf with this tonic.

INGREDIENTS:
1 cup of beer
1 cup of regular cola (not diet)
½ cup of dishwashing liquid
¼ cup of ammonia
Warm water

INSTRUCTIONS: Mix the beer, cola, dishwashing liquid, and ammonia in a 20 gallon hose-end sprayer, filling the balance of the jar with warm water. Saturate the entire turf area, even where thatch isn't a problem. Repeat once a month during summer, when grass is actively growing, and that nasty thatch will soon be a thing of the past!

◆ DEEP THOUGHTS

A good rule of thumb is to remove thatch from your lawn when the layer is more than ¾ inch thick. How can you determine its thickness? It's easy: Simply take a sharp knife and cut out a small plug of turf. Pull it out, measure the depth of the thatch, and then replace the plug in its hole.

MAKING CENTS

The best way to tackle a serious thatch problem in a hurry is with a motorized dethatcher. But don't blow your whole lawn-care budget buying one, because dethatching isn't something you'll need to do often. When it comes to power, renting is definitely the way to go! Better yet, encourage a neighbor to go in halves on the rental cost.

Tire-Track Remover Tonic

Trying to get rid of tire tracks in your lawn, but feeling like you're spinning your wheels? Let me share my secret on how to curb tread damage in a hurry. First, wait for the damaged area to dry out a bit, then punch holes in the turf or walk over it with aerating lawn sandals. This will allow the soil to expand. Follow up by sprinkling gypsum over the damaged area at the recommended rate and overspraying it with my special track remover tonic.

INGREDIENTS:

1 cup of ammonia
1 cup of beer
$1/2$ cup of baby shampoo
$1/4$ cup of weak tea water*
Warm water

INSTRUCTIONS: Mix the ammonia, beer, shampoo, and weak tea water in a 20 gallon hose-end sprayer, filling the balance of the jar with warm water. Apply to the point of run-off. Repeat this treatment every three weeks. Quicker than you can say "Jumpin' Jack Flash," your lawn will be on the road to recovery!

Soak a used tea bag and 1 teaspoon of dishwashing liquid in a gallon of warm water until the mix is light brown.

◆ RUT REMEDIES

What if you're faced with deep ruts in your turf, or if a car sat there for a while and compacted the area? Simply churn the soil with a spade to loosen it up again, then fill it in with good, clean (weed-free) topsoil. Rake it smooth, water the soil lightly to settle it, then sow grass seed or cover the area with a fresh piece of sod. Water lightly for a week to 10 days.

GREAT IDEA!

Have careless drivers left shallow ruts in your lawn?

Simply sprinkle some new topsoil on the low or damaged area. The grass will grow right up through the topsoil in no time at all.

Turf Builder Tonic

After applying my Spring Wake-Up Tonic (see **page 45**) to your lawn, overspray it with this tonic to energize it.

INSTRUCTIONS: Mix these ingredients in a 20 gallon hose-end sprayer, and apply to the point of run-off. This tonic will really get all that good stuff working to help your grass off to a great start—so get ready for the best lawn in town!

INGREDIENTS:

1 cup of baby shampoo
1 cup of ammonia
1 cup of regular cola (not diet)
4 tbsp. of instant tea granules

◆ A Little Off the Top

I've seen way too many well-meaning homeowners make a mess out of an otherwise healthy lawn by not knowing how to trim or edge properly around beds, walkways, trees, and buildings. To avoid making those same mistakes, buy a well-balanced, well-built trimmer, then learn how to properly use and maintain it. If it's a gas-powered trimmer, be sure to add clean gasoline and the proper amount of oil. Clean your trimmer after every use. And most importantly, remember that this tool *is not* for pushing, pounding, prying, digging, or pulling!

GRANDMA PUTT'S POINTERS ☞ Why do I suggest applying fertilizers by walking north to south, then east to west? It's a trick I learned from Grandma Putt back when I was a boy. Using this crisscross pattern guarantees that every inch of your turf gets fed, and you're not left with any obvious light green spots where the grass didn't get the proper amount of nourishment.

Weed Killer Prep Tonic

Sometimes, you need to call in the heavy artillery to tackle a major weed invasion—and that's where chemical herbicides come in. These materials work best when plants are actively growing, which is in the middle of the day, especially in spring. So time your treatments accordingly. And to really zing a lot of weeds in a large area, overspray your turf with this tonic first.

INGREDIENTS:

1 cup of dishwashing liquid
1 cup of ammonia
4 tbsp. of instant tea granules
Warm water

INSTRUCTIONS: Mix the dishwashing liquid, ammonia, and tea in a 20 gallon hose-end sprayer, filling the balance of the jar with warm water. Apply to the point of run-off, then spread or spray on the herbicide. This one-two punch will make those wily weeds wither away before you know it! And one more tip: DON'T water the grass for at least six hours following the herbicide application.

◆ BUYER BEWARE

When you decide to buy a chemical herbicide, *don't* buy in bulk: Get the smallest size necessary to do the job. You'll save money and avoid having to store a large quantity of poisonous products.

ASK JERRY

Q *Help! After months of digging, I've finally gotten all the dandelions out of my lawn. How can I keep them from coming back without resorting to chemical herbicides?*

A Treat your lawn to a dose of corn gluten! It's a natural, preemergent herbicide that'll wipe out dandelion seed pronto—and then go on to polish off crabgrass seeds, too. Best of all, corn gluten is a kissin' cousin to corn syrup, so it's safe to use, even with kids and pets on the scene.

Winter Walkway Protection Tonic

Plain and simple—salt kills grass! It doesn't matter whether the salt comes on coastal breezes or from a bag used to melt snow and ice on the driveway and sidewalk; either way, you get the same results. No matter how carefully you apply deicing salts, it's likely that some salt will spill onto the lawn bordering your driveway and walkways, or the run-off will seep into the turf.

So what do you do? In late fall, liberally sprinkle gypsum in a 5-foot-wide band all over the grass that's within spittin' distance of where you're even thinking about using salt. Then, overspray the gypsum with this simple solution.

INGREDIENTS:

1 cup of dishwashing liquid
$\frac{1}{2}$ cup of ammonia
$\frac{1}{2}$ cup of beer

INSTRUCTIONS: Mix these ingredients in a 20 gallon hose-end sprayer, and then apply it over the gypsum to the point of run-off. Your soil and turf will then be in great shape for winter.

GREAT IDEA!

This winter, why not try some terrific natural alternatives to melting the ice?

Clean cat litter and sand both provide traction on slippery surfaces, and they're cheap, effective, and lawn-friendly. There's also a whole slew of new ice melters that are salt-free. Some even contain fertilizers that provide nutrients to your lawn as they wash away the ice—so check 'em out!

Worms-Away Tonic

Like all of God's other creatures, earthworms deserve respect, too. These wiggling wonders loosen the soil and feed your grass with their droppings (called castings). But sometimes, too many worms can render a fine lawn unsightly. If you're lucky enough to have this problem, try this worm-chaser tonic.

INGREDIENTS:

2 lbs. of dry mustard
1 bucket of water

INSTRUCTIONS: Put the mustard into a coarse canvas bag, cheesecloth, or old pantyhose, and soak it in the water. Then, drain off the mustard water, and sprinkle it over your lawn. This will bring the worms to the surface, where you can easily gather them up for your compost pile— or use them for some mighty good fishin'!

◆ TO THE RESCUE

When the rain keeps fallin' and the soil gets waterlogged, earthworms move to the surface to avoid drowning. There they become easy prey for robins and other early birds. Grandma Putt knew the important work worms do in adding organic matter to the soil and opening up drainage holes, and there was no way she was going to let a single one of her helpers perish. So after a rain, she'd go out and scoop up all the worms she could find. Then she'd give 'em a safe haven in her compost pile.

ASK JERRY

Q *Some of my neighbors have lots of earthworms in their yards, and some don't. Got any idea why?*

A Believe it or not, the type of fertilizer you use can make a big difference in whether worms find your lawn hospitable or not. If you use organic fertilizers or my tonics, it's like hanging out a welcome sign for worms!

CHAPTER 2

TERRIFIC TREES & SHRUBS

THERE'S WAY MORE TO an eye-pleasing yard than just a nice lawn—trees, shrubs, and evergreens count, too! I like to think of them as the framework for any great landscape. If you've ever moved into a newly built home in the middle of a bare lot, then you know how empty the surroundings seem until the landscape gets growing. For you folks, I've come up with a bounty of root-boosting tonics to get your new trees and shrubs off to a rousing start. You'll have beautiful blooms and nice, cooling shade before you know it!

And for those folks with an already established yard—well, I've got all kinds of perfect potions for you, too. From the first days of spring to the return appearance of Old Man Winter, my terrific tonics take all of the guesswork out of keeping your trees, shrubs, and evergreens in tip-top form.

Not exactly sure what to do for your trees and shrubs? Use this handy guide to plan feeding, pruning, and pest control treatments. Just follow these simple steps, and your lush and lovely landscape will be the envy of all your neighbors!

Spring

◆ **Step 1:** As soon as you can get outside, wash down all of your trees, shrubs, and evergreens with my All-Purpose Bug and Thug Spray (see **page 63**):

3 tbsp. of baking soda
2 tbsp. of Murphy's Oil Soap®
2 tbsp. of canola oil
2 tbsp. of vinegar
2 gal. of warm water

Mix these ingredients in a bucket, pour into a hand-held sprayer, and mist-spray your plants until they are dripping wet. Apply in early spring, just when the bugs and thugs are waking up from their long winter's nap soon, and you'll say "So long!" to those bad boys.

◆ **Step 2:** To keep ALL of your flowering shrubs in top-notch form, mix up a batch of my Fantastic Flowering Shrub Tonic (see **page 77**):

1 tbsp. of baby shampoo
1 tsp. of hydrated lime
1 tsp. of iron sulfate
1 gal. of water

Mix these ingredients in a bucket, and apply with a 20 gallon hose-end sprayer. In the South and West, early February is the time to treat flowering shrubs. In the cooler areas of the country, apply this tonic just after the forsythias bloom.

◆ **Step 3:** Early spring is a super time to add new trees and shrubs to your green scene. Give bare-root plants a taste of my Bare-Root Revival Tonic #1 (see **page 67**) before they go into the ground:

1/4 cup of brewed tea
1 tbsp. of dishwashing liquid
1 tbsp. of Epsom salts
1 gal. of water

Mix these ingredients in a bucket, and let the plants soak in the tonic for up to 24 hours. While they are soaking, dig wide holes with ample room to spread out the roots, then proceed to Step 4.

◆ **Step 4:** Follow up Step 3 by enriching the planting hole with my Bare-Root Revival Tonic #2 (**see page 68**):

3 cups of bonemeal
1 cup of Epsom salts
1 handful of hair
1 tsp. of medicated
    baby powder

Mix these ingredients in a bucket, and sprinkle a handful on the bottom and sides of the planting hole. Set the plant in the hole, cover the roots with some soil, and pack it down carefully to remove any air pockets. Finish refilling the hole, water thoroughly, and mulch with a thick layer of shredded bark.

◆ **Step 5:** Give all of your trees and shrubs an energizing jump start with a dose of my Terrific Tree Chow (see **page 89**) and Shrub Grub (see **page 81**):

25 lbs. of all-purpose plant food
1 lb. of sugar
1/2 lb. of Epsom salts

Feed your trees by drilling holes in the ground out at the weep line (a ring around the tree out at the tip of the farthest branches). Make the holes 8 to 10 inches deep and 18 to 24 inches apart. Fill each hole with 2 tablespoons of the above mixture, and sprinkle the remainder over the soil. To feed your shrubs, work this mixture into the soil around them once a year. (Pull back the mulch first, scatter the mixture over the soil around the shrub, and replace the mulch.)

◆ **Step 6:** Follow up with my Tree Chow Energizing Tonic (see **page 93**) to kick the dry chow/grub into gear:

1 can of beer
1 cup of liquid lawn food
1/4 cup of dishwashing liquid
1/4 cup of ammonia
Regular cola (not diet)

GRANDMA PUTT'S POINTERS ☞ When it's time to set out new trees and shrubs, take Grandma Putt's advice: Never plant them just after a heavy rain, when the soil is very wet. It will form clumps that refuse to crumble, and soil that won't break apart won't be in good contact with the roots. And very dry soil makes for difficult planting, too, because it's so hard to dig. The lesson to be learned is to water dry soil very deeply two days before planting to soften it and make it easier to cultivate at planting time.

Mix the beer, lawn food, dishwashing liquid, and ammonia in a 20 gallon hose-end sprayer, filling the balance of the jar with the cola. Then saturate the ground underneath your trees and shrubs.

◆ **Step 7:** Use my Timely Tree Tonic (see **page 90**) to REALLY get your trees growin' like gangbusters:

$^1\!/_2$ **can of beer**
4 tbsp. of instant tea granules
1 tbsp. of baby shampoo
1 tbsp. of ammonia
1 tbsp. of whiskey
1 tbsp. of hydrogen peroxide
1 tbsp. of gelatin
2 gal. of warm water

Mix these ingredients in a large watering can, and give each tree a good long drink once in the spring and again on June 15. (Figure on about $1^1\!/_2$ quarts of tonic per tree.) This double-shot feeding will keep your trees at their peak all season long.

◆ **Step 8:** If you want your evergreens to grow big and strong, sprinkle a mix of $^1\!/_4$ pound of Epsom salts and 1 pound of gypsum (per 3 feet of height) under each plant. Follow this up with my Evergreen Growth Tonic (see **page 73**):

1 cup of dishwashing liquid
1 cup of tobacco tea*
4 tbsp. of instant tea granules
2 tbsp. of bourbon
2 tbsp. of fish emulsion
2 gal. of warm water

Mix these ingredients in a large watering can, and sprinkle about a quart of the tonic around each plant. Then water in well. You'll be absolutely AMAZED at the results!

*To make tobacco tea, place half a handful of chewing tobacco in an old nylon stocking and soak it in a gallon of hot water until the mixture is dark brown.

 Summer

◆ **Step 9:** My All-Season Clean-Up Tonic (see **page 65**) is the one tonic that you ABSOLUTELY need to use religiously throughout the growing season for super-sized results:

1 cup of baby shampoo
1 cup of antiseptic mouthwash
1 cup of tobacco tea*

Mix these ingredients in a 20 gallon hose-end sprayer, and give everything in your yard a good shower in the early evening every two weeks throughout the growing season. You'll have the healthiest trees and shrubs in town—GUARANTEED!

*To make tobacco tea, place half a handful of chewing tobacco in an old nylon stocking and soak it in a gallon of hot water until the mixture is dark brown.

◆ **Step 10:** Looking for a surefire way to help your trees and shrubs sail right through the hot weather? Give them a taste of my All-Season Green-Up Tonic (see **page 66**), and they'll stay in tip-top shape all summer long!

1 can of beer
1 cup of ammonia
$\frac{1}{2}$ cup of dishwashing liquid
$\frac{1}{2}$ cup of liquid lawn food
$\frac{1}{2}$ cup of molasses or clear corn syrup

Mix these ingredients in a large bucket, pour into a 20 gallon hose-end sprayer, and spray everything in sight—not just your trees and shrubs, but also your lawn, flowers, and even vegetables. Apply this tonic every three weeks right up through the first hard frost.

◆ **Step 11:** If needed, prune flowering trees and shrubs as soon as they are done blooming. But first, whip up a batch of this Tree Wound Sterilizer Tonic (see **page 95**):

$\frac{1}{2}$ cup of antiseptic
    mouthwash
$\frac{1}{4}$ cup of ammonia
$\frac{1}{4}$ cup of dishwashing liquid
1 gal. of warm water

Mix these ingredients in a bucket, and pour into a hand-held sprayer. Drench the spots where you've pruned limbs from trees or shrubs to the point of run-off to keep pests and diseases away.

◆ **Step 12:** Sap-sucking pests like aphids, leafhoppers, and spider mites can do a real number on your trees and shrubs. To send these pernicious pests on their way, blast 'em with my Simple Soap and Oil Spray (see **page 86**):

1 cup of vegetable oil
1 tbsp. of dishwashing liquid
1 cup of water

Mix the vegetable oil and dishwashing liquid, then add 1 to 2 teaspoons of the mixture to the water in a hand-held sprayer. Shake well, then drench affected plants thoroughly—especially the under-sides of the leaves, where sap-sucking pests particularly like to hide.

Fall

◆ **Step 13:** By the middle or end of August, you need to think about getting your trees and shrubs ready for winter. To help them along, give them a good dose of my Tree Snack Mix (see **page 94**) to fortify the soil:

5 lbs. of bonemeal
1 lb. of Epsom salts
1 lb. of gypsum
$\frac{1}{2}$ cup of mothballs

Mix these ingredients in a bucket, and apply with a broadcast spreader in a broad band beneath your trees. One batch is just right for one mature shade tree or two smaller flowering trees.

◆ **Step 14:** Thinking of moving an established tree or shrub within the next year? The job will go a whole lot easier if you root prune it now (see **page 79** for directions). After root pruning, scatter about ¼ pound of Epsom salts over the soil all around the plant, then follow up with a dose of my Root Pruning Tonic (see **page 79**):

1 can of beer
4 tbsp. of instant tea granules
1 tbsp. of baby shampoo
1 tbsp. of ammonia
1 tbsp. of hydrogen peroxide
1 tbsp. of whiskey
2 gal. of warm water

Mix these ingredients in a large watering can, then pour about a quart of the tonic into the soil where you've cut your plant's roots. This will encourage new roots to form quickly.

◆ **Step 15:** Fall is an ideal time to transplant trees and shrubs, because the warm soil and regular rainfall encourage lots of new root growth. Finish up with a dose of my Tree and Shrub Transplanting Tonic (see **page 92**):

⅓ cup of hydrogen peroxide
¼ cup of whiskey
¼ cup of baby shampoo
4 tbsp.of instant tea granules
2 tbsp. of fish emulsion
1 gal. of warm water

Mix these ingredients in a bucket, and pour the mixture around the trunk when you transplant a tree or shrub. About a quart of this mixture, dribbled onto the soil to reach the roots, will help get that young tree or shrub off to a stress-free start and it'll be rarin' to grow!

◆ **Step 16:** Before Old Man Winter makes a return appearance, apply my Fall Wash-Down Spray (see **page 76**) to get rid of any bad bugs that are hiding in and around your trees and shrubs:

1 cup of tobacco tea*
½ cup of baby shampoo
6 tbsp. of fruit tree spray
4 tbsp. of antiseptic mouthwash
2 tbsp. of witch hazel

Mix these ingredients in a 20 gallon hose-end sprayer, and douse your plants to the point of run-off, making sure you thoroughly soak the plants and the soil underneath them.

To make tobacco tea, place half a handful of chewing tobacco in an old nylon stocking and soak it in a gallon of hot water until the mixture is dark brown.

Acid-Loving Shrub Formula

Azaleas, camellias, gardenias, hollies, and rhododendrons all need acidic plant food to grow and bloom their very best. To keep them in tip-top shape, blend up a batch of this super shrub formula.

INSTRUCTIONS: Mix these ingredients in a bucket, and let them sit for a few days. Strain, and use the resulting liquid by sprinkling 1 cup of it on the ground around each bush. Pretty soon, your acid-loving shrubs will be as happy as clams! To keep them in top-notch form, mulch them with chopped leaves or pine straw so they'll produce new growth that's a rich, deep green and plenty of beautiful blooms.

> **INGREDIENTS:**
> 1 bushel of dried oak leaves
> Coffee grounds, as much as you can find
> Boiling water to cover the dry ingredients

◆ KEEP THE COFFEE COMIN'

March is prime time for feeding most flowering shrubs, but don't feed your azaleas and rhododendrons just yet! Wait until after they bloom, then give them a fertilizer that's specially formulated for plants that prefer acidic soil. And don't forget to throw your coffee grounds around these blooming beauties, too!

ASK JERRY

Q *I have a steep slope in my yard that keeps washing out every time it rains. What can I do?*

A Take my advice, and cover that slope with spreading shrubs, such as junipers or forsythias. Their branches and foliage will break up hard rainfall that can start a mud slide, and below ground, the shrubs' spreading, fibrous roots will hold the soil in place. Your worries will soon be over!

All-Purpose Bug and Thug Spray

Very cold winter weather can strike a big blow against the bad bugs that plague your yard, but you can't depend on it to kill all of them. However, you CAN depend on this bug and thug spray to do the job!

INSTRUCTIONS: Mix these ingredients in a bucket, pour into a hand-held sprayer, and mist-spray your plants until they are dripping wet. Apply in early spring, just when the bugs and thugs are waking up from their long winter's nap, and you'll say "So long!" to those bad boys.

INGREDIENTS:

3 tbsp. of baking soda

2 tbsp. of Murphy's Oil Soap®

2 tbsp. of canola oil

2 tbsp. of vinegar

2 gal. of warm water

◆ THE INSIDE SCOOP

My All-Purpose Bug and Thug Spray (above) delivers a one-two knockout punch that'll take care of any malingerers. First, it protects your trees and shrubs from diseases, so they can defend themselves better against insect invasions. Second, it suffocates lots of itty-bitty bugs that lurk in stem crevices through the winter. So, if you had serious insect problems on a particular plant last summer, spray it extra good to prevent a repeat performance this year.

TERRIFIC TIME⧗SAVERS

Lady beetles, a.k.a. ladybugs, are big-time predators of many types of tree and shrub pests. Growing lots of flowers—especially those with small or daisy-like flowers—is a great way to attract these hard-working ladies to your yard, and *keep* them there!

All-Purpose Varmint Prevention Potion

Voles, which are close kin to mice, can do extensive damage to young trees in the winter. They chew on the tender bark, often under the snow, sometimes completely killing the plant. To protect your young trees from those fiendish teeth, try circling the trunks with fine-mesh wire or hardware cloth from the ground up to above the snow line. For added protection, drench the area all around young trees with this anti-varmint potion just before the snow flies.

INGREDIENTS:

1 cup of ammonia
½ cup of dishwashing liquid
½ cup of urine
¼ cup of castor oil

INSTRUCTIONS: Mix these ingredients in a 20 gallon hose-end sprayer, and thoroughly saturate all the animal runs and burrows you can find. Voles—and gophers, moles, and skunks, too—will turn tail and run away when they get a whiff of this powerful potion!

◆ BE A MULCH MANAGER

Come wintertime, there's almost nothing a mouse or vole likes better than snuggling under a nice deep blanket of mulch. To keep

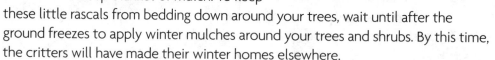

these little rascals from bedding down around your trees, wait until after the ground freezes to apply winter mulches around your trees and shrubs. By this time, the critters will have made their winter homes elsewhere.

GRANDMA PUTT'S POINTERS ☞ If you hang your bird feeder from a tree, you know that keeping cats and squirrels away can be a real hassle! Grandma Putt kept them from climbing up by placing a 12-inch-wide piece of sheet metal or aluminum around the trunk, about 6 feet or so off the ground. That'll do it for you, too!

All-Season Clean-Up Tonic

This is the one tonic that you ABSOLUTELY need to use religiously throughout the growing season. The shampoo cleans the plants and helps the other ingredients stick better; the mouthwash kills bad bacteria and discourages insects; and the tobacco tea contains nicotine, which does a double whammy on those pesky pests.

INSTRUCTIONS: Mix these ingredients in a 20 gallon hose-end sprayer, and give everything in your yard a good shower in the early evening every two weeks throughout the growing season. You'll have the healthiest trees and shrubs in town —GUARANTEED!

> **INGREDIENTS:**
>
> 1 cup of baby shampoo
> 1 cup of antiseptic mouth-
>   wash
> 1 cup of tobacco tea*

To make tobacco tea, place half a handful of chewing tobacco in an old nylon stocking and soak it in a gallon of hot water until the mixture is dark brown.

◆ IT PAYS TO PLAN AHEAD

It's easy to have a good-looking yard in summer, but what about in winter? Pines and spruces are classics for winter color, but you can also spice up your mixed borders with more compact, broad-leaved evergreens, such as hollies (*Ilex*), rhododendrons, and leatherleaf viburnum (*Viburnum rhytidophyllum*). For even more excitement, toss in red-twig dogwood (*Cornus alba* 'Sibirica') and paperbark maple (*Acer griseum*) for their colorful bark.

GREAT IDEA!

Sick of looking at sparse, weedy grass under your trees?

Replace that mess with a bed of bright-leaved hostas and other shade-loving perennials! Add shade-appreciating annuals like impatiens, and you'll have cheerful color to enjoy all summer long.

All-Season Green-Up Tonic

Looking for a surefire way to help your trees and shrubs sail right through the tough summer months? Then, give them a taste of this sweet snack every three weeks right up to hard frost, and they'll be lean, mean, and green growing machines!

INSTRUCTIONS: Mix these ingredients in a large bucket, pour into a 20 gallon hose-end sprayer, and spray everything in sight—not just your trees and shrubs, but also your lawn, flowers, and even vegetables. Your plants will come through the hot summer months with flying colors!

INGREDIENTS:

1 can of beer
1 cup of ammonia
1/2 cup of dishwashing liquid
1/2 cup of liquid lawn food
1/2 cup of molasses or clear corn syrup

◆ **DOWN BY THE SEASIDE**

In gardens by the seashore, salt and wind can be as much of a challenge as the sand is. To cut down on wind-borne salt and create a sheltered haven for your flowers at the same time, surround your garden with hedges of salt-tolerant shrubs. Try some of the following, all of which grow well in sandy soil: American holly (*Ilex opaca*), bigleaf hydrangea (*Hydrangea macrophylla*), forsythias, inkberry (*I. glabra*), junipers, northern bayberry (*Myrica pensylvanica*), and rugosa roses (*Rosa rugosa*).

TERRIFIC TIME⬥SAVERS

Shrubs that get too big for their britches can make even a big house look small. It's not being snooty to want your house to look at least as large as it really is, and one way to do this is to control the size of your foundation shrubs. But instead of carving them up into nice, neat cubes, let them have a looser, more natural shape. They won't need pruning nearly as often, and that means a *lot* less work for you!

Bare-Root Revival Tonic #1

If you're used to buying only balled-and-burlapped trees, planting a bare-root tree may seem a bit scary. Not to worry: It's easier than you think! As soon as you get the tree, soak it in a solution of my Bare-Root Revival Tonic #1 to rev up those tired roots and get them ready to grow—in a flash!

INGREDIENTS:
$\frac{1}{4}$ cup of brewed tea
1 tbsp. of dishwashing liquid
1 tbsp. of Epsom salts
1 gal. of water

INSTRUCTIONS: Mix these ingredients in a bucket, and let the tree soak in the tonic for up to 24 hours. While it is soaking, dig a wide hole with ample room to spread out the tree's roots. For best results, follow up with Bare-Root Revival Tonic #2 (see **page 68**).

◆ DON'T DELAY

Spring is the prime season for planting trees with bare roots, or those that have been plucked from nursery fields and sold with their roots wrapped in burlap. Either condition is traumatic to the tree, so the sooner you get it planted, the better off you'll both be!

◆ TLC FOR BABY TREES

Young trees need special care for several years after planting—and that includes paying close attention to the water supply. That's because it usually takes about three years for the roots to stretch out far enough to meet the tree's needs for moisture and nutrients.

MAKING CENTS

No need to spend a fortune buying big trees. I've always gotten the best results by planting trees that are less than 8 feet tall. Besides being easier to handle than larger trees, young trees are quick to develop roots and rarely need to be staked to keep them standing upright.

Bare-Root Revival Tonic #2

To get your newly planted bare-root trees off to a rip-roaring start, treat them to this marvelous mix at planting time.

INSTRUCTIONS: Mix these ingredients in a bucket, and sprinkle a handful on the bottom and sides of the planting hole. Set the tree in the hole, cover the roots with some soil, and pack it down carefully to remove any air pockets. Finish refilling the hole, then water thoroughly and mulch with a thick layer of shredded bark. This'll do the trick!

INGREDIENTS:

3 cups of bonemeal
1 cup of Epsom salts
1 handful of hair
1 tsp. of medicated baby powder

◆ PERFECT PLANNING—1, 2, 3!

Ever plan a garden that looked...well, sort of lop-sided? I did, until I learned these three simple steps that give gardens a professionally designed look every time!

◆ **Step 1:** Plant three shrubs for each tree. Group the shrubs near the base of the tree, but set them a few feet away from the trunk to avoid the tree's roots.

◆ **Step 2:** Include at least three to five perennials—some larger and some smaller—for each shrub.

◆ **Step 3:** Finish off around the edges with as many low-growing perennials and annuals as you need to fill the space that's available. It's that easy!

ASK JERRY

Q *I recently planted a 1-inch-diameter maple tree, and I was wondering, do I need to stake it?*

A Most young trees do not need staking to hold them upright. In fact, staking trees can traumatize tender trunks, doing more harm than good. Support your young tree *only* if it is exposed to strong winds or if it insists on leaning sideways.

Bye-Bye, Birdie Tonic

Berry-bearing trees and shrubs—like crabapples, hollies, and viburnums—are true beauties for all-winter interest in your landscape. So it's a big disappointment when your fabulous fruiting plants are suddenly stripped clean by a flock of busy birds. To discourage these winged warriors, spritz your plants with my Bye-Bye, Birdie Tonic.

INSTRUCTIONS: Mix these ingredients in a bucket, pour into a hand-held sprayer, and liberally spray on your trees and shrubs when they're full of fruit. Make sure that you reapply the tonic after every rain. This will keep pesky birds from getting to your fruiting trees and bushes before you can enjoy the sight of those bountiful berries!

INGREDIENTS:

1 tbsp. of baby shampoo
1 tbsp. of ammonia
1 gal. of water

◆ BOOZY BERRIES

Don't be surprised if birds ignore shrub berries for a long time, and then feast on them in mid- to late winter. Berries of holly and juniper, for example, are simply unpalatable to birds until they have been frozen several times, and actually begin to ferment. Some wildlife experts suspect that birds enjoy the alcohol that is present in well-weathered berries.

GREAT IDEA!

Want to prevent sunscald on your beautiful, ornamental fruit trees?

In winter, when frozen trunks are warmed by bright sunlight, ruptures sometimes develop on the south or west sides of the trunks. This problem is called sunscald. The best way to prevent it is to loosely wrap the trunks with tree wrap (sold at garden centers) in late fall, then remove the wrap each spring.

Caterpillar Killer Tonic

Several kinds of caterpillars can do a real number on your trees, chomping on the leaves and creating ugly webs. While the trees can produce a second set of leaves, the effort will weaken them severely. To protect all of your trees, blast the buggers with this potent potion.

INSTRUCTIONS: Simmer the wormwood leaves in 2 cups of water for 30 minutes. Strain out the leaves, then add the Murphy's Oil Soap and 2 more cups of water. Pour the solution into a 6 gallon hose-end sprayer, and apply to your plants to the point of run-off. Repeat as often as necessary until the caterpillars are history.

INGREDIENTS:

$^{1}/_{2}$ lb. of wormwood leaves
2 tbsp. of Murphy's Oil Soap®
4 cups of water

◆ GO ON CATERPILLAR PATROL

Starting in early spring, check your trees every 7 to 10 days for signs of gypsy moth caterpillars, tent caterpillars, and other creepy crawlers. When you spot them, remove them and their webs with a stick or high-pressure hose, and drop them into a coffee can with about 2 inches of oil in the bottom. Or, if you'd rather spray first and whack later, give these wily worms a blast of my Caterpillar Killer Tonic (above).

TERRIFIC TIME⌛SAVERS

Are caterpillars chomping on your trees and shrubs? Enlist some *real* professional help in the form of chickadees and tufted titmice—two small songbirds that gobble up caterpillars and their eggs like nobody's business. To place a help-wanted ad, simply stock a feeder with peanut butter, sunflower seeds, or thistle, and station it close to infested trees and shrubs. The winged warriors will beat a path to your buffet and hang around to polish off the pests!

Compost Feeder Tonic

It's normal for tree leaves, sticks, wood chips, and sawdust to take several months to decompose, but you can speed things along by mixing a little high-nitrogen fertilizer into your heap. Microorganisms that have been waiting for a good supply of nitrogen will get busy, and you should have finished compost in only a few weeks. In the meantime, don't forget to keep your whole pile energized; my Compost Feeder Tonic works wonders.

INGREDIENTS:

1 can of beer
1 cup of dishwashing liquid
1 can of regular cola (not diet)

INSTRUCTIONS: Mix these ingredients in a bucket, pour into a 20 gallon hose-end sprayer, and apply generously to your compost pile once a month to keep things cookin'.

◆ PILE IT ON!

Fall leaf clean-up provides ample fixin's for a new compost pile. Build up one or more piles in autumn, then let 'em sit over the winter. Come spring, when your compost pile thaws, get after it with a digging fork, and turn it as best you can. When combined with rising temperatures, the slicing, dicing, and mixing should get your compost going like gangbusters. For an extra boost, overspray it with my Compost Feeder Tonic (above).

ASK JERRY

Q *I took your advice and started a compost pile. But how do I know when it's ready to use?*

A When the compost is done, or finished, it becomes dark and crumbly. When a batch nears this point, start a new one, and dole the good stuff out to all of your plants in generous servings. Compost is not fertilizer, but it is very rich in enzymes and beneficial bacteria—and it's a first-class banquet of trace nutrients that plants need. That's why I call it black gold!

Deer-Buster Eggnog Tonic

I'll be the first to agree that deer are beautiful animals, but in some places, there are just too darn many of them! If the problem isn't bad enough to warrant a fence, but deer do come around to browse on certain plants again and again, you can probably get good results using deterrents that rely on the critters' sense of smell. This deer-busting tonic fits that bill to a "T"!

INGREDIENTS:

2 eggs
2 cloves of garlic
2 tbsp. of Tabasco® sauce
2 tbsp. of cayenne pepper
2 cups of water

INSTRUCTIONS: Put these ingredients in a blender and purée them. Allow the mixture to sit for two days, then pour or spray it around all of the plants you need to protect. Reapply it every other week or so (or after a rain) to keep the odor fresh, and deer will head for friendlier territory.

◆ GOOD-BYE, BAMBI!

Thickets made of spiny shrubs, such as barberries, can deter all kinds of unwanted visitors, including burglars and deer. So, a thicket planted just outside your back fence is a fine way to put out a thorny and prickly unwelcome mat.

It's one thing to gamble with perennials—they're pretty inexpensive to replace, after all—but you don't want to take chances with the main shrubs in your landscape. So stick to plants that are dependably winter-hardy. To be extra safe, it's a good idea to pick shrubs that are rated a whole zone colder than where you live—if you live in Zone 5, for example, choose shrubs that are hardy to Zone 4. That way, your shrubs should sail right through the winter, even if it's extra-cold one year!

Evergreen Growth Tonic

If you want your evergreens to grow up big and strong, then you've got to feed them in spring and early summer. On the soil surface, beneath the foliage and beyond, sprinkle a mix of $\frac{1}{4}$ pound of Epsom salts and 1 pound of gypsum (per 3 feet of height) under each plant. Then follow up with this tonic.

INSTRUCTIONS: Mix these ingredients in a large watering can, and sprinkle about a quart of the tonic around each plant, then water in well. You'll be absolutely amazed at the results!

INGREDIENTS:

1 cup of dishwashing liquid
1 cup of tobacco tea*
4 tbsp. of instant tea granules
2 tbsp. of bourbon
2 tbsp. of fish emulsion
2 gal. of warm water

*To make tobacco tea, place half a handful of chewing tobacco in an old nylon stocking and soak it in a gallon of hot water until the mixture is dark brown.

◆ MIX 'EM UP

If your main reason for wanting evergreen trees is to block an ugly view, consider using two or three types with varying forms and textures. For example, a stiffly formal blue spruce looks even better when it's beside a gentle white pine. From Zone 7 southward, evergreen magnolias, such as the scaled-down 'Little Gem', make great company for evergreens with needled leaves.

GRANDMA PUTT'S POINTERS ☞

Some evergreens, like arborvitae and junipers, have multiple stems. To prevent snow from bending them down and breaking them apart, do what Grandma Putt did: Gently gather the tops together with long strips of cloth or nylon pantyhose before it snows.

Evergreen Wake-Up Tonic

Whatever you do, don't feed newly planted evergreens right away. Let them get used to their new homes for a couple of weeks, and then give them a light snack of this wake-up tonic. It'll perk 'em up the same way a cup of coffee does to you and me! Apply it early in the morning, every three weeks, throughout the growing season.

INSTRUCTIONS: Mix these ingredients in a bucket, pour into a 20 gallon hose-end sprayer, and apply to the point of run-off. After the first application of the year, feed them a month later with a low-nitrogen, dry plant food (like 4-12-4 or 5-10-5) to stimulate root growth.

INGREDIENTS:

1 can of beer
1 cup of baby shampoo
1 cup of liquid lawn food
$\frac{1}{2}$ cup of molasses
2 tbsp. of fish emulsion

◆ GROW A ROW

There are times when a row of evergreen trees of the same species is just the ticket— say when you want a solid backdrop for your house or a flowering border. In mild climates, Leyland cypress fills the bill. Up North, look for cold-weather lovers such as arborvitae and Canada hemlock.

ASK JERRY

Q *Two years ago, I planted a white pine, which looked fine until this year. Now the color has faded to yellow-green, and there is very little new growth. What's wrong?*

A First, I want you to check your soil's pH. If it's above 6.5, it's too alkaline for white pine, and you'll need to apply sulfur to the soil to increase its acidity. Also, spray your tree with Liquid Iron™ and spread 5 pounds of all-purpose plant food evenly over the root zone of your tree to restore its color.

Fabulous Foundation Food

Planning on setting out some new shrubs around your home's foundation? Take the opportunity to build up the soil's fertility and organic matter at the same time with this foundation feast.

INGREDIENTS:

10 parts compost
2 parts bonemeal
2 parts bloodmeal
1 part kelp meal

INSTRUCTIONS: Mix these ingredients in a garden cart or wheelbarrow, and spread a 2- to 3-inch-thick layer over the soil and dig or till it in before planting. Each year, add a new 1/2-inch-thick layer around established shrubs, and scratch it lightly into the soil. Top it with shredded bark or other mulch, and your foundation shrubs will stay happy and healthy for many years to come!

◆ THE ACID TEST

Even if you've never bothered testing the soil's pH in the rest of your yard, I heartily recommend you do it for your foundation plantings. Most plants grow well where the soil's somewhere between 6.5 and 7.0. But foundation soil tends to be higher than that because of the lime that leaches out of the foundation walls. A simple pH test takes just a few minutes (you can find inexpensive test kits at your local garden center), and most come with guidelines to help you make any needed adjustments to your soil.

TERRIFIC TIME⊠SAVERS

Bored with battling the weeds that always seem to spring up around your foundation shrubs? Here's a handy hint: Fill in the gaps with low-growing groundcovers, like lesser periwinkle (*Vinca minor*), or with vigorous perennials. Plant hardy, spring-blooming bulbs, like daffodils and crocuses, to come up right through the groundcover, and you'll get twice the beauty from the same amount of space!

Fall Wash-Down Spray

Before Old Man Winter makes a return appearance, apply my Fall Wash-Down Spray to get rid of any bad bugs that are hiding in and around your trees and shrubs.

INSTRUCTIONS: Mix these ingredients in a 20 gallon hose-end sprayer, and douse your plants to the point of run-off, making sure you hit the plants and the soil underneath them. That'll knock out any pesky pests that were planning to spend the winter on your trees and shrubs!

INGREDIENTS:

1 cup of tobacco tea*
1/2 cup of baby shampoo
6 tbsp. of fruit tree spray
4 tbsp. of antiseptic mouthwash
2 tbsp. of witch hazel

To make tobacco tea, place half a handful of chewing tobacco in an old nylon stocking and soak it in a gallon of hot water until the mixture is dark brown.

◆ DON'T FORGET TO WATER, TOO!

Who says plants don't need water in winter? The roots of many deciduous and evergreen plants continue to function and absorb moisture from the soil all year-round. Evergreens lose water through their leaves, too, so their roots have to work even harder in winter. To make sure your trees and shrubs have all the moisture they need, give them a good drenching in late fall.

GREAT IDEA!

Want to help all of your trees and shrubs get through the winter with flying colors?

Then give them a good, thorough application of an antitranspirant, like my Weatherproof™, in late fall. It seals in moisture, while locking out destructive elements like wind, sun, dirt, salt, and pollution.

Fantastic Flowering Shrub Tonic

In warm weather—which in the South and West is all year long—shrubs need a substantial amount of iron in their diet. If they don't get it, they'll suffer from chlorosis, which means that their leaves turn yellow. For a quick fix, I want you to apply my Liquid Iron™ at the recommended rate, making sure that you give the plants a thorough drenching. To prevent future problems—and to keep ALL of your flowering shrubs in top-notch form— mix up a batch of this terrific tonic.

INGREDIENTS:

1 tbsp. of baby shampoo
1 tsp. of hydrated lime
1 tsp. of iron sulfate
1 gal. of water

INSTRUCTIONS: Mix these ingredients in a bucket, and apply with a 20 gallon hose-end sprayer. In the South and West, early February is the time to treat flowering shrubs. In the cooler areas of the country, apply this tonic just after the forsythias bloom. It'll get your beautiful bloomers off and running for their spectacular spring extravaganza!

◆ IMPROVE YOUR VIEW

If you have huge, old shrubs that are blocking your windows, arm yourself with a pruning saw and pruning loppers, and cut back those bushes by about one-third of their size. You can be even more aggressive if you like, but I've found that the one-third guideline is good to begin with.

TERRIFIC TIME⌛SAVERS

A late freeze that kills the flowers on your spring-blooming trees and shrubs means more warm-weather work for you. Protect them by spraying them lightly with water in the evening, so the buds will be coated with a thin layer of ice. You may still lose some blossoms, but later ones should emerge in all of their splendor.

No-Jive Chive Spray

Scale insects form tiny bumps on twigs as they suck the plant's sap, causing weak or stunted growth. If you spot them, spray your plants right away with a good horticultural oil, which will suffocate some of the scale. The remaining scale insects will come to life in spring and start moving around, which is the best time to hit them with this super spray.

INGREDIENTS:

¼ cup of dried chives
Water
Dishwashing liquid

INSTRUCTIONS: Pour 2 cups of boiling water over the chives, and let them sit for one hour. Strain out the leaves, then mix 1 part of the liquid with 2 parts water. Add a few drops of dishwashing liquid. Pour into a hand-held sprayer, shake, and apply to the point of run-off. Then say "So long!" to your scale problem.

◆ FOIL 'EM WITH OIL

To keep tent caterpillars from attacking your trees, fight back with this neat trick: Wrap the lower section of each trunk with aluminum foil, and fasten the foil to the trunk at both the top and bottom with electrical tape. Paint a ring of motor oil around the center of the foil strip, and you'll stop the caterpillars from climbing up to chow down!

ASK JERRY

Q My tree has a disgusting patch of greenish gray stuff on the trunk. Is it sick or something?

A That's not a disease: It's a patch of either lichen or moss. Both are harmless to the tree, but if you want to clean it up, mix up a solution of ½ cup of bleach and ½ cup of dishwashing liquid in 1 gallon of warm water. Spray the area thoroughly several times until the moss dies and falls away.

Root Pruning Tonic

Thinking of moving an established tree or shrub within the next year? The job will go a whole lot easier then if you try a trick called root pruning now! Simply dig a narrow, circular trench about 18 inches deep all the way around the plant. (The outer edge of the trench should be a few inches inside the outer limit of the branch tips.) Saw through any big roots, and cut smaller ones with clippers, then replace the soil. Scatter about ¼ pound of Epsom salts over the soil all around the plant, then follow up with a dose of this tonic.

INGREDIENTS:

1 can of beer
4 tbsp. of instant tea granules
1 tbsp. of baby shampoo
1 tbsp. of ammonia
1 tbsp. of hydrogen peroxide
1 tbsp. of whiskey
2 gal. of warm water

INSTRUCTIONS: Mix these ingredients in a large watering can, then pour about a quart of the elixir into the soil where you've cut the roots. This will encourage lots of new root growth, and the transplanting process will go a whole lot easier!

◆ LOCATION IS EVERYTHING

If your house is tall and rather imposing, large trees near it will make it appear less intimidating without taking away from its grandeur. If, on the other hand, your house is on the small side, trees that barely reach the roofline will tend to make it look a little larger, and much more impressive.

GRANDMA PUTT'S POINTERS ☞

Try this old-time trick: Beat tree trunks with a stick or rolled-up newspaper from the ground all the way up to the first branch to stimulate sap flow (and flowering) in early spring. Sounds strange, I know, but Grandma Putt swore it worked—and so do I!

Shrub Greening Tonic

It's not easy being green—unless you're a plant, that is! And, even then, sometimes it's difficult to retain that glorious, deep green color. So if your leafy shrubs are fading fast, green them up with this terrific tonic.

INGREDIENTS:

1 tsp. of baking soda
1 tsp. of Epsom salts
$1/2$ tsp. of ammonia
1 gal. of water

INSTRUCTIONS: Mix these ingredients in a bucket, and dribble about a quart of the mixture around the base of each of your shrubs. They'll be lush and lovely again before you know it! To keep them that way, put them on a regular feeding program, such as my Shrub Grub (at right).

◆ You'll Love These Leaves!

Some shrubs have such good-looking leaves, they don't even need flowers! To get the biggest and brightest foliage on these beautiful bushes, try this tough-love tip: Whack 'em down to a foot or so above the ground every spring. Sounds harsh, I know, but you won't believe how quick they bounce back, and they'll look all the better for it! This trick works great with purple-leaved smoke bush (*Cotinus coggygria*), elderberries (*Sambucus*), and ninebarks (*Physocarpus*), too.

GREAT IDEA!

Want to know a great trick for getting your spring-blooming shrubs to do double duty?

Train vines to grow over them! Create an amazing display with summer-blooming annual vines, like morning glories or hyacinth beans. Or, for plant-it-once color, try hardy vines instead, such as clematis or honeysuckle. Set the vine just outside of the farthest reach of the shrub's stems, so it'll get all the sun and rain it needs to thrive. Once the vine starts to climb, simply stand back, and enjoy the show!

Shrub Grub

Once shrubs mature, they need hardly any care to look their best. It's still a good idea to feed them once a year, though. You can feed spring-blooming shrubs in late fall or late winter, but wait until early spring to feed evergreens and shrubs that bloom in summer or fall. My Shrub Grub is a power-packed, once-a-year meal that'll make all kinds of shrubs grow like gangbusters!

INSTRUCTIONS: Once a year, work this mixture into the soil around your shrubs. (Pull back the mulch first, scatter the mixture over the soil around the shrub, and replace the mulch.) Follow up with my Shrub Grub Activator (see **page 82**).

> ## INGREDIENTS:
> **25 lbs. of all-purpose plant food**
> **1 lb. of sugar**
> **½ lb. of Epsom salts**

◆ VARIETY MAKES LIFE EASIER!

Some folks think they need to keep their foundation shrubs all the same type or all the same size. But why make all that work for yourself—trimming and pruning to keep it all the same? Changes in height and plant texture make foundation plantings all the more interesting, so mix it up!

Don't throw out those leftover coffee grounds—they make a fantastic (and *free*) fertilizer! Sprinkle them on the soil all around your shrubs, and believe you me, you'll soon have the healthiest, most vigorous shrubs in the neighborhood. And when those plants bloom, they'll bloom *big* time!

Shrub Grub Activator

Once you've treated all of your shrubs to a taste of my Shrub Grub (see **page 81**), follow up with a good, long drink of this activator to get 'em energized!

INSTRUCTIONS: Mix these ingredients in a 20 gallon hose-end sprayer, and overspray your newly fed shrubs to rouse those roots and get new growth growin' strong.

INGREDIENTS:
1 can of beer
½ cup of liquid lawn food
½ cup of dishwashing liquid
½ cup of ammonia
½ cup of regular cola (not diet)

◆ A FEAST FOR YOUR FEATHERED FRIENDS

If you want to draw songbirds to your yard like a magnet, plant shrubs that produce berries, such as Oregon grape-hollies (*Mahonia*), cotoneasters, and viburnums. Besides giving them food, shrubs provide birds with shelter and nesting sites. You benefit, too, because most of the birds that flock to your shrubs will also devour insects that might otherwise feast on your plants, or even you!

◆ TIMING IS EVERYTHING

Prune spring-flowering shrubs right after they bloom, and prune later-flowering shrubs in spring. But if you really need to cut back any shrub, do it in late winter or early spring, regardless of when it blooms. You might miss out on the flowers that year, but at least the job will be done, and the shrub will have a whole growing season to recover its strength.

GRANDMA PUTT'S POINTERS ☞ Here's an old trick my Grandma Putt taught me: When planting a tree or shrub, line the planting hole with baking potatoes. They'll hold in moisture and provide nutrients to the plant as they decay.

Shrub Pest-Preventer Tonic

Fall is prime time for cleaning up your yard—and I don't just mean raking up dropped leaves. It's also the time to wash your shrubs down with my Shrub Pest-Preventer Tonic. This soapy solution will get rid of any pesky pests and dastardly diseases that were planning to spend their long winter vacation snuggled up in your shrubs.

INSTRUCTIONS: Mix the shampoo, mouthwash, tobacco tea, and chamomile tea in a bucket, and then add 2 cups of it to a 20 gallon hose-end sprayer, filling the balance of the jar with water. Overspray your shrubs until they are dripping wet whenever the temperature is above 50°F. This will send them into the winter clean and healthy.

*To make tobacco tea, place half a handful of chewing tobacco in an old nylon stocking and soak it in a gallon of hot water until the mixture is dark brown.

INGREDIENTS:
1 cup of baby shampoo
1 cup of antiseptic mouthwash
1 cup of tobacco tea*
1 cup of chamomile tea
Water

◆ FALL IS FOR PLANTING

In the mild-winter climates of Zones 7 and 8, October is prime time for setting out container-grown trees and shrubs. Evergreens, in particular, benefit from winter rains and from the chance to develop extensive roots before summer. And to fend off trouble, give each plant a dose of my Shrub Pest-Preventer Tonic (above) after planting.

TERRIFIC TIME⬛SAVERS

If you want truly trouble-free shrubs, plant ones that are native to your part of the country, where they're born to perform like troupers. Ask your Cooperative Extension Service to suggest some good candidates, or have fun exploring local arboretums and botanical gardens, where all the rooted residents are clearly labeled.

Shrub-Planting Booster Mix

Whenever you set out new shrubs, toss a handful of this booster mix into the planting hole to help get the roots off to a good start.

INSTRUCTIONS: Mix these ingredients in a bucket and add a handful to the planting hole. This will energize the soil and give your shrub something tasty to snack on as it gets growing.

> **INGREDIENTS:**
> 4 parts bonemeal
> 1 part Epsom salts
> 1 part gypsum

◆ KEEP 'EM ON THE LEVEL

When you plant a shrub, always make sure you're planting it at the same depth it was growing in the pot. Sure, it takes a few extra seconds, but it'll make a *big* difference in the long run! And it's easy to do: Simply dig the hole, set the plant in place, and then lay the handle of your shovel across the hole. Look at the plant carefully from the side. The handle should rest on the soil line on both sides of the hole and touch the base of the plant in the center.

If you need to, adjust the depth of the plant by digging deeper, or by adding soil under the root ball. If you do end up putting some soil under the roots, add enough to raise the root ball about a quarter-inch above the soil line, because it'll settle a bit after you water.

Newly planted shrubs need water daily for the first three or four days, and the best way to deliver that supply is with a soaker hose. You don't have to buy one, though: Just poke holes in an old hose and lay it out on the ground among the plants.

Shrub Stimulator Tonic

Newly planted shrubs will breathe a sigh of relief as you set their roots free into well-prepared soil. But don't be too quick to feed them; wait at least four weeks after planting. Sprinkle $1/4$ cup of Epsom salts onto the soil beneath each one, then water them in with this Shrub Stimulator Tonic to get those babies off to a flying start.

INSTRUCTIONS: Mix these ingredients in a large watering can, and sprinkle the mixture around the base of all of your recently planted shrubs to encourage vigorous new growth. Once your shrubs are established, follow up with a well-balanced plant food (such as 5-10-10) in late winter or early spring. If you live in the South, make another application in fall.

INGREDIENTS:

4 tbsp. of instant tea granules
4 tbsp. of bourbon or $1/2$ can of beer
2 tbsp. of dishwashing liquid
2 gal. of warm water

◆ POSTPLANTING PAMPERING

While it doesn't pay to baby shrubs when you're makin' their bed, it's good green-thumb sense to give 'em some TLC *after* you get 'em in the ground. First, use the leftover soil to form a raised ring around the edge of the planting hole. Using a gentle flow from a hose or watering can, fill the basin two or three times with water to give the roots a thorough soaking. Then finish up by covering the soil with a 2-inch layer of mulch, such as shredded bark or chopped leaves, to keep the soil moist.

ASK JERRY

Q *What's the proper spacing for planting shrubs? My wife and I argue about this all the time.*

A In most situations, you want your shrubs to barely grow together when they reach mature size. So if a shrub is expected to grow 4 feet wide, plant it at least 3 $1/2$ feet from its nearest neighbor. That'll give 'em some breathing room.

Simple Soap and Oil Spray

Sap-sucking pests like aphids, leafhoppers, and spider mites can really do a number on your trees and shrubs. These little terrors live their entire lives without ever eating solid food; instead, they sink their little mouthparts into tender stems and leaves, then settle in to drink their fill. These pests are so small that you can hardly see them, but you'll sure be able to spot the damage they cause: yellowing or speckled leaves, distorted shoots, and overall poor growth. To send these pernicious pests on their way, blast 'em with this simple spray.

INGREDIENTS:

1 cup of vegetable oil
1 tbsp. of dishwashing liquid
1 cup of water

INSTRUCTIONS: Mix the vegetable oil and dishwashing liquid, then add 1 to 2 teaspoons of the mixture to the water in a hand-held sprayer. Shake well, then drench affected plants thoroughly—especially the undersides of the leaves, where sap-sucking pests like to hide.

◆ COLOR MAGIC

To change pink hydrangea flowers to blue, mix iron filings into the soil, or water the plant with 1 teaspoon of alum or 3 ounces of aluminum sulfate dissolved in a gallon of water. But be careful! This doesn't work on white hydrangeas—they'll turn an unattractive slate color.

GREAT IDEA!

Thinking of planting shrubbery near your driveway entrance?

When you're planning plantings for the entrance to your driveway or anywhere near the street, choose ones that will never grow more than 30 inches tall. That way, you will always be able to see over them, and oncoming traffic can see you, too.

Super Shrub Restorer

This mixture is just the ticket for perking up old shrubs and starting them on their way to a robust new life.

INSTRUCTIONS: Mix these ingredients in a 20 gallon hose-end sprayer and drench your shrubs thoroughly each spring, including the undersides of leaves. They'll bounce back with lots of fresh new growth to thank you!

INGREDIENTS:
1 can of beer
1 cup of ammonia
$\frac{1}{2}$ cup of dishwashing liquid
$\frac{1}{2}$ cup of molasses or clear corn syrup

◆ NEW LIFE FOR OLD SHRUBS

Don't put up with that ugly old shrub—give it a new lease on life with renewal pruning! Every year for three years running, cut out one-third of the branches close to the ground. By the second spring, you'll already see lots of new growth eager for the room you're about to create with your pruning saw. By the third (and final) rejuvenation pruning, you'll be taking out the last of the old wood—and your vigorous new shrub will look lush and flower better than ever.

◆ KEEP 'EM CLEAN

When pruning, sterilize your tools before moving from one tree or shrub to another, especially if any of them show signs of disease. Use a mixture of 1 part rubbing alcohol or chlorine bleach to 9 parts water. Soak the tools for several minutes before wiping them dry and moving on.

TERRIFIC TIME✕SAVERS

Got so many coffee cans that you don't know what to do with 'em? Hide 'em behind your shrubs to hold dead flowers you pluck off and weeds you pull up during your morning strolls around your yard.

Super Shrub Tonic

To get all of your shrubs growing with plenty of vim and vigor, treat them to a taste of this super solution.

INSTRUCTIONS: Mix these ingredients in a 20 gallon hose-end sprayer, then spray your shrubs to the point of run-off in early spring and every three weeks during the growing season. You'll have the happiest, healthiest, humdingingest shrubs in town—GUARANTEED!

INGREDIENTS:
$^1/_2$ **can of beer**
$^1/_2$ **cup of fish emulsion**
$^1/_2$ **cup of ammonia**
$^1/_4$ **cup of baby shampoo**
1 tbsp. of hydrogen peroxide

◆ SUPER SHRUB COVERS

Snow may be a blessing to your garden in winter, but ice can be a real nightmare. It's so heavy that it often breaks off branches, and any attempts you make to lighten the load by knocking off the ice can only make matters worse. But you can help small, ice-encrusted shrubs by throwing lightweight covers over them so that when the sun shines through the ice, it doesn't burn the plant tissues inside. This is a perfect job for sheets or shower curtains that are too old for regular duty.

GREAT IDEA!

Keep spring-flowering shrubs, like forsythias and lilacs, in the pink of good health with an organic or controlled-release plant food and a dusting of lime, too.

Then for every 3 feet of plant height, sprinkle $^1/_4$ cup of Epsom salts on the ground out at the tips of the farthest branches. This will deepen the color, thicken the petals, and increase the root structure. You'll have the best-looking shrubs around, and folks will be wondering what kind of miracle food you've been using!

Terrific Tree Chow

Trees have extensive roots that usually do a fine job foraging for nutrients on their own. But if you have young trees that need a little extra help—or established trees that could use a boost—mix up a batch of this tremendous chow.

INSTRUCTIONS: Feed your trees in spring by drilling holes in the ground out at the weep line (a ring around the tree out at the tip of the farthest branches). Make the holes 8 to 10 inches deep and 18 to 24 inches apart. Fill each hole with 2 tablespoons of the mixture, and sprinkle the remainder over the soil. This mix will really give your trees something to grow on! Follow up with my Tree Chow Energizing Tonic (see **page 93**) to help the dry food work its magic.

> **INGREDIENTS:**
> 25 lbs. of all-purpose plant food
> 1 lb. of sugar
> ½ lb. of Epsom salts

◆ DON'T BE LATE

Never feed your trees, shrubs, or ever-greens after August 15: You'll encourage new growth that may not have sufficient time to mature before winter.

ASK JERRY

Q *I love the trees in my yard, but I hate the roots that grow right at the surface. They make mowing almost impossible! Is it okay to cut them out?*

A Cutting out a few surface roots won't kill trees that are large and healthy, but I have a better idea: Make friends with those surface roots! Bring in some topsoil to fill in around the roots and level the area a bit, then plant an evergreen groundcover, like periwinkle or pachysandra. Or, mulch around the surface roots with finely shredded bark, so that your mower easily rides up and over them.

Timely Tree Tonic

Making loads of lush leaves and beautiful blooms takes a whole lot of energy out of your flowering trees! To build up their strength and keep them at their best, apply my Terrific Tree Chow (see **page 89**) in spring. Then follow up with this power-packed tonic.

INSTRUCTIONS: Mix these ingredients in a large watering can, and then give each tree a good long drink once in the spring and again on June 15. (Figure on about a 1½ quarts of tonic per tree.) This double-shot feeding will keep your trees at their peak all season long.

INGREDIENTS:

½ can of beer
4 tbsp. of instant tea granules
1 tbsp. of baby shampoo
1 tbsp. of ammonia
1 tbsp. of whiskey
1 tbsp. of hydrogen peroxide
1 tbsp. of gelatin
2 gal. of warm water

◆ GROVES ARE GROOVY!

Don't make all of your trees fly solo! Instead of planting one here and one there, try growing them in groups of three. Plant a weed-smothering groundcover underneath to link them together, and you've got yourself a gorgeous grove effect. And you can go even one better by using four-season trees like river birch (*Betula nigra*) or dogwoods (*Cornus*). That simple grouping suddenly becomes an awesome year-round accent—with no extra work on your part!

GRANDMA PUTT'S POINTERS
One of Grandma's least favorite garden chores was trimming the straggly grass around tree trunks. If you feel the same, do what she did: Build beds around the base of each tree and fill them with multi-season perennials or groundcovers. Besides adding year-round interest, these little gardens will cut your trimming chores down to practically nothing!

Toodle-oo Tick Spray

Ticks can make life miserable for humans and pets alike. If these germ-totin' terrors are hanging out in your shrubs—one of their favorite hideouts—send 'em packin' with this spray. Just make sure you wait 'til evening to blast the culprits—the alcohol will burn your plants if it's used in the sun.

INGREDIENTS:

1 tbsp. of dishwashing liquid
2 cups of isopropyl (rubbing) alcohol
1 gal. of rainwater or soft tap water

INSTRUCTIONS: Mix these ingredients in a bucket, pour into a 6 gallon hose-end sprayer, and spray your plants from top to bottom. Make sure you get under all the leaves where these rascals like to hang out. Repeat whenever necessary to keep ticks from spoiling your outdoor fun.

◆ DON'T GET STUMPED

Want to get rid of a stump without digging it up? Cut the stump at or below soil level, then drill a bunch of holes in it—the more, the merrier. Make them as large and as deep as you can drill. Now fill them with a commercial stump remover that contains potassium nitrate, and plug up the holes. Let it sit for one year. At the end of the year, remove the plugs, pour in kerosene, let it sit for an hour or so, then light it. The stump will smolder away to ashes.

TERRIFIC TIME◼SAVERS

When you're washing windows outdoors, don't fight with your shrubs. Instead, haul out an old shirt, and tie lengths of rope to the wrists and tail. Then pull the shirt against the shrub and away from the house. Secure the ropes to a stake, and get to work washin' those windows!

Tree and Shrub Transplanting Tonic

Fall is an ideal time to transplant trees and shrubs, because the warm soil and regular rainfall encourage lots of new root growth. Come next spring, your plants will be ready and rarin' to grow! Simply set the tree or shrub into the planting hole, gently spread out the roots, then refill the planting hole halfway with soil. Flood it with water, finish refilling the hole with soil, and water again. Finish up with a nice dose of this transplanting tonic.

INGREDIENTS:
$^1/_3$ cup of hydrogen peroxide
$^1/_4$ cup of whiskey
$^1/_4$ cup of baby shampoo
4 tbsp. of instant tea granules
2 tbsp. of fish emulsion
1 gal. of warm water

__INSTRUCTIONS:__ Mix these ingredients in a bucket, and pour the mixture around the trunk when you transplant a tree or shrub. About a quart of this mixture, dribbled onto the soil to reach the roots, will help get that young tree or shrub off to a stress-free start.

◆ TRY THIS TRICK
Tired of looking at mushrooms growing under your trees? Sprinkle 2 cups of dry laundry detergent over the area with your hand-held spreader, and those toadstools will be history!

ASK JERRY

Q *I know watering newly planted trees and shrubs is critical, but it takes forever by hand. Any suggestions?*

A You'll *love* this quick trick: Punch five or six tiny nail holes in the bottom of a plastic milk jug, place it at the base of each tree, and fill it with water. The water will soak in with no run-off, so you can run off to do other things!

Tree Chow Energizing Tonic

Even established trees can really benefit from a few extra nutrients during the growing season. Once you've fed them with a dry fertilizer mix, such as my Terrific Tree Chow (see **page 89**), overspray the soil with this tonic to really get things growing.

INSTRUCTIONS: Mix the beer, lawn food, dishwashing liquid, and ammonia in a 20 gallon hose-end sprayer, filling the balance of the jar with the cola, and saturate the ground underneath your trees. This elixir will really energize the dry chow so your tree will have plenty of food to support a bounty of healthy new growth. For an extra energy boost, follow up with my Timely Tree Tonic (see **page 90**) applied a few times throughout the summer.

INGREDIENTS:

1 can of beer
1 cup of liquid lawn food
$\frac{1}{4}$ cup of dishwashing liquid
$\frac{1}{4}$ cup of ammonia
Regular cola (not diet)

◆ EVERGREENS TO THE RESCUE

If your home turf gets too much wind to suit you, give your yard some shelter with a row or two of evergreen trees. Better yet, double up by placing a second row of flowering shrubs or small flowering trees along the inside edge of your windbreak. Any plant with white or light-colored blooms looks like a million bucks when it's backed by an evergreen screen!

When you're tree shopping, remember this: That cute little tree in its neat little pot may be just the ticket for now, but within a few years, it can grow into a monster that will overshadow your house and garden, send its roots through your driveway, drop its leaves into your gutters, and who knows what else! So always buy a tree that will be the size you want when it's fully grown—not when you see it at the garden center.

Tree Snack Mix

By the middle or end of August, you need to think about getting your trees and shrubs ready for winter. To help them along, give them a taste of this snack. It will fortify the soil and keep critters away, too.

INSTRUCTIONS: Mix these ingredients in a bucket, and apply with a broadcast spreader in a broad band beneath your trees. One batch is just right for one mature shade tree or two smaller flowering trees. Your trees will stay in great shape through winter and be rarin' to grow come spring!

> **INGREDIENTS:**
>
> 5 lbs. of bonemeal
> 1 lb. of Epsom salts
> 1 lb. of gypsum
> ½ cup of mothballs

◆ THE ROOTS OF THE MATTER

Besides casting lots of shade, tall trees add another challenge: dense root systems that can suck the water and nutrients right out of any plants you put directly underneath 'em. If your trees have deep roots, like oaks do, you're in luck; shallow-rooted trees, though—like maples—are a real pain to plant under.

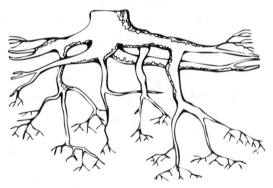

To figure out what's underfoot, use a small spade to gently dig around the trees in your yard. If a solid mass of roots impedes digging, your best option is to keep flower gardens farther out—beyond where the branch tips end. Believe you me, digging will be a whole lot easier out there!

TERRIFIC TIME⧗SAVERS

Are tree roots make digging too daunting? Potted plants are a perfect way to bring color to those tough sites in the shade. Choose long-blooming annuals like begonias and impatiens for loads of showy flowers, or coleus for a spectacular show of brightly colored leaves.

Tree Wound Sterilizer Tonic

To prune, or not to prune: That is the question. Many trees actually grow better if you just leave them alone, but sometimes, young trees can benefit from a bit of a trim. Always feel free to cut off any limbs damaged by wind or disease, as well as any branches that cross or grow very close together. After you've made your cuts, treat them with this sterilizer tonic.

INGREDIENTS:
$\frac{1}{2}$ cup of antiseptic mouthwash
$\frac{1}{4}$ cup of ammonia
$\frac{1}{4}$ cup of dishwashing liquid
1 gal. of warm water

INSTRUCTIONS: Mix these ingredients in a bucket, and pour into a hand-held sprayer. Drench the spots where you've pruned limbs from trees or shrubs to the point of run-off. This soothing solution will clean things up and allow for quick healing. Those wounds will be covered up before you know it!

◆ PLAN YOUR PRUNING SCHEDULE

Begin pruning trees and shrubs in February, on those rare days when you can smell spring in the air. But keep your hands off birches and maples for now, because they often bleed sap when pruned at this time of year. It's best to wait until late summer or early fall to trim those trees.

GREAT IDEA!

Looking for a way to control the size of your trees and shrubs?

Cutting back the tips of branches actually makes 'em grow faster, so that's the wrong thing to do if size control is your goal! Instead, cut out a few whole branches each year—back to a main stem, or all the way back to the ground.

Tree-Mendous Planting Booster Mix

Tree experts used to recommend planting trees in elaborately prepared holes, but not anymore. Instead, the idea is to choose a variety that's likely to grow well in your climate and soil, and make it stretch its roots in native turf right from the get-go. Start off by digging a hole as deep as the root ball and twice as wide. Use a spade to make jagged slices into the sides of the planting hole, especially if you have clay soil. Then energize the soil with my Tree-Mendous Planting Booster Mix.

INGREDIENTS:

4 lbs. of compost
2 lbs. of gypsum
1 lb. of Epsom salts
1 lb. of dry dog food
1 lb. of dry oatmeal

<u>**INSTRUCTIONS:**</u> Mix these ingredients in a bucket. Work a handful or two into the bottom of the planting hole—sprinkle some over the top after planting, too—and your tree will get off to a tremendous start.

◆ TLC FOR TENDER TRUNKS

Young trees—especially dogwoods, beeches, and maples—have very delicate bark that can easily get sunburned. To protect them from the sun, wrap the trunks from the base to the lowest branches with burlap, aluminum foil, or tree wrap. Spiral the wrap up the trunk, overlapping the layers by about an inch or so to keep water out. Leave the wrap on the tree for a year or two to give the trunk plenty of time to toughen up.

There's nothing mice and rabbits love more than newly planted trees, so protect your treasures with heavy-duty aluminum foil. Wrap it around the trunk from the top of the root ball up to about the 1-foot mark, and keep it there until the tree has established itself.

Winter Survival Strategies

Fall is a super time for planting, but your young trees and shrubs will need a bit of TLC to make it through their first winter in your yard. If you follow my advice, your newly planted friends will survive just fine and be rarin' to grow come spring.

INSTRUCTIONS: In late fall, spray your trees and shrubs with an all-season horticultural oil or dormant oil to stop napping pests dead in their tracks. Before the ground freezes, soak the soil well, and apply an extra layer of mulch to keep moisture in the ground. Coat the trees and shrubs with my Weatherproof or another antitranspirant to lock in moisture and seal out the harsh winter elements. Then wrap the tree trunks to prevent splitting, cracking, and sunscald. In exposed sites, stake young trees so they don't get whipped about in heavy winter winds. With these few basic precautions, your trees and shrubs will sail through the winter with flying colors!

INGREDIENTS:

All-season horticultural oil
   or dormant oil
Water
Mulch
Weatherproof™ or another
   antitranspirant spray
Tree wrap
Stakes

◆ WEEPERS DON'T LIKE COMPANY

Combining trees with different shapes is a great way to jazz up your winter garden—with one exception: *Never* crowd weeping trees with other companions. To look their best, the graceful, arching branches need plenty of room to spread out and do their thing.

TERRIFIC TIME⌛SAVERS

Need privacy in a hurry? Plant a row or grouping of large shrubs. They fill in faster than trees—and they're a whole lot less expensive than fences, to boot!

CHAPTER 3

FABULOUS FLOWERS

GUESS WHAT, FOLKS—Creating a fabulous, flower-filled yard is a whole lot easier than you think. Sure, you could spend years trying out different techniques and experimenting with your own homemade elixirs, but why bother? I've already done all of the hard work for you! I've rounded up my favorite tonics to cover everything you need for a fabulous flower garden, from nutrient-packed soil builders to fantastic feeding tonics that'll get your bloomers growin' like crazy. And if nasty bugs and germs rear their ugly little heads—well, I've got magical mixers to take care of them, too!

So, if you've got flower garden problems—or if you just want to give your bloomers a little extra boost—here's all of my very best flower formulas right at your fingertips. Now, you, too, can grow the biggest, brightest, bloomingest beds on the block—DAZZLING daisies, MAGNIFICENT marigolds, and STUNNING snapdragons—that'll make your yard the Blue Ribbon winner in town!

No need to puzzle over what to do in your flower garden—just follow these simple steps to surefire flower-growing success.

 ## Spring

◆ **Step 1:** Ready to get a jump start on the growing season? Begin by building up the soil in your beds and borders with my power-packed Bed Energizing Mix (see **page 114**):

50 lbs. of peat moss
25 lbs. of gypsum
10 lbs. of organic plant food
    (such as 5-10-5)
4 bushels of compost

Mix these ingredients in a large wheelbarrow, then work the mixture into the soil before you plant. This amount is enough to cover about 100 sq. ft. It'll energize the soil to take all kinds of beautiful bloomers to new heights!

◆ **Step 2:** Early spring is prime time for planting bare-root perennials. So give 'em a good soak in my Bare-Root Revival Tonic #1 (see **page 112**), then get 'em in the ground as soon as possible:

¼ cup of brewed tea
1 tbsp. of dishwashing liquid
1 tbsp. of Epsom salts
1 gal. of water

Mix these ingredients in a large bucket. Clip off any broken or discolored roots cleanly with sharp shears, then soak the remaining roots in this tonic for up to 24 hours. This will revive the plants and get them up and rarin' to grow!

◆ **Step 3:** When you bring your annual transplants home from the garden center, douse them with my Bedding Plant Starter Brew (see **page 115**) until you're ready to get them in the ground:

2 tsp. of fish emulsion
2 tsp. of dishwashing liquid
1 tsp. of whiskey
1 qt. of water

Mix these ingredients in a watering can, and then feed this formula to your adopted seedlings every other time you water them. Give them a good soak with it just before you set them out, too.

◆ **Step 4:** For feeding potted perennials until planting time, you can't do any better than my Container Perennial Tonic (see **page 121**):

1 tbsp. of 15-30-15 plant food
1/2 tsp. of gelatin
1/2 tsp. of dishwashing liquid
1/2 tsp. of clear corn syrup
1/2 tsp. of whiskey
1/4 tsp. of instant tea granules
Water

Mix the plant food, gelatin, dishwashing liquid, corn syrup, whiskey, and tea in a 1 gallon milk jug, filling the balance of the jug with water. Stir, and add 1/2 cup of the mixture to every gallon of water you use to water your perennials.

◆ **Step 5:** Wait for a cloudy day to set out annual bedding plants and potted perennials. Once you're done planting, spread a 2-inch-deep layer of chopped leaves or other organic mulch around your flowers to keep moisture in and weeds out. Then overspray your beds with my Mulch Moisturizer Tonic (see **page 142**):

1 can of regular cola (not diet)
1/2 cup of ammonia
1/2 cup of antiseptic mouthwash
1/2 cup of baby shampoo

Mix these ingredients in a 20 gallon hose-end sprayer, and give your mulch a nice long, cool drink. Add more mulch as needed through the season to keep it at the same depth, and treat it with this spray each time you re-mulch.

◆ **Step 6:** Get your container plants off to a great start in spring with my Potting Soil Booster Mix (see **page 152**):

2 cups of dry oatmeal
2 cups of dry dog food, crushed
Pinch of human hair
1 1/2 tsp. of sugar

Mix these ingredients in a bucket, and add 2 tablespoons of the mixture to each container of moistened, professional potting soil.

◆ **Step 7:** To discourage insects and diseases, use my All-Season Clean-Up Tonic (see **page 106**) every two weeks throughout the growing season:

1 cup of baby shampoo
1 cup of antiseptic mouthwash
1 cup of tobacco tea*

Mix these ingredients in a 20 gallon hose-end sprayer, and give everything in your yard a shower in the early evening.

To make tobacco tea, place half a handful of chewing tobacco in an old nylon stocking and soak it in a gallon of hot water until the mixture is dark brown.

✦ Summer

◆ Step 8: When used regularly, my All-Season Green-Up Tonic (see **page 107**) will turn your annuals and perennials into clean, lean blooming machines:

1 can of beer
1 cup of ammonia
1/2 cup of dishwashing liquid
1/2 cup of liquid lawn food
1/2 cup of molasses or clear corn syrup

Mix these ingredients in a large bucket, pour into a 20 gallon hose-end sprayer, and spray everything in sight—not just your flowers, but also your trees, shrubs, lawn, and even vegetables. Apply this tonic every three weeks right up through the first hard frost.

◆ Step 9: Are deer, mice, rabbits, or rodents chowing down on your beautiful bloomers? Whatever the culprit, I've got the cure—my All-Purpose Varmint Repellent (see **page 105**):

1/2 cup of Murphy's Oil Soap®
1/2 cup of lemon-scented dishwashing liquid
1/2 cup of castor oil
1/2 cup of lemon-scented ammonia
1/2 cup of hot, hot, hot pepper sauce
1/2 cup of urine

Mix these ingredients in a 20 gallon hose-end sprayer, then apply to the point of run-off to any area that needs protecting. Reapply every other week or so, or after a rain.

◆ Step 10: Summertime is the right time to get perennial seeds off to a rousing start. For even speedier results, soak your seeds in my Perennial Seed Send-Off Tonic (see **page 147**) before you sow them:

1 cup of vinegar
1 tbsp. of baby shampoo or dishwashing liquid
2 cups of warm water

Mix these ingredients in a small bucket, and soak your seeds in the solution overnight before planting them in well-prepared soil.

◆ Step 11: To keep your outdoor containers filled with flowers all season long, feed them regularly with my Potted Plant Picnic (see **page 151**):

2 tbsp. of brewed black coffee
2 tbsp. of whiskey
1 tsp. of fish emulsion
1/2 tsp. of gelatin
1/2 tsp. of baby shampoo
1/2 tsp. of ammonia
1 gal. of water

Mix these ingredients in a watering can, and water your potted plants with the mixture once a week to keep them happy, healthy, and full of flowers!

◆ **Step 12:** If your annuals seem to be on the brink of exhaustion in late summer, pinch them back a bit, then give them a dose of my Annual Pick-Me-Up Tonic (see **page 110**) to get 'em growing again:

¼ cup of beer
1 tbsp. of clear corn syrup
1 tbsp. of baby shampoo
1 tbsp. of 15-30-15 plant food
1 gal. of water

Mix these ingredients in a watering can, then slowly dribble the solution onto the soil around all of your annuals. Within two weeks, they'll be real comeback kids!

 *Fall*

◆ **Step 13:** Early fall is prime time for dividing crowded perennial clumps. My Perennial Transplant Tonic (see **page 148**) will get your new divisions back on their feet without missing a beat:

1 can of beer
4 tbsp. of instant tea granules
2 tbsp. of dishwashing liquid
2 gal. of warm water

Mix these ingredients in a bucket, and soak newly divided perennials in this tonic for about 10 minutes just before replanting them. When you're finished, dribble any leftover tonic around your newly settled divisions to get 'em off to a supercharged start.

◆ **Step 14:** In most areas, fall is the ideal time to get started on a new flower garden. To get the area in prime shape for spring planting, treat it to my Fall Bedtime Snack (see **page 130**) as soon as you are done digging:

25 lbs. of gypsum
10 lbs. of organic plant food
    (either 4-12-4 or 5-10-5)
5 lbs. of bonemeal

Mix these ingredients in a wheelbarrow, then apply the mix to every 100 sq. ft. of soil. Work it into the soil and cover with a thick blanket of leaves, straw, or other organic mulch.

◆ **Step 15:** Once the ground freezes, put established flower gardens to bed by covering them with finely mowed grass clippings or chopped leaves, then overspraying with my Flower Garden Nightcap (see **page 133**):

1 can of regular cola (not diet)
1 cup of baby shampoo
½ cup of ammonia
2 tbsp. of instant tea granules

Mix these ingredients in a 20 gallon hose-end sprayer, and saturate the mulch blanket. This tonic feeds your mulch, which in turn will feed your garden while it protects your perennials all through the winter.

All-Around Disease Defense Tonic

Most common flower garden diseases are caused by fungi—microscopic life forms that exist as parasites on our beloved plants. These funky fungi invade plant tissues, destroy cells, and drain the energy out of leaves, then release thousands of spores that germinate and infect them, too. The best way to stop mildews and leaf spots dead in their tracks is to keep a close eye on your flowering plants and douse them often with this tonic.

> **INGREDIENTS:**
> 1 cup of chamomile tea
> 1 tsp. of dishwashing liquid
> ½ tsp. of vegetable oil
> ½ tsp. of peppermint oil
> 1 gal. of warm water

INSTRUCTIONS: Mix these ingredients in a bucket, then pour into a hand-held sprayer. Spray your plants every week or so before the really hot weather (75°F or higher) sets in. This elixir is strong stuff, so test it on a few leaves first—then wait a day or two to make sure no damage has occurred—before applying it to any plant.

◆ WATER WISDOM 101

If I have to water my flower garden, I make sure I do it in the morning. That way, the plants are juiced up and ready to handle the heat of the day. It also means that the leaves have plenty of time to dry off before bedtime, so diseases are less likely to get started. You don't send your kids to bed with a wet head, so don't do it to your flowers, either!

GREAT IDEA!

Tripped up by that mess of kinky garden hose?

Here's a quick, easy, and cheap way to keep any hose from knotting and twisting—simply coil it loosely around the bottom of an old garbage can.

All-Purpose Perennial Fertilizer

Tired of planting the same old annuals year after year? Then it's time to give perennials a try! Set 'em out once to enjoy many seasons of beautiful blooms. Whether you're setting out new plants or feeding established clumps, this power-packed mix will keep perennials "in the pink."

INSTRUCTIONS: Mix these ingredients in a bucket or in a wheelbarrow. Apply 3 to 5 pounds of the mix per 100 sq. ft. of new perennial garden bed before planting, and work it into the soil. Or scatter 2 tablespoons around each clump of established perennials in spring and scratch it lightly into the soil with a hand fork.

INGREDIENTS:

3 parts bonemeal
3 parts greensand or wood ashes
1 part bloodmeal

◆ DON'T WAIT FOR THE WILT

If you wait until your plants are wilting before you water, it's almost too late! You're better off checking the soil instead. Pull back the mulch in a small area, then dig down a few inches with a trowel. If the top 2 inches of soil are dry, get out the hose, and get busy waterin'!

ASK JERRY

Q *I've heard that it's possible for some plants to get too much sun? Is this true?*

A It sure is! Sunburn shows up as tan, bronzed, or scorched-looking patches on the leaves or flowers. To prevent it, expose indoor-grown plants to sunshine gradually— a few hours more each day over a period of a week or so. If you see these symptoms on plants in the garden, give them a long, cool drink right away, and move them to a shadier spot.

All-Purpose Varmint Repellent

Like deer, rabbits and rodents will snack on just about anything in your flower garden. The only difference is that they eat a whole lot less than the big guys! But I've got just the cure: my All-Purpose Varmint Repellent!

INSTRUCTIONS: Mix these ingredients in a 20 gallon hose-end sprayer, then apply to the point of run-off to any area that needs protecting. Reapply every other week or so (or after a rain) to keep the odor fresh.

INGREDIENTS:

$^1/_2$ cup of Murphy's Oil Soap®

$^1/_2$ cup of lemon-scented dishwashing liquid

$^1/_2$ cup of castor oil

$^1/_2$ cup of lemon-scented ammonia

$^1/_2$ cup of hot, hot, hot pepper sauce

$^1/_2$ cup of urine

◆ WHAT'S THE PROBLEM?

If you're not sure who's coming to dinner in your flower garden, do a little detective work and examine the damage. Here's how to decipher these telltale signs:

- ◆ Annuals or perennials that completely disappear overnight are one possible sign of deer damage; others include plants with stem tips, flowers, or flower buds missing; hoofprints in soft soil; and broken stems or leaves.

- ◆ Seedlings and young plants that vanish were likely attacked by rabbits. They also chew holes in foliage, or eat entire leaves.

- ◆ Perennials that are completely missing in spring were probably victims of vole damage over the winter.

GREAT IDEA!

Are mice, voles, and other rodents a problem in your garden?

Then avoid spreading winter mulch. A layer of mulch makes a snug mouse house during the colder months—complete with the crowns and roots of tasty perennials and bulbs for snacking!

All-Season Clean-Up Tonic

This is the one tonic that you ABSOLUTELY need to use religiously throughout the growing season. The shampoo cleans the plants and helps the other ingredients stick better; the mouthwash kills bad bacteria and discourages insects; and the tobacco tea contains nicotine, which does a double whammy on those pesky pests.

INSTRUCTIONS: Mix these ingredients in a 20 gallon hose-end sprayer, and give everything in your yard a good shower in the early evening every two weeks throughout the growing season. You'll have the healthiest flowers in town—GUARANTEED!

INGREDIENTS:

1 cup of baby shampoo
1 cup of antiseptic mouthwash
1 cup of tobacco tea*

To make tobacco tea, place half a handful of chewing tobacco in an old nylon stocking and soak it in a gallon of hot water until the mixture is dark brown.

◆ BUILD YOUR BEDS WITH ANNUALS

Here's a terrific tip I learned from Grandma Putt: If you've got crummy soil, don't sweat it—let annuals do the work for you! First, dig a 1-inch layer of compost into the soil as best you can the first spring, then plant your annuals. Dig some more compost into the soil that fall when you put the garden to bed for the winter. Repeat the following season. By the end of the second year, the combination of digging, compost, and annual roots will leave you with loose, rich soil that's just perfect for perennials!

TERRIFIC TIME⌛SAVERS

Psst! Wanna know the absolutely easiest way to get rid of any plant pest, *pronto?* Simply pinch or prune off the branches or leaves where the buggers are hanging out! Drop the infested plant parts in a plastic grocery bag, tie it up, and throw it away.

All-Season Green-Up Tonic

If your flowering plants are looking a bit peaked, give them a taste of this sweet snack. It's rich in nutrients and packed with energizers, too—just what your plants need to keep the flowers comin' along all summer long. Your bloomers will green up in a jiffy!

INGREDIENTS:

1 can of beer
1 cup of ammonia
$\frac{1}{2}$ cup of dishwashing liquid
$\frac{1}{2}$ cup of liquid lawn food
$\frac{1}{2}$ cup of molasses or clear
   corn syrup

INSTRUCTIONS: Mix these ingredients in a large bucket, pour into a 20 gallon hose-end sprayer, and spray everything in sight—not just your flowers, but also your trees, shrubs, lawn, and even vegetables. Apply this tonic every three weeks right up through the first hard frost, and your flowers will come through the hot summer months with flying colors!

◆ GOT GOOD GROWTH?

If your answer to that question is no, then it's time to do some detective work! Stunted, slow-growing annuals might just need some fertilizer, like a dose of my All-Season Green-Up Tonic (above). No better in a few days? Then check the soil pH. If the soil is on the acidic side (below 6.5), scatter some lime around the plants and water thoroughly.

◆ FIGHT ICE WITH WATER

If your flowering plants get hit by an unexpected heavy frost, water them lightly the next morning *before* the sun hits them. This will thaw them out quickly, and they'll have a much better chance of survival.

Don't throw away old, broken umbrellas. Tear away the material and use the metal ribs for long-lasting flower supports. Paint them green or black, and nobody will even notice them in your garden!

Amazing Aphid Antidote

Unlike fungi, viruses can't blow around in the wind or be carried from place to place in droplets of rainwater. They must have a live host—usually an insect—which spreads the virus from plant to plant as it feeds. Aphids, leafhoppers, and thrips are the usual culprits. Keeping these pests under control with my aphid antidote is the surest way to protect all of your flowers from vicious viruses.

INSTRUCTIONS: Put these ingredients into an old blender and blend on high. Let the mixture sit overnight, and then strain it through a coffee filter. Pour the liquid into a hand-held sprayer, and apply liberally at the first sign of pest problems to keep all of your beautiful bloomers at the peak of good health.

INGREDIENTS:

1 small onion, chopped finely
2 medium cloves of garlic, chopped finely
1 tbsp. of baby shampoo
2 cups of water

◆ WHEN FLOWERS GET THE FLU

Plants infected with viruses don't sneeze or suffer stopped-up noses. Instead, new growth becomes distorted, leaves show odd textures and colors, and plants that are supposed to grow tall look short and stunted. The cure? Remove and destroy any infected plants right away!

ASK JERRY

Q *A bunch of my flower seedlings were flopped over onto the soil this morning. What critter could have done it?*

A I suspect cutworms. These dastardly demons strike at night, cutting through stems at ground level. Prevent damage next time by cutting 1- to 2-inch-tall rings from those cardboard tubes inside paper towel or toilet tissue rolls. Slip a collar over each seedling at transplanting time, and push it into the soil a bit to keep the critters from slithering underneath it.

Annual Flower Feeder Tonic

Lively annuals burn up a great deal of energy with their constant flowering, so they need to eat heartily to keep it up. For consistent color all through the growing season, stick with a liquid food that your plants can use right away, such as this feeder tonic.

INSTRUCTIONS: Mix these ingredients together in a large bucket, then pour into a watering can. Feed all of the annuals in your yard with this mix every two weeks in the morning for glorious blooms all season long.

INGREDIENTS:

1 can of beer
2 tbsp. of fish emulsion
2 tbsp. of dishwashing liquid
2 tbsp. of ammonia
2 tbsp. of hydrogen peroxide
2 tbsp. of whiskey
1 tbsp. of clear corn syrup
1 tbsp. of gelatin
4 tsp. of instant tea granules
2 gal. of warm water

◆ IF ALL ELSE FAILS...

Whenever I get a new annual and I'm not sure what it likes, I stick it in full sun with rich, well-drained soil that's evenly moist. Most annuals thrive in these conditions, so if you get a new plant to try and don't know what it needs, there's a good chance it will be happy there!

GREAT IDEA!

Want to make the most out of every inch in your flower beds?

Fill in the bare spots around your perennials and shrubs with annuals. You can even plant them on top of clumps of spring bulbs that are starting to die back. The annuals will do a bang-up job covering those yellowing bulb leaves, and they'll fill in perfectly after the bulb foliage completely disappears.

Annual Pick-Me-Up Tonic

If summer's heat and humidity have gotten the best of your annual flowers, don't give them up for lost. You can enjoy several more weeks of blooms if you treat 'em right, right now! Cut them back by about half, water them thoroughly, and then douse them with a shot of my Annual Pick-Me-Up Tonic. They'll be back in bloom before you know it!

INSTRUCTIONS: Mix these ingredients in a watering can, then slowly dribble the solution onto the soil around all of your annuals. Within two weeks, they'll be real comeback kids—and you'll get to enjoy their lush leaves and beautiful blooms right up until mean old Jack Frost makes a return appearance in midfall.

> **INGREDIENTS:**
>
> ¼ cup of beer
> 1 tbsp. of clear corn syrup
> 1 tbsp. of baby shampoo
> 1 tbsp. of 15-30-15 plant food
> 1 gal. of water

◆ SWEETEN UP YOUR SOIL

Don't try to grow annuals (except marigolds, nicotiana, and verbena) in soil with a pH below 6.5 for the simple reason that they can't tolerate the acidity. To sweeten the soil, add lime at a rate of 15 to 25 pounds per 500 square feet of garden area.

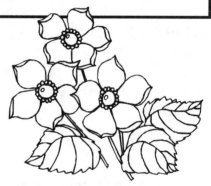

GRANDMA PUTT'S POINTERS ☞

Back when I was a boy, Grandma Putt often kept me busy by sending me out to pick the dead blooms out of her flower garden. She explained that snipping off spent blossoms kept the plants stronger, made them bloom better, and prevented them from making unwanted seedlings. And after years of doing this in my own yard, I know she was right!

Awesome Annual Potting Mix

There's no need to spend money on prepackaged potting soil, 'cause you can mix your own right at home. Here's one of my favorite recipes for keeping potted annuals in tip-top shape.

INGREDIENTS:

1 part topsoil
1 part peat moss
1 part vermiculite
1 part compost

INSTRUCTIONS: Mix these ingredients together in a wheelbarrow, and use it for potting up all kinds of annuals. Store any leftover mix in a closed bag, box, or can so you'll have it on hand for next year.

◆ SAY GOOD-BYE, BIRDIES!

Our fine feathered friends often mistake outdoor hanging baskets for ready-made condos. If you have birds making nests in your hanging baskets, don't despair: Cover the basket with a section of chicken wire, then pull the plants through it. That should stop the birds from feathering their nests with your flowers!

GREAT IDEA!

As pretty as annuals are out in your yard, nothing will impress your guests more than flower-filled planters flanking your front door.

But don't blow your bank account on fancy containers—just rummage around in your garage, attic, and kitchen. You're sure to find all kinds of fun possibilities, such as old wheelbarrows, sprinkling cans, wagons, and even soup kettles! (Whatever containers you choose, just be sure to poke drainage holes in the bottom before you tuck in your plants.)

Bare-Root Revival Tonic #1

Bare-root perennials may look downright unpromising, but give them a good start—AND a good soak in my Bare-Root Revival Tonic #1—and they'll repay you with tons of beautiful blooms for years to come.

INSTRUCTIONS: Mix these ingredients in a large bucket. Clip off any broken or discolored roots cleanly with sharp shears, then soak the remaining roots in the tonic for up to 24 hours. This will revive the plants and get them up and rarin' to grow!

> **INGREDIENTS:**
> ¼ cup of brewed tea
> 1 tbsp. of dishwashing liquid
> 1 tbsp. of Epsom salts
> 1 gal. of water

◆ PLAN AHEAD FOR PERENNIALS

One extra tip for success with bare-root perennials: Prepare their bed *before* they arrive, so you can get 'em in the ground immediately. Or, if you can't plant them within three days of their arrival, plant them in pots until you have time to find them a permanent home.

◆ SQUEEZE, PLEASE!

There's nothing like a warm spring day to make you want to get busy in the garden. But don't even *think* about digging in right away—unless your soil passes the squeeze test, that is! Simply trowel up a handful of soil from the site, and give it a good squeeze. If it crumbles apart when you open your hand, it's too dry. If it clumps into a solid shape, it's too wet. But if it holds together without packing, it's just right—and you can get on with your digging!

MAKING CENTS

Don't want to bother with bare-root perennials? Then try this super money-saving tip: Buy potted perennials at end-of-season sales, then bring them home and divide them *before* planting. By the next season, you'll have two, three, four, or even more great-looking perennials for less than the normal price of one clump!

Barnyard Booster Mix

This supercharged mix is one of my favorite brews for feeding flowers all season long. (And don't waste the material that's left in the "tea bag"; toss it onto your compost pile to make more good food for your bloomers!)

INSTRUCTIONS: Put these ingredients in a piece of cheesecloth or burlap to create a "tea bag," and soak it in a bucket or tub of warm water until the water is dark brown. Dilute the liquid with water until it is the color of weak tea, then water your bloomers with it every two or three weeks throughout the growing season.

INGREDIENTS:

1 part manure
1 part peat moss
1 part gypsum
1 part plant food (such as 5-10-5)

◆ DON'T GO OVERBOARD

Annuals and perennials need a lot of nutrients to produce loads of gorgeous flowers all through the summer. But don't feed them a lot of inorganic fertilizers because they'll go hog-wild on all that food. Sure, they'll grow fast and lush, but once they use up the food, they'll be starving again in no time. Instead, feed them lightly, but often with one of my liquid tonics, such as my Barnyard Booster Mix (above), to provide a continuous supply of nutrients. Your plants will grow more steadily, bloom better, and stay healthier than you ever dreamed possible!

ASK JERRY

Q *Is there a way that I can put wood ashes to good use in my garden?*

A Apply potassium-packed ashes to your garden at the rate of one bushel per 50 square feet to encourage good root growth. And scatter some onto your compost pile, too!

Bed Energizing Mix

When the gardening bug bites in spring, there's nothing to do but grab a shovel and get your garden started. Whip up a batch of my Bed Energizing Mix, spread it over your flower beds-to-be, and then get busy digging!

INSTRUCTIONS: Mix these ingredients in a large wheelbarrow, then work the mixture into the soil before you plant. (This amount is enough to cover about 100 sq. ft.) This combination provides a steady supply of nutrients well suited for just about any annual or perennial you'll put in.

INGREDIENTS:

50 lbs. of peat moss

25 lbs. of gypsum

10 lbs. of organic plant food (such as 5-10-5)

4 bushels of compost

◆ BE SWEET TO SWEET PEAS

If you love growing sweet peas as much as I do, you'll *love* this power-packed mix: It'll get them growin' like nobody's business! To start off, dig a 2-foot-deep trench (it can be a narrow one). Now mix 1 part peat moss with 1 part sharp sand. To each bushel of this mixture, add 1 tablespoon of bonemeal, 1 tablespoon of super phosphate, and 1 teaspoon of potassium sulfate. For areas that are not alkaline, add 2 tablespoons each of ground dolomitic limestone and ground chalk limestone. Fill the trench with this mix, then plant your seeds. With soil preparation like this, you'll get *amazing* results!

GREAT IDEA!

Planning to put in a rock garden this year?

To create the perfect growing conditions for plants that like their soil lean and mean, mix equal parts coarse sand, compost or leaf mold, and gravel. Spread this mix over the soil and work it in before planting; toss an extra handful into each planting hole as well.

Bedding Plant Starter Brew

Once you're satisfied that you're getting the healthiest transplants possible (see "Making Cents," below), bring them home and treat them with this starter brew until you're ready to get them in the ground.

INSTRUCTIONS: Mix these ingredients in a watering can, and feed this formula to your adopted seedlings every other time you water them. Give them a good soak with it just before you set them out, too, then stand back and enjoy the best-looking bloomers on the block!

INGREDIENTS:

2 tsp. of fish emulsion
2 tsp. of dishwashing liquid
1 tsp. of whiskey
1 qt. of water

◆ A PINCH IN TIME

It may seem cruel, but pinching or snipping off the tops of the stems and removing any flowers will do your transplants a big favor. They'll put more energy into growing new roots, so they'll settle in quicker. Plus, they'll come back a whole lot bushier, with lots more blooms—and that's what flower gardening is all about!

When you're shopping for bedding plants in spring, don't be too quick to plunk down your hard-earned dough! Before you buy, take a close look at the flowers, stems, and leaves—both the tops and bottoms—for signs of pests or diseases. Carefully tip each plant out of its pot to make sure it has healthy white, yellow, or bright brown roots—not black or rotted, or wound around each other. And look at the overall plant to see if it has yellow foliage, or spindly stems with few leaves. A sickly plant is no bargain at any price!

Beetle Juice

Are beetles chomping at your beautiful bloomers? My Beetle Juice can save the day. This recipe sure isn't for the squeamish, but nothing beats it for fighting bad beetles!

INSTRUCTIONS: Collect the beetles and whirl 'em up in an old blender (one you'll never again use for food) with 2 cups of water. Strain the liquid through cheesecloth and mix in the dishwashing liquid. Pour about ¼ cup into a 1 gallon hand-held sprayer and fill the rest of the jar with water. Spray your plants from top to bottom, and make sure you coat both sides of the leaves. Wear gloves when handling this mixture, and be sure to clean your blender with hot, soapy water when you're done.

INGREDIENTS:
½ cup of beetles (both larvae and adult beetles, dead or alive)
1 tsp. of dishwashing liquid
Water

◆ BEAT THE BEETLES

Many beetles are actually good guys in the garden, eating bad bugs that spoil your flower fun. But there *are* a few that can cause problems—*big* problems—when they start feeding in your flower beds. If you spot beetles breakfasting on your bloomers, pick them off by hand and drop them into soapy water. (Early morning is a good time for beetle-hunting, by the way, because cooler temperatures make these pests sluggish and easier to catch.) Once you have a bunch of beetles, use them to whip up a batch of my Beetle Juice (above).

TERRIFIC TIME⊠SAVERS

Don't spend time scraping rust off your gardening tools! Simply store them in a pail of clean, dry sand. The sand will keep them rust-free when they're not in use.

Blossom-Pusher Tonic #1

When flowers fail to perform, it's typically because they're either dirty or tired (or both). Here's a great way to clean 'em up and green 'em up in a hurry. The first step is to perk up your soil with this simple dry mixture.

INSTRUCTIONS: Mix these ingredients in a bucket, and apply the mixture to your flower beds with a broadcast spreader. Follow up with my Blossom-Pusher Tonic #2 (see **page 118**) to really get things growin'!

INGREDIENTS:
$1/3$ lb. of sugar
$1/3$ lb. of Epsom salts
$1/3$ lb. of gypsum

◆ GIVE 'EM A PINCH

Would you believe that you can get better blooms by pinching *off* some flower buds? Sounds crazy, I know, but it works—honest! You see, pinching out the smaller side buds from a cluster directs all that stem's energy into the main bud, so you get a bigger bloom. That's how florists get those huge "football" mums, and it works great on dahlias, peonies, and roses, too.

If you'd rather have *more*, but slightly smaller, blooms, do just the opposite: Pinch out the main bud on the stem, and let the smaller side buds get all the growing energy.

GRANDMA PUTT'S POINTERS ☞ Ever wish your favorite flowers would last longer? With a little of Grandma Putt's garden magic, you can bring tired perennials back to life and enjoy blooms for months longer than everyone else! Simply cut back bushy plants like catmints by one-half to two-thirds after their main summer showing of flowers. They'll be back in bloom within a few weeks, and flower their fool heads off for the rest of the growing season.

Blossom-Pusher Tonic #2

Once you've used my Blossom-Pusher Tonic #1 (see **page 117**) to feed your faded flowers, it's time to get those leaves clean and shiny, so they can get back to their job of feeding your flowers.

INSTRUCTIONS: Mix these ingredients in a 20 gallon hose-end sprayer, and overspray your flower beds to the point of run-off. This'll wash the dirt right off those leaves—

AND help energize the dry mix at the same time. Before you know it, your flowers will be back to blooming like crazy!

INGREDIENTS:

1 cup of apple juice
1 cup of Gatorade®
$\frac{1}{2}$ **cup of ammonia**
$\frac{1}{2}$ **cup of Pedialite®**

◆ FLOWERS LIKE A COOL DRINK, TOO!

The dog days of summer can be a tough time to keep flowers looking fresh. What's the problem? Well, if your summer-blooming annuals or perennials tend to develop droopy-looking leaves and stop flowering as the mercury rises, bone-dry soil is often the culprit. Fortunately, regular watering can perk up plants in a jiffy, so be prepared to drench those spots once a week during dry weather, and you'll keep the color coming even through scorching summer spells.

ASK JERRY

Q *My flower garden tends to fizzle out by early fall. Got any suggestions for fall color?*

A Take a drive down a country road to get some inspiration. Roadside wildflowers are a super source of ideas for your fall flower garden. Asters top the list for autumn color, and boltonia bears clouds of daisy-like fall flowers in white or pink. Include some goldenrods, too—'Fireworks' has golden blooms that literally explode into flower in fall, just as its name suggests.

Chamomile Mildew Chaser

Believe it or not, you can protect your flowers from powdery mildew with a plant that may already be growing in your herb garden—chamomile! Simply apply the following mix at the first sign of trouble (or as a preventive measure in damp weather), and every week throughout the growing season.

INGREDIENTS:

4 chamomile tea bags
2 tbsp. of Murphy's Oil Soap®
1 qt. of boiling water

INSTRUCTIONS: Put the tea bags in a pot, pour the boiling water over them, and let the tea steep for an hour or so until the brew is good and strong. Let it cool, then mix in the Murphy's Oil Soap. Pour the tea into a 6 gallon hose-end sprayer, and spray all of your flower beds thoroughly. Try to apply this elixir early in the day, so your plants' leaves can dry by nightfall.

◆ MILDEW ALERT!

Of all the funky fungi that can affect your flowers, powdery mildew is probably the most common you'll run across. Symptoms include white to powdery gray patches on leaves, buds, or stems. Affected plant parts are distorted and eventually drop off. This dastardly disease runs rampant when days are warm and nights are cool and humid—common conditions in late summer and early fall, or sometimes in spring.

IDEA!

GREAT

Is powdery mildew making unsightly white spots on your asters, bee balm, or mums?

If so, then pruning is a good first line of defense. In spring or early summer, snip off one-third to one-half of the stems in the clump, right at ground level. This reduces crowding and improves air circulation, so that the funky fungi can't get a grip!

Compost Tea

Compost tea is the healthiest thing any plant could ask for. It delivers a well-balanced supply of all the important nutrients—major and minor—to keep your flowers blooming their very best. But compost tea isn't just a good fertilizer; applied every two to three weeks, it's also one of your best weapons in the fight against dastardly diseases that can spoil your gardening fun!

INSTRUCTIONS: Pour the water into a large bucket or garbage pail. Scoop the compost into a cotton, burlap, or pantyhose sack, tie the sack closed, and put it in the water. Cover the bucket, and let the mix steep for seven days. Pour some of the finished tea into a watering can and sprinkle it around the base of your plants as a mild fertilizer. Put the rest in a hand-held sprayer and spritz it onto leaves.

> **INGREDIENTS:**
> 1 gal. of fresh compost
> 4 gal. of warm water

◆ GREEN GRASS IS GOLD

...for your compost pile, that is. If you're removing grass from a new garden site, pile it upside down (roots up) on your compost pile. (You may need to turn it once or twice so it doesn't start growing again.) Once it dies and rots, it yields gardener's gold—nutrient-rich compost.

MAKING CENTS

If your town collects yard waste, it probably also offers free (or really cheap) compost. If that's available where you live, then make the most of it! Get as much compost as you can haul, and spread a thick layer right over the area where you'd like a new flower bed to be. Plant directly into the compost, or mix in some topsoil first for super results.

Container Perennial Tonic

If you're like me, your plant-shopping tendencies tend to get way ahead of your planting schedule. The great thing about container-grown perennials is that they don't mind sitting around for days or weeks on end while they're waiting for you to get them in the ground. To keep them happy in the meantime, treat them to this marvelous master mix of fortified water.

INGREDIENTS:

1 tbsp. of 15-30-15 plant food
½ tsp. of gelatin
½ tsp. of dishwashing liquid
½ tsp. of clear corn syrup
½ tsp. of whiskey
¼ tsp. of instant tea granules
Water

INSTRUCTIONS: Mix the plant food, gelatin, dishwashing liquid, corn syrup, whiskey, and tea in a 1 gallon milk jug, filling the balance of the jug with water. Stir, and add ½ cup of the mixture to every gallon of water you use to water your container-grown perennials. And do try to get them in the ground as soon as you can; they'll grow even better once they can sink their roots into real soil!

◆ BE A SMART SHOPPER

Flower-filled annuals and perennials are a pretty sight, but they're not necessarily the best buy. It takes a lot of energy to make all of those flowers, so flowering plants have less to spare for making the new roots they need to adapt to life in your garden. You'll get much better results in the long run if you buy those that have healthy stems and leaves, but few or no flowers.

✳ IDEA!

GREAT

Do you know how to buy good transplants for a great price at grocery and discount stores?

The secret is to shop smart. Ask a manager when the next plant delivery is scheduled, then show up to shop within a day or two after that.

Crazy Daisy Spray

Who'd have thought that pretty perennials could also pack a punch in the pest control department? Sun-loving painted daisies—also called pyrethrum daisies—are a snap to grow in any sunny, well-drained site, and their beautiful blooms contain a potent pest-fighting compound that you can easily extract right at home!

INSTRUCTIONS: Pour the alcohol over the flower heads and let sit overnight. Strain out the flowers, then store the extract in a labeled and sealed container. When you need it, mix the extract with 3 quarts of water, then pour into a hand-held sprayer. This tonic will control a wide range of garden pests.

INGREDIENTS:

$1/8$ cup of 70% isopropyl (rubbing) alcohol

1 cup of packed, fresh painted daisy flower heads

◆ NOT JUST FOR THE SUMMER

To have a steady supply of daisy spray all year-round, pick some extra flowers when they are fully open, and spread them on screens in a warm, dry, dark place. When they're dry, pack them into tightly sealed jars, and store in a cool, dark place. To make them into a spray, grind up a few flowers with a mortar and pestle. Mix the dust with a splash of dish-washing liquid, dilute it with a cup or two of water, pour the mixture into a hand-held sprayer, and spray wherever pests are a problem.

GRANDMA PUTT'S POINTERS ☞ When she needed a pest control helper that worked cheap, Grandma Putt would invite a toad to move into her garden! She knew that a single toad can eat between 10,000 and 20,000 insects and other creepy crawlies a year. To make a toad abode for your own yard, knock a doorway out of the rim of an old clay pot, then nestle it upside down in a shady spot.

Cut Flower–Saver Solution

I love having fresh-cut flowers indoors, but I definitely DON'T like paying a buck or more per bloom at a flower shop. And there's no reason to do that, when your backyard flower garden can provide all the blooms you could ever use! To keep your cut flowers in prime form from the get-go, take a pail of tepid water into the garden when you go out to harvest. And when you are ready to arrange them, mix up a batch of this flower-saver solution.

INGREDIENTS:

1 cup of regular lemon-lime
   soda (not diet)
¼ tsp. of bleach
3 cups of warm water (110°F)

INSTRUCTIONS: Mix these ingredients in an old container, and pour the solution into a clean vase. It'll make those posies perk right up. Add more solution as needed every few days to keep the water level topped off. You'll be AMAZED at how much better your cut flowers look!

◆ GIVE DRYING A TRY

Want to keep extra-special blooms looking great for months? Cut them on a sunny, dry morning—never right after a rain—when they look their very best. Then mix 3 cups of borax and 1 cup of cornmeal in a sealable container. Place the freshly picked flowers in the container and cover them with the mixture. Let stand for four to five days, then enjoy the dried blooms in bouquets or crafts.

TERRIFIC TIME⬛SAVERS

If you don't have any lemon-lime soda on hand to make my Cut Flower–Saver Solution (above), mix 2 tablespoons of vinegar and 1 teaspoon of sugar in 1 quart of warm water, and put this tonic in your vase before adding any flowers. The blooms will stay in great shape for a week or more!

Cutting Keeper Soil Mix

One of the best ways of making new plants from the ones you already have is to take cuttings. The resulting plants reach flowering size a whole lot quicker than seed-grown plants. All you do is snip off 3- to 5-inch-long stem tips. Then remove the leaves on the bottom half of each cutting, and insert the stem halfway into its own peat pot filled with this super soil mix.

INSTRUCTIONS: Mix the sand, soil, and peat moss in a bucket, and add water until the mixture is evenly moist. Fill each peat pot, tap the base of the pot on a table to settle the soil a bit, then insert a cutting. When you're done, water the new cuttings thoroughly, then set them in an old aquarium or clear plastic sweater box. They'll be rooted before you know it!

INGREDIENTS:

2 parts sand
2 parts soil
2 parts peat moss
Water

◆ AVOID THE BIG CHILL

The secret to growing big, healthy cuttings every time? Keep their toes warm! You see, keeping the tops of the cuttings on the cool side (65°F or so) slows down water loss from the leaves. That's important, because cuttings don't have roots to drink up any more water if they get thirsty—they'll just wilt. But warm *soil* gets cuttings to grow roots fast, and that means big plants in a jiffy.

ASK JERRY

Q You've sold me on the importance of giving cuttings "bottom heat," but just how do I do that?

A I like to use a heat mat, the kind sold for seed-starting. Set pots of cuttings in shallow trays, and set the trays on the heat mat. Then just plug it in, and get growing!

124   FABULOUS FLOWERS

Cutting Keeper Transplant Tonic

It's easy to tell when cuttings planted in peat pots have made new roots, because you can actually SEE the new roots coming out of the bottom of the pot. Once your cuttings reach this stage, it's time to move them up to larger clay or plastic pots. Set the newly potted cuttings on a shallow tray, then give them a dose of this tonic to help them adjust to their new homes.

INGREDIENTS:
$\frac{1}{2}$ tsp. of all-purpose plant food
$\frac{1}{2}$ tsp. of vitamin B_1 plant starter
$\frac{1}{2}$ cup of weak tea water*
1 gal. of warm water

INSTRUCTIONS: Mix these ingredients in a watering can, and gently pour the tonic through the soil. Allow it to drain for 15 minutes or so, then pour off any excess tonic in the tray and use it on your other plants.

Soak a used tea bag and 1 teaspoon of dishwashing liquid in a gallon of warm water until the mix is light brown.

◆ PERENNIALS FOR PENNIES

Big garden, but a small budget? Grow plants from cuttings, divisions, and seeds. That way, you can buy a single plant and make all the copies you want without spending another dime! To make caring for baby plants a snap, dig a small garden in a protected area near your house. (Make sure it's handy to the hose, too.) Grow them in rows until they're big enough to go into the yard.

GREAT IDEA!

How do you know when a plant is ready for cutting?

The best time to take cuttings is from early to midsummer, when tender new growth has had a chance to toughen. To see if a stem is ready, bend it over. If it snaps off cleanly, it's perfect cutting material.

Damping-Off Prevention Tonic

Don't let that darn damping-off disease destroy your seedlings! Keep those funky fungi at bay from the very beginning by using a sterile seed-starting medium and this terrific tonic.

INSTRUCTIONS: Mix these ingredients in a large bowl or bucket and let steep for at least an hour. Strain out the flowers (toss them in your compost pile), and let the remaining liquid cool. Mist-spray your seedlings with this tonic as soon as their little heads appear above the soil to keep dastardly damping-off fungi at bay.

INGREDIENTS:

4 tsp. of dry chamomile flowers
1 tsp. of dishwashing liquid
1 qt. of boiling water

◆ MOSS IS THE BOSS

Unlike garden-sown seeds, indoor-sown seeds don't have to deal with pesky pests, hungry critters, or bad weather. But they can still have disease problems, and damping-off is just one of them. To stop fatal fungi before they start, sprinkle milled sphagnum moss (available at garden centers) over the entire surface of each pot, either before or right after you sow your flower seeds. For extra protection, follow up with my Damping-Off Prevention Tonic (above).

TERRIFIC TIME⌛SAVERS

Instead of squinting to see super-tiny seeds—like begonias—as you sow, mix 'em with a pinch of unflavored, powdered gelatin. The light-colored gelatin makes it a cinch to see where you've sown the seeds. Plus, it contains a bit of nitrogen that the seedlings can use to grow strong!

Daylily Transplant Tonic

Are your daylily clumps looking a little crowded? You can divide these no-fail perennials pretty much any time during the growing season, but spring and fall are ideal. To get your new divisions off to a great start without skipping a beat, give them a taste of this tonic.

INSTRUCTIONS: Mix these ingredients in a large bucket. Then just before setting your divided daylilies into their new planting holes, dip out 2 cups of the mixture and pour it into each hole. Your transplants will be growing like gangbusters in no time!

INGREDIENTS:

$\frac{1}{2}$ can of beer
2 tbsp. of dishwashing liquid
2 tbsp. of ammonia
2 tbsp. of fish emulsion
1 tbsp. of hydrogen peroxide
$\frac{1}{4}$ tsp. of instant tea granules
2 gal. of warm water

◆ THE EYES HAVE IT

Before you chop up a clump of daylilies—or any other perennials—into many small pieces, count the "eyes," or buds. Ideally, each new piece should have three to five eyes, along with a good complement of roots, to boot. While divisions that have only a single eye will grow, it's easier to handle slightly larger pieces with more eyes, and they'll fill in far more quickly.

GRANDMA PUTT'S POINTERS
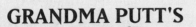 To make the kindest cuts when dividing perennials, be sure all your tools are clean and sharp. Spades and trowels with sharp blades cut through roots neatly, without ripping or tearing at them. One of Grandma Putt's favorite tools was an old kitchen knife. It had a long, serrated blade that never seemed to get dull, and it would slice through those clumps like butter!

Dog-Be-Gone Tonic

Whether it's a Border collie rolling in your begonias or a dachshund digging in your daisies, the pitter-patter of pet paws can do a real number on your flower beds. Either way, you end up with smashed plants, compacted soil, and lots of frustration. What's the solution? Try my Dog-Be-Gone Tonic to let Rover know he's not welcome there.

INSTRUCTIONS: Chop the garlic, onions, and jalapeño pepper finely, and then combine with the rest of the ingredients. Let the mixture sit and marinate for 24 hours, strain it through cheesecloth or old pantyhose, then sprinkle the resulting liquid on any areas where dogs are a problem. This spicy potion will keep man's best friend from becoming your garden's worst enemy!

INGREDIENTS:

2 cloves of garlic
2 small onions
1 jalapeño pepper
1 tbsp. of cayenne pepper
1 tbsp. of Tabasco® sauce
1 tbsp. of chili powder
1 tbsp. of dishwashing liquid
1 qt. of warm water

◆ GET ON THE BALL

Stake tips poking up through your flowers can be an accident waiting to happen. You lean over to sniff or pick a bloom, and "Ow!"—you get poked in the arm or eye. There's a simple and safe solution: old tennis or racquet balls. Simply cut a slit or small hole in each ball, and stick it over the top of a stake. If you don't like the color, spray paint the balls black or dark green before putting them in place.

TERRIFIC TIME⌛SAVERS

Instead of struggling to bag, burn, or shred thorny rose and berry stems, cut them up and scatter them around your prized plants and shrubs. They'll keep rabbits and other hungry critters away—cats, too!

Fabulous Foliar Formula

If you have sandy soil, you know it. It feels gritty when you rub it between your fingers, and you're constantly hauling water to plants that still turn yellow and grow poorly. The secret to successful sandy-soil gardening is simple: Bulk up your soil with lots of organic matter to help it hold more moisture and nutrients. And for bright, shiny leaves in even the sandiest soil, feed your plants this fantastic formula every three weeks.

INGREDIENTS:

1 can of beer
$\frac{1}{2}$ cup of fish emulsion
$\frac{1}{2}$ cup of ammonia
$\frac{1}{4}$ cup of blackstrap molasses
4 tbsp. of instant tea granules

INSTRUCTIONS: Mix these ingredients in a 20 gallon hose-end sprayer, and apply thoroughly until the mixture starts running off the leaves. This formula works best on annuals and perennials that aren't blooming. If your plants are already in flower, aim the spray at the foliage, and try to avoid wetting the blooms.

◆ THE SECRET TO A STUNNING GARDEN

What do you look at while you're waiting for your plants to bloom, or after they're finished flowering? The foliage! So when you pick out bloomers for your garden, look for those that have pretty leaves, too, and you're guaranteed to have the best-looking garden from spring to frost.

ASK JERRY

Q *I'd really like to attract more butterflies to my yard. Got any suggestions on how to do it?*

A I sure do! Remember that butterflies get thirsty, too, so make your birdbath do double duty: Fill it with rounded stones that stick out from the water surface. Then the butterflies can rest on the stones and drink without falling in.

Fall Bedtime Snack

In most areas, fall is the ideal time to get started on a new flower garden. There's not much else to do at this time of year, and the weather is usually quite pleasant. You can work at a comfortable pace, since you're not in a hurry to plant, and the soil will have time to settle before spring planting. To make sure your new planting area will be as loose and fertile as possible, treat it to this snack as soon as you are done digging.

INSTRUCTIONS: Mix these ingredients in a wheelbarrow, then apply the mix to every 100 sq. ft. of soil. Work it into the soil and cover with a thick blanket of leaves, straw, or other organic mulch. This rich mixture works miracles for lightening up heavy clay soil, but it's also a good booster for average and sandy soils, too.

> **INGREDIENTS:**
> 25 lbs. of gypsum
> 10 lbs. of organic plant food
> (either 4-12-4 or 5-10-5)
> 5 lbs. of bonemeal

◆ PUT YOUR BEDS TO BED

After frost hits, it's time for a quick bit of clean-up. Pull out dead annuals and cut back perennials, except for the ones that provide winter interest (like ornamental grasses) or food for birds (like asters). Add the trimmings to your compost pile, unless the plant they came from was bothered by pests or diseases; in that case, you're better off throwing them in the trash.

GREAT IDEA!

Do you know the best time for planting, dividing, or moving plants in your flower garden?

The answer is fall. While you're at it, ensure a good restart by adding a handful of dry oatmeal and human hair to the soil when replanting.

Flower Defender Tonic

Bad bugs feed on lots of different flowers, so it's smart to be ready for them with my Flower Defender Tonic. This power-packed mix will wipe out just about any garden bugs—GUARANTEED!

INSTRUCTIONS: Mix the dishwashing liquid, tobacco tea, mouthwash, and Tabasco sauce in a 20 gallon hose-end sprayer, filling the balance of the jar with warm water. Then bathe all of your bloomers with this bug-busting elixir to send those pesky pests running for the hills!

> **INGREDIENTS:**
> 1 cup of dishwashing liquid
> 1 cup of tobacco tea*
> 1 cup of antiseptic mouthwash
> 1/4 cup of Tabasco® sauce
> Warm water

To make tobacco tea, place half a handful of chewing tobacco in an old nylon stocking and soak it in a gallon of hot water until the mixture is dark brown.

◆ What's Bugging Your Bloomers?

Annuals with yellowed leaves may simply need a snack, but before you reach for the fertilizer, rule out other possible problems first. Whiteflies are the culprit if clouds of tiny white bugs fly up when you brush the foliage. Webbing on stems and under leaves and yellow-speckled leaves are signs of spider mites. Spraying with insecticidal soap or my Flower Defender Tonic (above) will send either of these pests packing!

TERRIFIC TIME⊠SAVERS

No matter what weedy foes you're fighting, baby weeds are always easier to pull than full-grown adults. They also haven't set seeds yet—and as the saying goes, "One year's seeding makes seven years' weeding." So make it a habit to always pull weed seedlings as soon as you spot them, and you'll save yourself a whole lot of work in the long run!

Flower Flea Fluid

"Flower fleas" was Grandma Putt's name for leafhoppers. When she spotted any of these feisty little guys bugging her prize asters and dahlias, she'd let the tiny culprits have it with this powerful potion.

INSTRUCTIONS: Mix these ingredients in a hand-held sprayer. Apply liberally to leaves until they're dripping wet on both sides to kill leafhoppers in a hurry. If hoppers are still around a few days later, spray 'em with a mixture of 2 tablespoons of vegetable oil and 1 tablespoon of baby shampoo mixed in a quart of water.

*To make tobacco tea, place half a handful of chewing tobacco in an old nylon stocking, and soak it in a gallon of hot water until the mixture is dark brown.

> **INGREDIENTS:**
> 1 cup of tobacco tea*
> 1 tbsp. of baby shampoo
> 1 qt. of water

◆ KEEP AHEAD OF HOPPERS

With their powerful rear legs, leafhoppers can jump around just like fleas. You'll know you have a leafhopper problem if you see brown, curled edges on the leaves of your flowering plants. As they feed, they can spread viruses, too—all the more reason to make sure you keep leafhoppers from gettin' ahead of you in the garden! In addition to using my Flower Flea Fluid (above), you can keep small infestations from mushrooming by giving your plants a blast with the garden hose. It'll kill most of the marauders, and any that are left will be targets for hungry birds.

MAKING CENTS

To rub out all kinds of pesky pests, simply keep a bottle of rubbing alcohol on hand in your garden shed. It's a cheap and easy way to get rid of all sorts of pests, including aphids, leafhoppers, mealybugs, spider mites, and whiteflies. Simply mix ½ cup of rubbing alcohol with a quart of water, and lightly mist-spray any infested plants.

Flower Garden Nightcap

When it's time to close up your flower beds for the season, cover the frozen ground with finely mowed grass clippings or chopped leaves, then overspray with this nightcap to settle them in for a long winter's nap.

INSTRUCTIONS: Mix these ingredients in a 20 gallon hose-end sprayer, and saturate the mulch blanket. This tonic feeds your mulch, which in turn will feed your garden while it protects your perennials all through the winter.

INGREDIENTS:

1 can of regular cola (not diet)
1 cup of baby shampoo
$\frac{1}{2}$ cup of ammonia
2 tbsp. of instant tea granules

◆ AVOID THE HEAVING JEEBIES

While *people* prefer to bundle up at the drop of the thermometer, your *plants* will be much happier if you don't cover them up until *after* the ground freezes. Why wait so long? Because your real enemy isn't chilly temperatures; it's those midwinter thaws that cause the ground to shift, resulting in root damage. Unprotected plants that are heaved out of the soil can die from exposure or may just dry out. But if you mulch soon after the ground freezes, you'll keep the ground colder, lessening the chance of heaving due to a warm spell.

ASK JERRY

Q *Is it worth buying perennials at end-of-season sales? And if so, should I plant them right away or wait until spring?*

A Late-summer and fall sales are a great time for gardeners to shop 'til they drop. If you get 'em early, plant bargains can go out in the garden up to six weeks before the first fall frost. Keep later-season purchases in a protected spot over the winter, then plant them in spring.

Fragrant Pest Fighter

People love perfumed perennials, but pests sure don't! The next time you're out in your herb garden, gather the ingredients for this aromatic pest control spray.

INSTRUCTIONS: Place the herbs in a 1 quart glass jar; fill with boiling water, cover, and let it sit until cool. Add ⅛ cup of the liquid to the 2 cups of room-temperature water and the Murphy's Oil Soap. Pour into a hand-held sprayer, and apply to your plants to keep pests at bay.

INGREDIENTS:

½ cup of fresh tansy or mugwort leaves

½ cup of fresh lavender flowers and/or leaves

½ cup of fresh sage leaves

Boiling water

2 cups of room-temperature water

1 tsp. of Murphy's Oil Soap®

◆ A GARDEN THAT MAKES SCENTS

To sample the fragrance of scented foliage plants, you need to rub or crush the leaves. That makes them a perfect choice for planting along paths, where legs will brush by them and feet will step on them. Some of my all-time favorites for perfumed paths include lavenders, lemon balm, lemon thyme, and southernwood. Scented geraniums are also great for edging a walkway.

Between stepping stones, plant mat-forming wild thyme and Roman chamomile, which release their scent as you step on them.

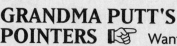

GRANDMA PUTT'S POINTERS ☞ Want to enjoy flowery fragrances from your garden even in winter? Try this trick I picked up from Grandma Putt: Save the dried stalks of fragrant herbs and other scented plants from your garden, and tie them up in small bundles with cotton string. Toss a bundle or two into your fireplace, and you'll enjoy a heavenly reminder of summer!

Fungus Fighter Tonic

When it comes to handling plant diseases, an ounce of prevention is worth a pound of fungicide. Fungal diseases thrive on wet leaves, so water plants early in the day to let the foliage dry before nightfall. And if diseases still appear despite your best preventive efforts, then mix up a batch of this molasses-rich brew.

INSTRUCTIONS: Mix the molasses, powdered milk, and baking soda into a paste. Place the mixture into the toe of an old nylon stocking, and let it steep in a gallon of warm water for several hours. Then strain, and apply the liquid with a hand-held sprayer as a fungus-fighting tonic for your garden every two weeks throughout the growing season.

INGREDIENTS:
$^1\!/_2$ cup of molasses
$^1\!/_2$ cup of powdered milk
1 tsp. of baking soda
1 gal. of warm water

◆ RAISING THE ROOTS

Too wet to dig down? Then it's time to grow up—with raised beds, that is! To try this approach, mix 1 part coarse builder's sand with 3 parts compost, rotted sawdust, and/or rotted manure. Spread it thickly over the area where you want to plant, rake it smooth, and let the site settle for three or four weeks. Then top off the area with bagged topsoil before planting.

Topsoil

ASK JERRY

Q For the past three years, I've had really bad luck with my annual flowers. I've tried giving them regular fertilizer, but it hasn't helped. Any suggestions?

A For each 100 square feet of flower bed, I want you to spread this mix over the soil, then spade it in well: 6 bags of shredded leaves, 2 bags of grass clippings, 1 cup of Epsom salts, and $^1\!/_4$ cup of sugar. That will really give your annuals something to grow big and strong on.

Go, Go, Geraniums! Tonic

Nothin' says "It's summertime!" like the bright blooms of these classic flower garden favorites. They're a breeze to grow, and they'll produce their rounded clusters of scarlet, pink, or white flowers all the way from spring until frost. If you bring your plants indoors in fall, they'll bloom all winter long, too! To keep your potted geraniums in tip-top shape, use the following formula to give 'em a quick jump start.

INGREDIENTS:

Epsom salts
1 cup of beer
4 tbsp. of instant tea granules
2 tsp. of baby shampoo
1 gal. of water

INSTRUCTIONS: Sprinkle the soil with 1 tablespoon of Epsom salts for each 3 inches of pot size. Then mix the remaining ingredients in a watering can, and use the solution to water the salts into the soil around your plants.

◆ JERRY'S GERANIUM BLOOM BOOSTER

To keep your geraniums growin' like gangbusters all year-round, mix 2 tablespoons of baking soda with 1 tablespoon of baby shampoo in 1 gallon of water. Treat your geraniums to a good taste of this liquid every two weeks throughout the growing season. You won't believe the big, bright blooms you'll get month after month after month!

GREAT IDEA!

Want to know the best way to feed your flowers?

Give 'em a daily dose of this fortified drink. Take any plant-based kitchen scraps—like table scraps (no meat or fats), eggshells, and potato peelings—and put 'em in an old blender. Fill it to the top with water, blend on high, then pour around the base of your bloomers.

Horsetail Anti-Fungus Spray

Horsetail loves wet soil in the garden, so it's great for soggy spots where nothing else will grow. This vigorous perennial spreads quickly, though, so keep it under control by picking lots of the stems to make this great fungus-fighting tonic.

INSTRUCTIONS: Put the stems and water in a large pot. Bring to a boil, then let simmer for at least 30 minutes. Let cool, then strain out the stems. Store the leftover liquid concentrate in a glass jar. To use, mix 1 part concentrate with 10 parts water. Spray disease-prone plants, such as bee balm and garden phlox, every four to seven days to prevent powdery mildew and other fungal problems from developing.

INGREDIENTS:

$1/8$ cup of dried horsetail stems

1 gal. of water

◆ GRIME IS A CRIME

For quick and easy clean-up once you're done working in your flower garden, place a bar of soap in the toe of an old nylon stocking or pantyhose leg, and hang it near an outdoor faucet. Instead of making a mess inside the house, you can scrub up outside without even having to take the soap out of the stocking. Believe you me, this simple secret has saved many a gardener's marriage!

ASK JERRY

Q *Why do my flowers look so dismal after I water them? Some even get a white powder on them.*

A The white stuff is powdery mildew, and it comes from improper watering. Water with a soaker hose early in the morning, and avoid sprinkling the flowers from above. This should keep your flowers happy and healthy. If you continue to have a problem, try my Horsetail Anti-Fungus Spray (above).

Hot Bite Brew

If you have plants that deer always like to sample, treat 'em with this spicy brew to discourage their browsing.

INSTRUCTIONS: Mix the cayenne pepper with the hot water in a bottle, and shake well. Let the mixture sit overnight, then pour off the liquid without disturbing the sediment. Mix the liquid with the remaining ingredients in a hand-held sprayer. Spritz critter-susceptible plants as often as you can to keep 'em hot, hot, hot! It's strong medicine, so make sure you wear rubber gloves while you're handling this brew.

INGREDIENTS:

3 tbsp. of cayenne pepper
1 tbsp. of Tabasco® sauce
1 tbsp. of ammonia
1 tbsp. of baby shampoo
2 cups of hot water

◆ OH, DEER!

Deer are probably the toughest animal pests to control in your garden. Once they develop a taste for your flowers, they're likely to come back again and again. So *before* your beds and borders become the next all-you-can-eat salad bar for the local herd, try sprinkling repellents such as bloodmeal or human hair trimmings on and around the plants. It can also help to hang bars of strongly scented deodorant soap at deer nose level.

GREAT IDEA!

How do you keep rabbits and other pesky critters from chomping your flowers to bits?

While you may see a neatly planted flower bed, believe you me, rabbits and their allies see a "Free Eats" sign! Transplants are most at risk from these hungry little fellas during their first week or two in the garden, so protect them from the get-go by covering them up with small cages made of poultry wire.

Iris Energizer Tonic

I scream, you scream, we all scream—for iris! It's hard to believe that such easy-to-grow plants can produce such exquisite flowers. I think of them as the orchids of the perennial garden! To keep all of your irises at their eye-catching best, treat them to a taste of this magical mix at planting time.

INSTRUCTIONS: Mix these ingredients in a watering can, then drench the soil around your newly planted irises. Once they are established, keep them in top-notch form with a mixture of 4 parts bonemeal and 6 parts hydrated lime. Sprinkle the mixture around established plants in early spring. Use a hand fork to scratch it lightly into the soil, then get ready for the best iris blooms you've ever seen!

INGREDIENTS:
$\frac{1}{2}$ **cup of beer**
Vitamin B$_1$ plant starter (mixed at 25% of the recommended rate)
2 tbsp. of dishwashing liquid
1 gal. of warm water

◆ DON'T GET BORED

It's a fact of life: If you grow bearded irises, sooner or later, you'll have borers. To keep these plump, pink caterpillars from irritating your irises, discard any rhizomes with rot or visible larvae when you divide the plants. Also, cut back and destroy old leaves at the end of the season, and rake up any debris around your plants.

ASK JERRY

Q *How often should I divide my irises? And is there a certain time of year that's best?*

A Dig up and divide bearded irises every three years, in midsummer or early fall. Divide most other perennial irises in spring or early fall—every three to five years is fine. Siberian iris is the one exception: It's happiest left undisturbed, so divide these plants only if they begin to have blooming problems.

Magical Mildew Control

Crowded perennial clumps can have poor air circulation around the leaves and stems, so their foliage stays wet longer and diseases can get an early start. To stop funky fungi in their tracks, set out your perennials at the proper spacings at planting time. For extra protection, treat them with this tonic at the first sign of mildew.

INSTRUCTIONS: Mix these ingredients in a bucket, then pour the solution into a hand-held sprayer. Thoroughly douse your plants when you see telltale signs of mildew: dusty white or gray patches on leaves, stems, and buds.

INGREDIENTS:

4 tbsp. of baking soda
2 tbsp. of Murphy's Oil Soap®
1 gal. of warm water

◆ 'SNO JOKE!

Believe it or not, snow makes great mulch, so pile it on any plants that need a little extra insulation. But don't shovel snow on beds if it's likely to contain deicing salts, because the salt can harm plant roots.

◆ THESE FLOWERS FIGHT BACK

Want to say good-bye to mildew forever? Replace disease-prone perennials with mildew-resistant cultivars, such as 'Jacob Cline' bee balm and 'David' phlox. New ones are coming on the market every year, so be sure to ask what your local garden center has to offer each spring. You'll save yourself a load of trouble this way!

TERRIFIC TIME⊠SAVERS

The days may be long, but your gardening time is short—so what's your best weeding strategy? Make a quick sweep through your garden with a bag in one hand and your pruners in the other. Clip off all the weed flowers you see, bag 'em, and toss 'em in the garbage. Sure, the roots'll still be there, but at least they won't be making any more seeds before you have time for a more thorough weeding job!

Miracle Mum Booster

Whenever Grandma Putt set out new mums in spring, she'd always give 'em a little extra TLC. She'd fill the hole with plenty of compost, and then follow that up with a handful of this mix to get those mums growin' up right!

INSTRUCTIONS: Mix these ingredients in a 5 gallon bucket, then work a handful of the mixture into the bottom of each hole before planting. Mums love this stuff, as do many other perennials—so why not give all your new plantings a taste?

INGREDIENTS:

2 lbs. of dry oatmeal
2 lbs. of dry dog food, crushed
1 handful of human hair
$\frac{1}{2}$ cup of sugar

◆ DON'T LIGHT UP THE NIGHT

Mums don't set flower buds at just any old time. They need short days and a long period of darkness at night for the process to begin. Normally, conditions are right for flower buds to start forming by late July. But if you plant them under a lamppost or streetlight where they get light for part or all of the night, they may never flower! So now you know better.

GRANDMA PUTT'S POINTERS ☞ Come fall, Grandma Putt's garden was just filled with mums. They all stood up straight and tall, even though she never bothered staking them. Her secret? She'd pinch off the stem tips twice between late spring and early summer. But she never pinched them after the Fourth of July, because she knew that late-pinched shoots wouldn't have time to make flowers before the cold weather set in.

Mulch Moisturizer Tonic

Mulching your flower garden in spring will go a long way toward minimizing maintenance chores for the rest of the growing season. To really kick things into action, overspray your mulch with this fantastic formula.

INSTRUCTIONS: Mix these ingredients in a 20 gallon hose-end sprayer, and give your mulch a nice long, cool drink. Add more mulch as needed through the season to keep it at the same depth. Treat it with this spray each time you re-mulch, then get ready to have the most bloom-filled flower beds on your block!

INGREDIENTS:

1 can of regular cola (not diet)
½ cup of ammonia
½ cup of antiseptic mouthwash
½ cup of baby shampoo

◆ SPREAD THE WEALTH

There's no doubt that mulch is great for your garden—*if* you apply it properly! What I *don't* want you to do is pile it up around the base of your plants, so it looks like they're rising out of mini mulch mountains. It'll hold moisture against your plants' leaves and stems, and that's an open invitation for fungi, as well as borers, mice, and various other critters. Prevent these problems by keeping a mulch-free zone that's 2 or 3 inches wide around each plant.

GREAT IDEA!

Want to get the most out of your mulch?

Use it in the fight against weeds. Mulch will smother most weeds, and the few that do pop up can be easily pulled from the loose soil. For extra benefit, spread a 1-inch layer of compost first (this will help improve your soil). Top that with another 1 to 2 inches of shredded bark, pine needles, or chopped leaves. Then overspray the whole area with my Mulch Moisturizer Tonic (above) to give it a little extra kick.

Natural Nutrients for Neglected Soil

Unless you're SURE that your soil is naturally very fertile, it makes sense to take every opportunity to build it up for your flowers. This all-natural, home-blended fertilizer is just what you need to keep all your flowers looking great and growing their very best.

INGREDIENTS:

6 parts greensand or wood ashes

3 parts cottonseed meal

3 parts bonemeal

Gypsum

Limestone

INSTRUCTIONS: Mix the greensand or wood ashes, cottonseed meal, and bonemeal together. Add 2 cups of gypsum and 1 cup of limestone per gallon-size container of the resulting mixture. Apply 5 pounds of the mixture per 100 sq. ft. of garden area a few weeks before planting, or work it into the soil around established perennials.

◆ SPRING INTO ACTION

If you live in a hot-summer area, consider digging your new flower garden in late winter or early spring, then letting the site sit until fall. That way, the perennials can settle in when the weather's mild and moist, rather than hot and dry.

ASK JERRY

Q *Is there a way to test my soil to determine if it's too wet or too dry for flowers?*

A It's easy: First, water the area very thoroughly—really drench it. Then wait two days, dig a 6-inch-deep hole, and feel the soil at the bottom. If it's dry, your soil doesn't hold enough water to keep flowers happy. If it's still sopping wet, poor drainage is a problem. The solution for both sites: Work lots of organic matter, like chopped leaves, into the soil.

Nifty Hummingbird Nectar

Want to really bring your flower beds to life? Hummingbirds are nothing short of magic in the garden! These aerial daredevils can dart from flower to flower with more control than a fighter pilot, hover in midair, actually back up in midflight, and then zoom away at speeds of 50 to 60 miles per hour. Hummers will visit a feeder all summer long, once they get the idea it's filled with nectar. Sure, you can buy packets of nectar mix, but making your own is easy and inexpensive.

INGREDIENTS:

1 part white sugar (not honey, which hosts bacteria harmful to hummers)

4 parts water

A few drops of red food coloring (optional)

INSTRUCTIONS: Mix the ingredients in a saucepan and bring to a boil. Let it cool before filling your feeder.

Once hummers start coming, decrease the solution to about 1 part sugar to 8 parts water. No, this isn't the old bait-and-switch tactic—there's a good reason for diluting the solution. Hummingbirds can sometimes suffer a fatal liver disorder if they get too much sugar.

◆ KEEP IT CLEAN, PLEASE!

Replace the nectar in your hummingbird feeder every three days or so—every other day if temperatures are above 60°F. Wash the feeder with soap and scalding hot water, then rinse thoroughly before refilling. Old nectar and/or a dirty feeder can host hummingbird-harming bacteria.

IDEA!

GREAT

Baths are nice, but give hummingbirds a shower.

Hummers will visit birdbaths, but to really make them happy, install a fountain that sends up a fine mist. You can find these at places that specialize in supplies for feeding wild birds. The hummers will fly right through the mist to bathe in midair!

No Mo' Nematodes Tonic

When is a disease not due to a fungus, bacteria, or a virus? When it's caused by little critters called nematodes. These colorless, microscopic worms usually live in the soil, although some can climb up on plants. Say "No!" to pesky nematodes with this simple solution.

INSTRUCTIONS: Mix these ingredients in a 20 gallon hose-end sprayer, and thoroughly soak any area where nasty nematodes are doing their dirty work. It'll stop these pests in their tracks.

INGREDIENTS:

1 can of beer
1 cup of molasses

◆ BUBBLE BATH FOR YOUR BLOOMERS

I can't say this often enough—giving your plants a good washing before applying liquid fertilizers, weed killers, or pest controls can mean the difference between a garden that's just getting by and one that is healthy and growing. Why? Soap removes dust, dirt, and pollution from foliage pores, enabling plants to better take up the good stuff that follows. So before you apply fertilizers or controls, give your bloomers a bath with 1 cup of dishwashing liquid applied with a 20 gallon hose-end sprayer, or use my Plant Shampoo™.

ASK JERRY

Q *My plants look wilted, even though they're getting plenty of water. How can I tell if nematodes are to blame?*

A Above ground, the only symptom you may see of root-feeding nematodes is stunted or wilted leaves and shoots. But when you dig up the plants, you'll notice tiny galls all over the roots. Or, if foliar nematodes are at work, you'll see wedge-shaped sections of leaf that turn yellowish brown between the veins. It's usually best to dig up and destroy seriously affected plants. But if you catch the damage early, my No Mo' Nematodes Tonic (above) may help get rid of those wily worms for you.

Perennial Planting Potion

Ready to get your potted perennials in the ground? Start off by setting them to soak—pot and all—in a bucket of water for about 30 minutes. While they're soaking, whip up a batch of this powerful potion to get them off to a grand start.

INSTRUCTIONS: Mix these ingredients in a bucket, and pour ½ cup into each planting hole. One at a time, slip the perennials out of their pots, place them in the holes, and half-fill around the roots with soil. Add enough water to make a "soup," then let the water soak in for a few minutes. Finish filling the holes with soil, water again generously, and sprinkle any remaining Perennial Planting Potion around your new plants to toast their flower-filled future!

> **INGREDIENTS:**
> ½ can of beer
> ¼ cup of ammonia
> 2 tbsp. of hydrogen peroxide
> 1 tbsp. of dishwashing liquid
> 2 gal. of warm water

◆ SPRING OR FALL? IT'S YOUR CALL!

In most areas, early spring and early fall are ideal planting times for perennials. The best fall-planting conditions are a long, warm fall followed by a hard, freezing winter. But if your area tends to see a lot of freezing and thawing in winter, spring planting's a *much* better bet for you—*and* your plants!

GRANDMA PUTT'S POINTERS ☞

If she tipped a young plant out of its pot and saw a root ball that was all wrapped up, Grandma Putt knew it was time for some tough love! She'd use a knife or screwdriver to make shallow cuts along the sides of the root ball, then plant it as usual. This harsh treatment encouraged the roots to branch out, so they'd grow out into the soil and not continue their circling ways.

Perennial Seed Send-Off Tonic

Summer is a super time to start perennials from seed for blooms next spring. The ground is warm, so they'll germinate quickly, and they'll have plenty of time to produce good growth before cold winter weather returns. To give your perennial seeds an extra boost for super-quick sprouting, give them a bath in this send-off tonic.

INGREDIENTS:

1 cup of vinegar
1 tbsp. of baby shampoo or
   dishwashing liquid
2 cups of warm water

INSTRUCTIONS: Mix these ingredients in a small bucket, and soak your seeds in the solution overnight before planting them in well-prepared soil. This nourishing soak is sure to start 'em out strong and sturdy.

◆ SPICE UP SEED SOWING

Empty herb and spice jars—the ones with those plastic shaker lids that have holes in them—are absolutely perfect for sowing seeds. Drop a seed through one of the holes to make sure they'll fit through, then fill the jar with seeds and shake to sow! (Mixing some white play sand with the seeds before sowing makes it super-easy to see where you've already sprinkled.) After sowing, lightly cover the seeds and gently pat down the soil. And don't forget to add a label, so you'll remember what you sowed where!

TERRIFIC TIME⌛SAVERS

Not enough time to set out perennial seedlings in fall? Then use your basement window wells as handy winter cold frames. Simply cover the well with clear or white plastic (be sure the sunlight can get through), and seal around the edges with tape or caulk. You can water from inside the basement by lifting up one corner. That way, there'll be no need to go tramping through the snow to tend to your seedlings!

Perennial Transplant Tonic

Over the years, I've learned that some flowers are a little TOO vigorous, and they'll take over the whole backyard if you don't divide 'em. Others grow better after dividing because you get rid of the old, weak growth, which flowers poorly and attracts pests and diseases. Best of all, dividing is a great way to get loads of new flowers for free! So get out there and start chopping up those overgrown clumps, then soak 'em in my transplant tonic before replanting them.

INGREDIENTS:

1 can of beer
4 tbsp. of instant tea granules
2 tbsp. of dishwashing liquid
2 gal. of warm water

INSTRUCTIONS: Mix these ingredients in a bucket, and soak newly divided perennials in this tonic for about 10 minutes just before replanting them. When you're finished, dribble any leftover tonic around your newly settled divisions. It'll get 'em off on the right root and growin' like gangbusters—GUARANTEED!

◆ TIME TO DIVIDE THE DOUGHNUTS

Clumps of perennials that start looking like doughnuts are prime candidates for division. The doughnut syndrome—where a ring of healthy growth surrounds a dead-looking center—starts because the center is filled with old, sickly, or woody growth. Fortunately, there's an easy fix! Dig up the entire clump, and toss out any old growth from the middle. Cut the healthy growth into chunks, and replant.

GRANDMA PUTT'S POINTERS ☞ Can't remember what to divide when? Try Grandma Putt's simple rule of thumb: Divide spring-blooming plants in fall, and fall-blooming plants in spring. She made a few exceptions to this rule, because she knew that Oriental poppies and bearded irises are best off when divided in mid- to late summer.

Perfect Partners Planting Mix

Who says you can only plant annuals with annuals and perennials with perennials? Not me, that's for sure! Annuals are ideal for quick color and all-season bloom, while perennials provide dependable, easy-care flowers and foliage year after year from just one planting. Whether you're using annuals as a temporary filler around new perennials or as beautiful bedmates every year, my Perfect Partners Planting Mix will get the soil in great shape for ALL of your flowers.

INGREDIENTS:

4 cups of bonemeal
2 cups of gypsum
2 cups of Epsom salts
1 cup of wood ashes
1 cup of lime
4 tbsp. of medicated baby powder
1 tbsp. of baking powder
Peat moss

INSTRUCTIONS: Mix the bonemeal, gypsum, Epsom salts, wood ashes, lime, baby powder, and baking powder in a wheelbarrow with a bucketful of dried peat moss. Toss a handful into each planting hole, and scatter some over the soil around established clumps, too. Lightly scratch it into the soil, then water it in well before applying a 2- to 3-inch-thick layer of mulch over the whole area.

◆ DON'T KILL 'EM WITH KINDNESS

Lots of foliage, but few flowers? Most annuals enjoy rich soil, but it's possible for them to get too much of a good thing! Hold off on high-nitrogen fertilizers, and avoid working fresh farm animal manures into the soil just before planting.

Self-sowing annuals are a cheap and easy option for filling in between perennials. Plant 'em the first spring your perennials are in the ground, then let 'em sow around; they'll gradually die out once the perennials have filled in. Good choices include love-in-a-mist, Brazilian vervain, and larkspur.

Perfect Perennial Potting Soil

To get all of your potted perennials off to a great start, blend up a batch of this potting soil at planting time.

INSTRUCTIONS: Mix the sand, loam, and compost, peat moss, or potting soil in a large tub or wheelbarrow. For each cubic foot of soil mixture, add 1 ½ cups of Epsom salts, ¾ cup of coffee grounds, and 12 dried eggshells, crushed to a powder. Mix the ingredients together, and use the mixture to make your perennials feel comfy and cozy in their new pots.

INGREDIENTS:

1 part sharp sand
1 part clay loam
1 part compost, peat moss, or potting soil
Epsom salts
Coffee grounds (rinsed)
Eggshells (dried)

◆ FILL YOUR LIFE WITH FLOWERS

Growing perennials in pots is a super way to show them off. You can get up close to admire their beautiful colors and fragrances without having to get down on your knees—plus, soil preparation and planting are a breeze! So even if you don't have the space, time, or energy for an in-ground garden, you can still enjoy growing a wide variety of pretty perennials in pots right on your deck, porch, or patio.

You don't need to bother changing the soil for your potted perennials every year, 'cause I've found the perfect trick to pep up that tired soil. Just add 1 can of beer or one shot of bourbon, scotch, vodka, or gin—plus 1 ounce of dishwashing liquid—to 1 gallon of water. Use this formula to replace plain water when you mix up your favorite plant food, and it'll liven things up like nobody's business!

Potted Plant Picnic

A sprinkle here and a splash there won't do anything for thirsty flowers—especially when they're growing in containers. When you water, keep it up until water starts coming out of the holes in the bottom of the pot. This kind of thorough watering will definitely set your potted plants up right. But remember, the water that runs out of the pot carries some of the soil's nutrients along with it, so you need to keep up a regular feeding program, too! Here's a meal your flower-filled containers are sure to appreciate.

INSTRUCTIONS: Mix these ingredients in a watering can, and water your potted plants with the mixture once a week to keep them happy, healthy, and full of flowers!

INGREDIENTS:

2 tbsp. of brewed
    black coffee
2 tbsp. of whiskey
1 tsp. of fish emulsion
$\frac{1}{2}$ tsp. of gelatin
$\frac{1}{2}$ tsp. of baby shampoo
$\frac{1}{2}$ tsp. of ammonia
1 gal. of water

◆ GIMME SHELTER

Believe you me—scorching summer sun can dry out even well-watered pots in a New York minute! If you aren't home during the day, set your pots in a spot where they'll be shaded during the afternoon hours. That way, if they do dry out, the plants won't shrivel before you have a chance to water them in the early evening.

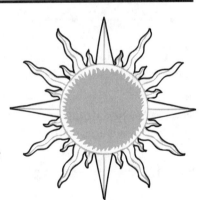

GREAT IDEA!

Big planters weigh a ton, even before they're filled with soil.

To really lighten the load, fill the bottom third of each pot with Styrofoam® "peanuts," then fill the rest of the container with potting mix. Water thoroughly, and add more mix so it comes to within an inch or two of the rim. Gently pat it down, then you're all set to plant.

Potting Soil Booster Mix

Believe it or not, dry dog food contains many of the same nutrients found in organic fertilizers, such as bloodmeal and bonemeal! It's great for all parts of your garden, either worked into the soil or scattered around growing plants, but my favorite use for it is fortifying pre-packed potting soil. It seems like these soils just never have enough nutrients to really push the bloom on flowering plants. So before you fill your pots this year, I want you to make a batch of this booster mix.

INGREDIENTS:

2 cups of dry oatmeal

2 cups of dry dog food, crushed

Pinch of human hair

1 ½ tsp. of sugar

INSTRUCTIONS: Mix these ingredients in a bucket, and add 2 tablespoons of the mixture to each container of moistened, professional potting soil. Follow up with my Potted Plant Picnic (see **page 151**) applied throughout the summer to keep the color coming all season long.

◆ WAGONS, HO!

If you can't find a suitable site for your flowers, put 'em on wheels! That's right—make a movable bed out of an old toy wagon. Drill drainage holes, add a thin layer of gravel, top with potting soil, and plant. When you need to move your bloomers, simply roll them where you want them to go!

TERRIFIC TIME⊠SAVERS

Want to speed the sprouting time of your seeds? Soak them in a mix of 1 teaspoon of dishwashing liquid, 1 teaspoon of ammonia, and 1 teaspoon of instant tea granules in 1 quart of warm water for 24 hours. Then place the seeds in a piece of old nylon stocking tied up with a twist tie. Let the seeds dry out, remove them from the stocking, and plant them. They'll be up and growing before you know it!

Pre-Plant Perennial Garden Tonic

Experienced gardeners know that you simply can't have good growth above ground unless you have great roots down below. Here's one of my favorite root-boosting feeding formulas for new perennial plantings.

INSTRUCTIONS: Mix these ingredients in a wheelbarrow, and work a handful of the mixture into the bottom of each planting hole. If you have some left over when you're done, scatter it on top of the soil around your new plantings to give them an extra nutrient boost.

INGREDIENTS:

5 lbs. of dry peat moss
4 cups of bonemeal
2 cups of gypsum
2 cups of Epsom salts
1 cup of wood ashes
1 cup of lime
4 tsp. of baby powder
1 tsp. of baking powder

◆ HANDLE WITH CARE

To water perennials properly, you should actually be watering the soil surrounding the plants, not sprinkling the leaves. One way to do this without straining your back is to attach a broom handle along its length to your hose, starting just behind the nozzle. The handle helps direct the water to the roots, and you won't have to bend over to make sure it gets where it needs to go.

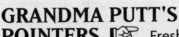

GRANDMA PUTT'S POINTERS ☞ Freshly dug soil is light and fluffy, but it settles back down during the first few weeks. So if you're planting immediately after digging, try this trick I learned from Grandma Putt—set your transplants slightly higher in the soil than you normally would. Once the soil settles, they'll end up at the same depth they were growing when they were in their pots— just right for great growth!

Quassia Slug Spray

There's no getting around it: Slugs love flowers! You'll know they are around if you see large, ragged holes in leaves or flowers, or shiny, slimy trails on leaves and on the ground around your bloomers. Their favorite hangout is in damp shade, where they chomp on the leaves of hostas, begonias, and many other shade-loving plants. But during rainy or humid weather, just about any flower is fair game, so it's smart to be prepared for these slimy slitherers with this spray.

INGREDIENTS:

4 oz. of quassia chips (bark of the quassia tree; available at health food stores)
1 gal. of water

INSTRUCTIONS: Crush, grind, or chop the chips, then add them to the water in a bucket. Let steep for 12 to 24 hours. Strain through cheesecloth, then spray the remaining liquid on slug-prone plants, such as hostas, bellflowers, and seedlings of all kinds. This spray also helps control aphids, but it will not hurt good guys like lady beetles and honeybees.

◆ START FROM SCRATCH

Don't throw away those used sandpaper disks—they make great slug busters! Cut a slit up to the center of the disk, and put the disk on the ground around the stem of your plant, like a collar. Slugs don't dare cross the scratchy surface!

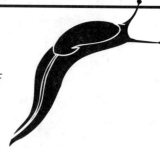

ASK JERRY

Q A few months ago, I used beer in margarine tubs sunk into the ground to trap slugs. It worked like a charm, but buying all that beer can get expensive! Is there a cheaper alternative that I can use?

A Yes, there is—and it's grape juice. Believe it or not, it works just as well, and costs a whole lot less than beer!

Scare-'Em-All Tonic

Everybody likes a little spice in their lives, right? Well, that may be true for people, but it's sure not the case where garden pests are concerned! When you blend onions and garlic together, you come up with a potent potion that'll keep all kinds of bad bugs at bay—and help protect your beautiful flowers against funky fungi, too.

INSTRUCTIONS: Place the garlic cloves, onion, and 1 quart of water in an old blender. Blend at high speed for 1 minute. Strain the mixture through cheesecloth or pantyhose. Mix the garlic-onion liquid with 1 gallon of water. Add the dishwashing liquid and glycerin, and pour into a hand-held sprayer. Spray on all your plants as needed to send pests and diseases packing.

INGREDIENTS:

20 cloves of garlic, peeled
1 medium onion, finely chopped
1 tbsp. of dishwashing liquid
3 tsp. of glycerin
1 qt. plus 1 gal. of water

◆ BABY THOSE BABIES

Floating row covers—the kind used in vegetable gardens—can be a huge help in the flower garden, too! They protect young plants from chilly, drying winds, help hold in moisture, and protect the soil surface from pounding raindrops, which can cause a crust to form. They'll also keep hungry birds from gobbling up your flower seeds, and prevent rascally rabbits from snacking on your seedlings.

MAKING CENTS

Believe it or not, old pantyhose make perfect plant ties! They're soft and stretchy, and a ruined pair or two yields all the ties you'll need for a whole year. Cut across each leg piece to get a bunch of 1- to 2-inch-wide loops. Slide the loops onto your wrist as you head out to the garden, and you've got a supply of plant ties close at hand.

Seedling Strengthener Solution

While you're getting your seedlings used to the great outdoors, mist-spray them every few days with this super solution. This terrific tonic will get all your flower seedlings off to a healthy, disease-free start.

INSTRUCTIONS: Put the manure and tea in the toe of an old nylon stocking, and let them steep in 5 gallons of water for several days. Dilute the mixture with 4 parts of warm water (for example, 4 cups of water for every cup of mix) before spritzing your seedlings with a hand-held sprayer.

INGREDIENTS:

2 cups of manure
½ cup of instant tea granules
Warm water

◆ TOUGH LOVE FOR TENDER SEEDLINGS

Flower seedlings that have been coddled in your home or in a greenhouse need toughening up before they're ready for the garden. Give 'em a good drink, then set them outside in a shady, protected spot. Leave them outdoors for an hour or so the first day, then bring them back in.

Gradually increase the amount of sun they receive and the number of hours they're outdoors over the course of a week. Once your youngsters can stay outdoors all day without drooping, they're ready for transplanting!

✳ IDEA!

GREAT

Want to get a head start on spring planting chores?

Then prepare your seedbeds in late summer or fall. Come spring, they'll be ready to sow whenever you are! Spread an inch or two of compost over the area, then dig or till it into the top 6 to 8 inches of soil. Rake the bed smooth—removing any rocks, breaking up dirt clods, and disposing of the weeds—then you're good to go.

Tansy Pest Repellent

Believe it or not, some "weeds" can actually be good for your garden! Tansy is wonderful for attracting beneficial insects, which help keep pesky pests from getting the upper hand. Plus, it makes a super spray for getting rid of leaf-eating bugs. This pretty, yellow-flowered perennial grows quickly, so feel free to harvest as much as you need; you won't hurt the plant!

INSTRUCTIONS: Pour the boiling water over the leaves, cover, and let stand until cool. Strain out the leaves, then dilute the remaining liquid with 2 cups of room-temperature water. Pour into a hand-held sprayer. Spray your plants thoroughly—make sure you get the undersides of the leaves, too—to protect them from hungry bugs.

INGREDIENTS:

3 cups of fresh tansy leaves
2 cups of boiling water
2 cups of room-temperature water

◆ A BERRY SMART IDEA

Here's the secret to making professional-looking floral arrangements right at home—use a plastic mesh berry basket to support the stems of the blooms! Turn the basket upside down, and place it in a bowl or large vase with water. Insert the stems of your cut flowers into the openings. If your container is shallow, you can drape moss over the top and sides of the berry basket to make it less noticeable.

ASK JERRY

Q *Can I use fresh-sheared sheep's wool for garden mulch? If not, can I compost it?*

A Whether it's straight off the sheep's back or an old wool rug, wool is slow to decompose. So if you're going to try to compost it, cut it into small pieces or clumps, then saturate the heck out of it with a sugar source like regular cola (not diet) to speed up the process.

Ultra-Light Potting Soil

Large planters can weigh a ton when filled with soil and plants, so it's smart to place them where you want them BEFORE you fill them up. Using my Ultra-Light Potting Soil will also help to keep your pot and planters from becoming back-breakers.

INSTRUCTIONS: Mix these ingredients in a wheelbarrow, then use the mixture to fill your containers. This mix dries out very quickly, particularly in the hot summer sun, so be sure to keep an eye on your plants and water them as needed.

INGREDIENTS:

4 parts perlite, moistened
4 parts compost
1 part potting soil
$\frac{1}{2}$ part cow manure

◆ THINK BIG

Pretty pots overflowing with annual and perennial flowers are perfect for bringing a bit of your garden right up to your deck or patio. And here's a little secret the pros use to create showstopping container plantings: Start with the biggest pots you can manage. Large containers hold more soil, so they provide plenty of room for healthy root growth, and that translates into abundant foliage and flowering. Plus, they need to be watered less often than smaller pots do, which means a lot less work for you.

Here's an egg-cellent idea! Dry eggshells in the microwave or oven and crush them underfoot on your garage floor. Then add them to any planting mix for a quick calcium fix. You can also soak them in water, and water your plants with the enriched liquid for outstanding results.

Undercover Mulch Booster

After mulching your flower beds with wood chips, shredded bark, sawdust, or any other wood-based mulch, overspray them with this mulch booster to feed the roots underneath.

INSTRUCTIONS: Mix these ingredients in a large bucket, then pour into a 20 gallon hose-end sprayer. Apply liberally over all of your flower beds to thoroughly saturate the mulch and wet the soil underneath as well. This'll keep the wood-based mulch from stealing nutrients from the soil (and in turn, from your flowers) as it gradually decomposes. Your plants will stay happier AND healthier with just one application!

INGREDIENTS:

1 can of beer
1 can of regular cola (not diet)
1 cup of dishwashing liquid
1 cup of antiseptic mouthwash
$1/4$ tsp. of instant tea granules

◆ RAINY DAY MULCHING

Mulch can do great things for your flowers—*if* you know the secret to applying it. The best time to mulch is after a heavy rain, before the weather gets too hot. Never apply mulch when the ground is dry. If you do, the mulch will absorb any rainwater that happens to come along and allow it to evaporate before it can soak into the soil.

GREAT ✳IDEA!

It doesn't matter what type of wood chips, bark chunks, or shavings you use to mulch your flower beds...

as long as you put shredded cedar or eucalyptus mulch underneath them! For some reason, these aromatic woods seem to discourage insects from setting up shop when they're either worked into the soil or laid on top of it.

Wonderful Weed Killer

Garden paths don't have problems with pests and diseases the way flowers do, but that doesn't mean they are totally carefree. Cracks make perfect homes for pesky weeds, which can spoil the looks of your beautiful flower garden before you know it. So fix up those paths as soon as you can, and in the meantime, use my Wonderful Weed Killer to tidy things up!

INSTRUCTIONS: Mix these ingredients in a bucket until the salt has dissolved. Pour the solution along cracks to kill weeds between bricks or stones in walkways. **Caution:** Don't spray it on plants that you want to keep, and don't pour it on soil that you plan to garden in someday!

INGREDIENTS:

1 gal. of vinegar
1 cup of table salt
1 tbsp. of dishwashing
   liquid

◆ SEND WEEDS TO A WATERY GRAVE

Weeds growing up between paving stones or in gravel paths can drive you crazy. Here's a super-simple solution: Boil up a tea kettle full of water, and give those pesky weeds a good dousing. One treatment will do in young seedlings, but for older, more stubborn types, repeat once a week until they stop comin' back.

GRANDMA PUTT'S POINTERS ☞
Whenever I see Gene Kelly dancing to "Singin' in the Rain," I think of my Grandma Putt. We always weeded in the rain—well, actually, *after* a rain. You see, weed roots come up easily when the soil is moist, so the best time to attack them is after a rain. And singin' while you're weedin' makes the work go that much faster!

Year-Round Refresher Tonic

To keep ALL of the members of your flower beds bursting with bloom, use this elixir every three weeks from spring through fall. (In warm climates, you can use it year-round.)

INSTRUCTIONS: Mix the beer, shampoo, lawn food, molasses, and fish emulsion in a 20 gallon hose-end sprayer. Fill the balance of the sprayer jar with ammonia, then apply liberally to your flower beds to the point of run-off. This nutrient-packed potion will keep all your flowers blooming their fool heads off!

INGREDIENTS:

1 cup of beer
1 cup of baby shampoo
1 cup of liquid lawn food
$\frac{1}{2}$ cup of molasses
2 tbsp. of fish emulsion
Ammonia

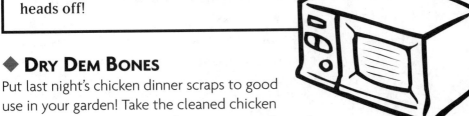

◆ DRY DEM BONES

Put last night's chicken dinner scraps to good use in your garden! Take the cleaned chicken bones and dry them out in the microwave. Place them in a heavy-duty plastic bag, and pound them to smithereens with a hammer. Sprinkle the bone shards around your plants, and work them into the soil to give your bloomers a nice nutrient boost.

Tree and shrub prunings are a super source of free supports for floppy flowers. Simply stick several stems into the ground—cut end down, twiggy end up—around each clump of plants. Snap the branch tips over toward the center of the clump—don't break them off completely—for extra stem support, and get rid of any pointy ends sticking up. Your supply of stakes will be never-ending—and best of all, *free!*

CHAPTER 4

RAVISHING ROSES

ROSES AREN'T JUST for old-fashioned rose gardens anymore! There's no law that says you need to keep these beauties stuck off in a corner bed by themselves, so get 'em out there front and center in your garden, and let 'em mingle with your other flowers. When roses are in their glory, your beds and borders will look as pretty as a postcard, and once they're done, the annuals and perennials will still be there to carry on with the show!

Besides making your plantings look great, mixing roses with other flowers makes it a lot harder for pesky pests and dastardly diseases to run rampant. But if these bad boys do rear their ugly little heads, don't despair—I've got plenty of magical mixers to send them runnin' for the hills. And don't forget to give my power-packed feeding tonics a try, too—they'll keep your roses burstin' with blooms, GUARANTEED!

AROUND *the* YEAR

I'll never understand why roses have such a bad reputation for being hard to grow. Sure, they like a little pampering (who doesn't?), but when you consider the fantastic flowers you get in return, it's well worth the effort! Simply follow my easy, step-by-step system to rose-growing success.

 ## Spring

◆ **Step 1:** Planning on adding some roses to your yard this year? It's never too early to start the soil-building process with my super-duper Bed Builder Mix (see **page 170**):

40 lbs. of bagged topsoil
10 lbs. of compost
5 lbs. of bonemeal
1 lb. of Epsom salts

Mix these ingredients in a wheelbarrow, spread a 2- to 3-inch layer over the entire site, and then top the bed with mulch. Add the plants whenever you're ready!

◆ **Step 2:** Midspring's a super time to plant container-grown rosebushes. My Super Start-Up Tonic (see **page 192**) is chock-full of good stuff to get 'em growing on the right root:

1 tbsp. of dishwashing liquid
1 tbsp. of hydrogen peroxide
1 tsp. of whiskey
1 tsp. of vitamin B_1 plant starter
$1/2$ gal. of warm brewed tea

Mix these ingredients in a bucket or watering can, then pour the liquid all around the root zone of each of your prize rose plants for a quick nutrient boost.

◆ **Step 3:** Established roses need lots of food, too, so treat 'em all to a taste of my Baker's Best Rose Chow (see **page 169**):

4 cups of bonemeal
1 cup of 5-10-5 plant food
1 cup of Epsom salts

Mix these ingredients in a bucket, then give each bush 1 heaping tablespoon in mid- to late spring, or work in 4 pounds per 100 sq. ft. of rose bed. Follow up with my All-Season Green-Up Tonic (see **page 167**) or my Rose Ambrosia (see **page 186**) to really energize this dry mix.

Summer

◆ **Step 4:** Don't let bad bugs and dastardly diseases spoil your rose-growing fun! Fight back and keep your roses blooming with regular doses of my All-Season Clean-Up Tonic (see **page 166**):

1 cup of baby shampoo
1 cup of antiseptic mouthwash
1 cup of tobacco tea*

Mix these ingredients in a 20 gallon hose-end sprayer, and give everything in your yard a good shower in the early evening every two weeks throughout the growing season. You'll have the healthiest roses in town—GUARANTEED!

To make tobacco tea, place half a handful of chewing tobacco in an old nylon stocking and soak it in a gallon of hot water until the mixture is dark brown.

◆ **Step 5:** To keep those beautiful blooms comin' along all summer, my All-Season Green-Up Tonic (see **page 167**) is just the ticket:

1 can of beer
1 cup of ammonia
$1/2$ cup of dishwashing liquid
$1/2$ cup of liquid lawn food
$1/2$ cup of molasses or clear corn syrup

Mix these ingredients in a large bucket, pour into a 20 gallon hose-end sprayer, and spray everything in sight—not just your roses, but also your trees, shrubs, flowers, lawn, and even vegetables. Apply this tonic every three weeks right up through the first hard frost, and your roses will come through the hot summer months with flying colors!

GREAT IDEA!

Want to get a jump on next spring's rose show?

Late fall's a great time to get bare-root roses in the ground. When you get these babies home, immediately take 'em out of their packaging, then plunk the roots in a bucket of warm water or my Rose Revival Tonic (see **page 189**) for four hours to get them juiced up again. Get 'em in the ground as soon as you can—ideally, within a day or two after you bring 'em home.

Fall

◆ **Step 6:** If you buy bare-root roses from a mail-order nursery, chances are, your plants will arrive in late fall. To get them off to a great start, wash your newly purchased bare-root bushes, roots and all, in a bucket of warm water with 1 tablespoon of dishwashing liquid and $\frac{1}{4}$ teaspoon of liquid bleach mixed in. Then before planting, soak your bare-root rosebushes in my Rose Revival Tonic (see **page 189**):

2 tbsp. of clear corn syrup
1 tsp. of dishwashing liquid
1 tsp. of ammonia
1 gal. of warm water

Mix the ingredients in a clean bucket, and let the roots soak for about half an hour before planting. This will help lessen the transplant shock and encourage healthy new roots to form. (This tonic is also great for locally purchased bare-root roses planted in late winter or early spring.)

◆ **Step 7:** Before you put all your roses to bed for the winter, treat them with my Rose Clean-Up Tonic (see **page 188**) to get rid of any lingering pests and diseases:

1 cup of Murphy's Oil Soap®
1 cup of antiseptic mouthwash
1 cup of tobacco tea*
$\frac{1}{2}$ cup of hot, hot, hot sauce
$\frac{1}{2}$ cup of urine

Mix these ingredients in a 20 gallon hose-end sprayer, and spray your plants well from top to bottom. That'll get your bushes squeaky clean for the winter and will ensure that they get off to a healthy start next spring.

To make tobacco tea, place half a handful of chewing tobacco in an old nylon stocking and soak it in a gallon of hot water until the mixture is dark brown.

GRANDMA PUTT'S POINTERS ☞ When Japanese beetles were chowing down on her rose blossoms, Grandma Putt would go out first thing in the morning and jiggle the beetles into a bowl of soapy water. The season for these bad boys lasts only about six weeks, so with a little midsummer attention, your roses will still have plenty of time to spring into bloom in late summer.

All-Season Clean-Up Tonic

This is the one tonic that you ABSOLUTELY need to use religiously throughout the growing season on all of your plants. The shampoo cleans the plants and helps the other ingredients stick better; the mouthwash kills bad bacteria and discourages insects; and the tobacco tea contains nicotine, which does a double whammy on those pesky pests.

INGREDIENTS:

1 cup of baby shampoo
1 cup of antiseptic mouthwash
1 cup of tobacco tea*

INSTRUCTIONS: Mix these ingredients in a 20 gallon hose-end sprayer, and give everything in your yard a good shower in the early evening every two weeks throughout the growing season. You'll have the healthiest roses in town!

To make tobacco tea, place half a handful of chewing tobacco in an old nylon stocking and soak it in a gallon of hot water until the mixture is dark brown.

◆ GET THE SITE RIGHT

What do roses and real estate have in common? It's all about *location, location, location!* Planting roses in an open, airy site will go a long way toward keeping dastardly diseases from getting a foothold. But you don't want 'em exposed to strong *northwest* winds, 'cause these chilly breezes can dry out the canes in a flash during rough winter weather. So what's the answer? A south- or east-facing site, with some sort of shelter or windbreak to the northwest side, is the perfect spot for growing great roses!

GRANDMA PUTT'S POINTERS ☞

To keep your everblooming roses flowering through the summer, try this terrific trick that Grandma Putt swore by: Dissolve 3 tablespoons of brewer's yeast in 2 gallons of water, and use it to soak the roots of each bush after their first big flush of flowers.

All-Season Green-Up Tonic

Roses need plenty of food to keep those beautiful blooms comin' along, so help 'em out with regular doses of my All-Season Green-Up Tonic. This power-packed formula has all the good stuff roses require to stay lush and lovely through the growing season.

INSTRUCTIONS: Mix these ingredients in a large bucket, pour into a 20 gallon hose-end sprayer, and spray everything in sight—not just your roses, but also your trees, shrubs, flowers, lawn, and even vegetables. Apply this tonic every three weeks right up through the first hard frost, and your roses will come through the hot summer months with flying colors!

INGREDIENTS:

1 can of beer
1 cup of ammonia
$1/2$ cup of dishwashing liquid
$1/2$ cup of liquid lawn food
$1/2$ cup of molasses or clear corn syrup

◆ THANKS FOR YOUR SUPPORT

Despite their name, climbing roses don't actually climb on their own—they need to be tied to a support to grow properly. They'll flower better if you tie them to a horizontal support, such as a fence or trellis, while the canes are still young and flexible. Or, to encourage even *more* blooms, you can train them in the shape of an arch (with the stem tips lower than the middle of the canes).

TERRIFIC TIME⌗SAVERS

A mulch of ground corncobs, spent hops, or well-rotted manure will do great things for all of your roses if you apply it soon after growth starts in spring. It'll maintain moisture and reduce weeds, so your roses will look and grow better than ever!

Aphid Antidote

A few aphids on your roses aren't a big problem, but if you don't watch out, they can turn into one quick! These tiny critters tend to congregate on tender new shoots and buds, sucking out the sap and leaving mangled, discolored growth behind. It's often simplest to pinch off leaves and stems that are covered with aphids, because they probably won't recover anyway. To protect the rest of your rosebush, give it a thorough drenching with this antidote.

INGREDIENTS:

1 medium onion
1 tsp. of dishwashing liquid
Water

INSTRUCTIONS: In a blender, thoroughly blend the onion in a quart of water. Strain off the clear juice, and mix 2 tablespoons of it per gallon of water with the dishwashing liquid. Pour into a hand-held sprayer, and apply to any aphid-prone plants to keep these little suckers from dining on your pride and joy.

◆ ONIONS RUN RINGS AROUND ROSE WOES

Companion planting experts swear that onions and their relatives protect roses from black spot and mildew (two pesky fungal diseases), as well as aphids. Ordinary onions aren't pretty enough to add to flower beds, but many of their relatives are real eye-catchers. Chives, for instance, make a handsome edging for beds containing roses. Other low-growing, ornamental onions that make rousing rose companions include yellow-flowered lily leek (*Allium moly*) and rose-purple to pink-flowered nodding onion (*A. cernuum*).

GREAT ✳IDEA!

Rose pruning doesn't have to be complicated!

Just remember my simple "3-D Rule": In early to midspring, trim out any dead, diseased, or damaged stems, cutting back to healthy, white-centered wood.

Baker's Best Rose Chow

Roses are the hardest-working flowering plants in your garden. These beauties bloom only for the sake of showing off as much as they can, for as long as they can. When you follow this simple feeding routine, your roses will have everything they need to keep those blooms comin' on strong!

INSTRUCTIONS: Mix these ingredients in a bucket, then give each bush 1 heaping tablespoon in mid- to late spring, or work in 4 pounds per 100 sq. ft. of rose bed. Follow up with my Rose Ambrosia (see **page 186**) to really energize this dry mix.

INGREDIENTS:

4 cups of bonemeal
1 cup of 5-10-5 plant food
1 cup of Epsom salts

◆ A LOT OFF THE TOP, PLEASE!

To keep your Hybrid Tea and Grandiflora roses healthy and full of flowers, heavy pruning is the key. Each spring, cut off all but three to six of the youngest, healthiest canes. In the North, cut the remaining canes back to 12 to 14 inches; in the South, leave them 18 to 24 inches tall. Floribunda and Polyantha roses do better if you leave a few more stems, so I suggest keeping six to eight of the youngest canes; then prune as you would for Hybrid Teas.

ASK JERRY

Q *How often should I water my roses, and is it OK to stop watering in the fall?*

A That depends on what kind of soil your roses are growing in. Where the soil is well drained or sandy, water twice a week if rain is lacking. In clay soil, water very lightly once a week. Either way, keep it up until the first deep freeze of winter.

Bed Builder Mix

If you have a site that you'd like to fill with roses someday, it's never too soon to start the soil-building process. Scrape off the weeds and grass with a sharp spade, then add a bunch of my Bed Builder Mix.

INSTRUCTIONS: Mix these ingredients in a wheelbarrow, spread a 2- to 3-inch layer over the entire site, and top the bed with mulch. Then all you've got to do is add the plants whenever you're ready!

INGREDIENTS:

40 lbs. of bagged topsoil
10 lbs. of compost
5 lbs. of bonemeal
1 lb. of Epsom salts

◆ BE A SMART SHOPPER

If you're looking to add some new roses to your yard, midspring is a super time to shop for them. But don't be tempted to buy bagged or boxed roses now, because they won't have time to make a good root system before summer heat arrives. Potted roses are a *much* better bet for midspring planting!

◆ REST IN PEACE

If you've had a rosebush die, it's tempting to buy another one to fill that very same spot. But planting a new rose in a dead rose's grave isn't a good idea. Why? Diseases, insects, or other problems in that spot probably will attack the new plant just as they did the old one. So sure, go out and buy a new plant to replace the one you lost, but look for a brand-new spot it can call home.

TERRIFIC TIME⌛SAVERS

Faced with soggy soil or heavy clay? Don't waste your weekends digging and tilling to get poor soil in better shape; instead, build a few raised beds! Fill 'em with a mix of good-quality topsoil, compost, and my Bed Builder Mix (above). In return for just a few hours' work, you'll enjoy a lifetime of happy, healthy roses.

Black Spot Remover Tonic

Just like its name suggests, black spot disease causes circular black spots (often surrounded by a yellow halo) on rose leaves. You can set these funky fungi way back by painting every last speckled leaf with my Black Spot Remover Tonic. If you love roses, it's well worth the trouble, even if you have to borrow some tomato leaves from a veggie-growing neighbor to make this brew.

INSTRUCTIONS: Chop the tomato leaves and onions until finely minced, and steep them in the alcohol overnight. Then use a small, sponge-type paintbrush to apply the brew to both the tops and bottoms of any infected rose leaves.

INGREDIENTS:

15 tomato leaves
2 small onions
$\frac{1}{4}$ cup of isopropyl (rubbing) alcohol

◆ NO MOO MILDEW

Tired of powdery mildew on your roses—you know, those dirty white spots that start on the leaves and spread to the whole plant? I've got an *amazing* secret weapon for you, and it's as close as your refrigerator! Simply stir up a 50-50 mix of milk and water, then spray away with a hand-held sprayer; once a week is about right. Sounds too good to be true, I know, but it really works!

ASK JERRY

Q *I'd love to try my hand at growing roses, but I sure don't want to spend my summer weekends spraying, pinching, and pruning. Can you recommend a fuss-free rose for me?*

A I sure can—give 'Knock Out' a try! This bulletproof rose is a real beauty, with bright, reddish pink flowers from late spring through frost. Best of all, it's practically immune to black spot and other funky fungi that can make rose growing a real hassle—and that means no spraying!

Bust 'Em Baking Soda Spray

No need to spend a bundle buying chemical sprays to treat rose pests and diseases. This simple spray does it all—and the ingredients are as close as your kitchen!

INSTRUCTIONS: Mix the baking soda, dishwashing liquid, and oil with 1 cup of water. Then add the vinegar last because the mixture may bubble over. Pour the mix into a pump sprayer, and add the remaining water. Thoroughly spray your roses, covering the tops and bottoms of leaves to the point of run-off.

INGREDIENTS:

1 ¹/₂ tbsp. of baking soda
1 tbsp. of dishwashing liquid
1 tbsp. of canola oil
1 cup plus 1 gal. of water
1 tbsp. of vinegar

◆ FUSS-FREE ROSES—1, 2, 3!

Roses are notorious for being disease magnets, but you don't have to be a slave to your sprayer. Here's my three-step program for keeping rose woes to a minimum:

◆ **Step 1:** Start with disease-resistant plants, and give 'em the best possible site—well-drained soil, full sun, and good air circulation.

◆ **Step 2:** Keep the leaves dry when you water. Soaker hoses wet the soil, not the plants, so they're a much smarter irrigation option than sprinklers.

◆ **Step 3:** If you see only a few diseased leaves, pick them off and destroy them; that way, you might stop the problem before it starts. But if the fungi have gotten a head start, don't wait to spray; stop the spores from spreading to still-healthy shoots ASAP.

Want to give your roses a super summer pick-me-up? Tuck all of your used tea bags into the mulch around the base of the bushes. The tannic acid in the tea makes the soil slightly acidic, which will make your roses pleased as punch!

Buttermilk Blast

Spider mites are so small that you can barely see them without a magnifying glass, but they can cause BIG problems for your roses! They suck the sap out of the leaves, at first causing tiny, pale speckling; eventually, the leaves turn brown, curl, and drop off. These pests multiply quickly during hot, dry weather, so be prepared to control them with my Buttermilk Blast.

INGREDIENTS:

2 cups of wheat flour
$\frac{1}{4}$ cup of buttermilk
2 gal. of water

INSTRUCTIONS: Mix these ingredients thoroughly in a bucket. Then pour the mixture into a hand-held sprayer, and douse your mite-plagued plants from top to bottom. The little suckers'll never know what hit 'em!

◆ A Clever Cover-Up

Rose blooms may be the queens of the flower garden, but the plants themselves aren't all that much to look at. Hybrid Teas, Floribundas, and Grandifloras—three of the most commonly grown kinds of roses—are particularly prone to losing their lower leaves. So what's the answer? Cover up those bare ankles with lower-growing flowers! Aromatic-leaved herbs, such as catmints and lavenders, are especially nice; in addition to adding beautiful, purple-blue flowers that look great with all colors of roses, their fragrant leaves may help send pests packing.

GRANDMA PUTT'S POINTERS ☞ Want to get twice the flower power from your rosebush? Then try this trick I learned from Grandma Putt: Plant a clematis next to it! The clematis will climb up and over the rose, so it'll look like the rose has two different kinds of flowers. You can pair a clematis and rose that bloom at the same time for one spectacular show, or choose ones that flower at different times for extended blooming.

Bye-Bye, Beetles Spray

This hot toddy will say a loud, strong "Get lost!" to any Japanese beetle that starts to munch on your roses.

INSTRUCTIONS: Add the peppers to the water, bring it to a boil, and let it simmer for half an hour. (Make sure you keep the pan covered or the peppery steam will make you cry a river of tears!) Let the mixture cool, then strain out the solids. Pour the liquid into a hand-held sprayer, and spritz your rosebushes from top to bottom.

INGREDIENTS:

$1/2$ cup of dried cayenne peppers
$1/2$ cup of jalapeño peppers
1 gal. of water

◆ TRY THESE TOUGHIES

Not all roses are garden prima donnas; in fact, a fair number of them do just fine with the same good care you give other garden shrubs! So if you don't want to be a slave to your garden, look for these easy-care roses:

- ◆ **Modern Shrub roses.** A catch-all category of sturdy plants with abundant flowers and attractive shapes; they do fine with minimal pruning.

- ◆ **Polyantha roses.** Tough, disease-resistant, easy-to-grow roses with large clusters of small flowers borne in flushes from spring through fall. Pink-flowered 'The Fairy' is one of the best.

- ◆ **Rugosa roses.** Rugged, disease-resistant roses with showy, fragrant flowers through the summer—and showy red fruits, too!

GREAT IDEA!

Don't let your roses die on the vine!

Dead blooms are an open invitation to pests and diseases. Always cut them off about $1/4$ inch above a leaf to encourage new growth.

Dead Bug Brew

Are your ravishing roses being bugged by bugs? Don't let these bad boys take the bloom off your roses; fight back hard with this proven, old-time repellent.

INSTRUCTIONS: Put all of these ingredients in an old blender (and I mean really old—one you'll never again use for food), and purée the heck out of them. Strain out the pulp using cheesecloth or pantyhose. Dilute the remaining brew at a rate of ¼ cup of brew per 1 cup of water. Apply with a hand-held sprayer to your roses to the point of run-off.

INGREDIENTS:

½ cup of dead insects (the more, the merrier!)

1 tbsp. of dishwashing liquid

1 tbsp. of cayenne pepper

2 cups of water

◆ Dig It!

When extra-vigorous canes shoot up from grafted roses, take a close look at 'em. Root suckers usually have leaves and thorns that look different from the grafted part of the plant, along with slender, more arching canes. They'll also have different flowers. To keep these suckers from taking over, you need to get rid of them, *pronto!* Dig next to the plant to see where they're attached, then pull or snap them off by hand. Never cut off root suckers right at the soil line—this simply encourages 'em to grow right back!

Don't throw out those banana skins—they make a fantastic *free* rose fertilizer! Simply work whole banana skins (or whole rotten bananas) into the soil near the base of your bushes. The potassium in the skins will give them a power-packed boost that helps the plants fend off pests and diseases, and delivers up a boatload of beautiful blossoms, to boot!

Double-Punch Garlic Tea

If thrips, aphids, and other bugs are driving your roses buggy, don't pull any punches. Deliver a knock-out blow to those rose rustlers with this powerful potion.

INSTRUCTIONS: Place the chopped garlic in a heat-proof bowl, and pour the boiling water over it. Allow it to steep overnight. Strain through a coffee filter, and then mix it with the other ingredients in a hand-held sprayer. Thoroughly drench your plants to thwart those pesky pests.

INGREDIENTS:
5 unpeeled cloves of garlic, coarsely chopped
2 cups of boiling water
$1/2$ cup of tobacco tea*
1 tsp. of instant tea granules
1 tsp. of baby shampoo

To make tobacco tea, place half a handful of chewing tobacco in an old nylon stocking and soak it in a gallon of hot water until the mixture is dark brown.

◆ THE GARDEN DETECTIVE

Are you seeing brown streaks on your pale roses? Cut off one of the marred blossoms, and lay it on a piece of white paper. After a few minutes, shake it hard. If little brown things fall out, they're rose thrips. They love to feed on white and pastel roses—but they *don't* like garlic! So snip off all the old blossoms and put them in the garbage. Then spray every new one with my Double-Punch Garlic Tea (above). Put up a good fight this year, and you may never see thrip damage on your roses again!

✳ IDEA!

GREAT

Do you prefer to apply powdered pest control dust rather than sprays?

If so, then apply the dust early in the morning or late in the evening. At that time of day, the air is still and the dew on the leaves will help the dust stick better. You get more control and less dust.

Fantastic Rose-Feeding Tonic

To keep Hybrid Tea roses in tip-top shape, alternate their diet, beginning with my Super Start-Up Tonic (see **page 192**). Next, use liquid rose and flower food mixed in a weak solution of instant tea, adding 1 tablespoon of dishwashing liquid per gallon of water. Then follow up with this terrific tonic.

INSTRUCTIONS: Mix these ingredients in a bucket and treat each rosebush to a quart of this mixture every three weeks through the summer.

INGREDIENTS:

2 tbsp. of instant tea granules
$\frac{1}{2}$ tbsp. of fish emulsion
1 tbsp. of dry red wine
1 tsp. of baking powder
1 tsp. of iron
1 gal. of warm water

◆ PACK A SNACK

Never feed roses after August 15 in an area where temperatures drop below 20°F in winter. If you do, your roses will produce tender new growth, which won't have time to mature before winter sets in. You *should,* however, apply a mixture of 1 cup of bonemeal and ½ cup of Epsom salts around the base of each bush before mulching it for the winter. This is like packing your roses an organic breakfast to wake up to in the spring.

ASK JERRY

Q *My neighbor says I shouldn't water my roses by spraying them with the hose. Why not?*

A Wet foliage helps spread diseases like black spot. A much better way to water roses is to use a soaker hose placed on the ground near the bushes. That way, the water can seep out near the roots, where it will do the most good.

Hot Bug Brew

People enjoy having a little spice in their life, but bugs sure don't! This power-packed tonic is guaranteed to chase all of those bad bugs out of your roses—PRONTO! (It works great on all your other flowers, too.

INSTRUCTIONS: Purée the peppers, garlic, and onion in a blender. Pour the purée into a jar, and add the dishwashing liquid and water. Let stand for 24 hours. Then strain out the pulp, and use a hand-held sprayer to apply the remaining liquid to bug-infested roses, making sure to thoroughly coat the tops and undersides of all the leaves.

INGREDIENTS:

3 hot green peppers (canned or fresh)

3 medium cloves of garlic

1 small onion

1 tbsp. of dishwashing liquid

3 cups of water

◆ THE KINDEST CUT

On roses, knowing *how* to make a good pruning cut is just as important as knowing *where* to make it! So do what the pros do: Always cut just above a bud, and slope the cut at a 45-degree angle *away* from the bud. And don't forget this bonus tip: A touch of fingernail polish or white craft glue on new cuts prevents bothersome borers from chewing into the cut cane ends.

GRANDMA PUTT'S POINTERS ☞

Grandma Putt really loved her roses, so she made a habit of snipping off the faded flowers all through the summer to encourage more blooms. Come fall, though, she'd put her pruners away—and so should you! Letting your roses form "hips" (fruits) tells them to stop growing and get ready for cold weather, so they'll get through the winter better. The colorful hips look pretty, too—plus, they make tasty winter treats for hungry birds.

Mildew Relief Tonic

Powdery mildew is a fungal disease that can really do a number on your roses. While there are several commercial products on the market to control this disease, you can do it yourself with this organic formula: Mix $1/4$ cup of baking soda and 1 tablespoon of vegetable oil in 2 quarts of water. Spray on roses (zinnias and lilacs, too) early in the morning at the first sign of trouble, and every two weeks from then on to keep the disease under control. Or, try my Mildew Relief Tonic.

INGREDIENTS:
1 tbsp. of baby shampoo
1 tbsp. of hydrogen peroxide
1 tsp. of instant tea granules
2 cups of water

INSTRUCTIONS: Mix these ingredients in a hand-held sprayer and apply to any infected leaves and buds. Midafternoon on a cloudy day is the best time to apply it.

◆ BE A WATER WIZARD

Roses need *lots* of water to stay healthy and bloom their best. Even where rainfall is plentiful, they benefit from occasional watering. Roses thrive when they receive the equivalent of 1 inch of water every 7 to 10 days throughout the growing season. Use a drip irrigation or soaker hose, or direct a small, very slow-moving stream of water from a garden hose around the bases of the plants. A heavy stream is wasteful—most of the water runs off before it can soak into the soil.

GREAT ✷IDEA!

Want to avoid using chemicals on your roses?

Here's a lesson I learned a long time ago—if you give your roses a bath once a week with a solution of 1 tablespoon of dishwashing liquid mixed with 2 gallons of warm water, odds are, you won't need to use ANY chemical controls!

Oil's Well That Ends Well Tonic

This oily potion is just the ticket for wipin' out scale, aphids, and other little pests that suck the sap from your roses.

INSTRUCTIONS: Mix these ingredients in a hand-held sprayer, and apply to your roses from top to bottom. (Shake the bottle now and then to make sure the oil and water stay mixed.) Repeat the process in seven days. It'll do a bang-up job getting rid of pests for good!

> **INGREDIENTS:**
> 1 tbsp. of Basic Oil Mixture*
> 2 cups of water

To make the Basic Oil Mixture, pour 1 cup of vegetable oil and 1 tablespoon of Murphy's Oil Soap® into a plastic squeeze bottle (an empty ketchup or mustard bottle is perfect). Then measure out whatever you need for this tonic, and store the rest for later.

◆ ROSES ON THEIR OWN

Hey, cold-climate rose lovers—have I got a tip for you! Whenever you can, buy roses that are grown from cuttings (called *own-root* roses), instead of grafted ones. You see, if cold winter weather kills the top of a grafted rose, any new shoots you get will be from the roots, not the desirable top growth you chose the rose for. But if an own-root rose dies back, the new shoots will be the same rose you started with! For extra protection from severe winter weather, set the crown of own-root roses (the point where the roots and stems join) 1 inch below the soil surface.

Would you believe that you can control weeds with a 50-cent bag of peanuts? That's right! Just sprinkle a 4-inch layer of peanut shells as mulch around your newly planted roses, and you won't have to worry about weeds!

Organic Rose Food

Slow and steady—that's the kind of feeding that's sure to keep your roses happy, healthy, and full of flowers. This rose food is just the ticket for boosting blooms and producing sturdy new growth that's naturally pest- and disease-resistant.

INSTRUCTIONS: Mix these ingredients in a large bucket. Every month during the growing season, apply 1 to 2 cups of the fertilizer in a circle around each plant. Work the food into the soil and then water well. (If your roses are flourishing, 1 cup of fertilizer is enough. But if your plants are struggling, give them 2 cups of the mix.)

INGREDIENTS:

2 parts fish meal
2 parts dried blood
1 part cottonseed meal
1 part rock phosphate
1 part greensand

◆ ROUGH AND RUGGED

Think you can't grow roses unless you fuss with sprays? Then give rugosa rose (*Rosa rugosa*) a try—this trouble-free shrub *hates* being sprayed. Give it full sun and well-drained soil, and it'll thank you with a bounty of fragrant, white, clear pink, or purplish pink flowers from late spring into fall, followed by large, tomato-red "hips."

◆ GIVE 'EM A PINCH

Want to enjoy the biggest possible blooms from your roses? Pinch off all but the topmost bud on each stem while the buds are still very small. That tip bud will then develop into a much larger flower than it would on its own.

ASK JERRY

Q *Last year, my roses were small, and the leaves were yellow. What went wrong?*

A The plant was probably starving to death! You need to feed it one of my tonics, such as my Organic Rose Food (above), every three to four weeks up until August 15 in snow country.

Peppermint Soap Spray

This herbal brew is a nightmare-come-true for hard-bodied insects like weevils. The secret ingredient? Peppermint oil. It cuts right through a bug's waxy shell, so the soap can get in and work its fatal magic.

INGREDIENTS:
2 tbsp. of dishwashing liquid
2 tsp. of peppermint oil
1 gal. of warm water

INSTRUCTIONS: Mix the dishwashing liquid and water together, then stir in the peppermint oil. Pour the solution into a hand-held sprayer, shake well, take aim, and fire! Those weevils will never know what hit 'em!

◆ CUTTING REMARKS

Have a treasured old rose you'd love to share with family and friends? Try taking cuttings! Simply snip off 6- to 8-inch-long stem tips after the flowers have fallen in summer, and remove all of the leaves except for one or two at the top. Stick the cut end into a potato, then plant the cutting (potato and all) with half of its length below the ground. Water thoroughly, then invert a small jar over it. Remove the jar the following spring, and you'll have a new little rosebush, complete with roots!

◆ A NO-PEST NIGHTCAP

Preventing pests and diseases isn't just a spring-to-fall task—your roses need year-round attention to stay healthy. So when it's time to put them to bed for the winter, rake up all fallen leaves and petals from beneath them to minimize lingering bugs or diseases. Then hang a piece of No-Pest® strip from the canes, cover the plants with straw, and say "nitey-nite" for the winter.

GREAT IDEA!

Want to preserve the beauty of your best rose blooms?

Cut the flowers, then bundle the stems with a rubber band and hang them upside down in a warm, dark, dry place.

Perfect Rose Planting Mix

If you're planting just one or two roses, it's fine to dig individual planting holes. Just be sure to use this planting mix to enrich the soil you take out as you dig, so your new beauties will have perfect growing conditions and get off to a rip-roarin' start.

INSTRUCTIONS: Mix these ingredients in a wheelbarrow, then use this special blend to fill in around the roots as you backfill the holes. Your roses will absolutely love the loose, fertile soil you've given them!

> **INGREDIENTS:**
>
> 1 part peat moss or leaf mold
> 1 part manure
> 5 parts garden soil

◆ THE GRAFT CRAFT

Most times, the roses you buy will be grafted plants—the top growth of a desirable rose growing on the roots of another rose. You can tell when you look at the base of the plant, 'cause grafted roses have a knobby-looking area just above the roots. It's important to know where the graft union is, since it'll tell you how deep to set the plant in the ground. In the North (Zone 6 and colder), set the graft union 3 inches below the soil surface. In the South, set it 1½ inches *above* the soil line.

◆ A SCENT-SIBLE IDEA

Old-time gardeners swore that parsley makes roses more fragrant. So why not plant some around your favorite bushes to enhance the sweet smell of success?

TERRIFIC TIME⧗SAVERS

Planting more than a few roses in one area? Instead of spending hours digging individual holes, prepare a bed big enough to hold all of them. Improve the soil in the whole area by digging or tilling in a 2- to 4-inch-deep layer of organic matter. Planting will be a snap in that perfectly prepared soil!

Quick Thrip Control

Thrips are tiny insects that bug your roses, hanging out in the flowers and discoloring the petals or stopping the roses from opening. Use this formula to attract beneficial green lacewings to your rose garden—these good guys absolutely LOVE to eat nasty thrips.

INGREDIENTS:
1 part yeast
1 part sugar
Water

INSTRUCTIONS: Mix the yeast and sugar with just enough water to make a thin paste, and dab a little bit of the mixture onto each rosebud early in the morning.

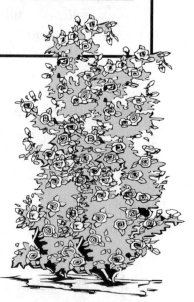

◆ THIS ROSE'LL GROW ON YOU!

When you're ready for a rose that's more than just a pretty face, give red-leaved rose (*Rosa glauca*) a try. This 6- to 8-foot-tall shrub looks great all year long, with single, pink blooms in early summer and purple-tinged, gray-green leaves. My favorite feature shows up in fall, when the clustered, oval fruits turn from green to orange to red, then stay on the plant well into winter. Best of all, this rose doesn't need fancy pruning, fertilizing, *or* spraying. Treat it more like a regular shrub than a rose, and it'll treat you to multi-season beauty year after year!

GRANDMA PUTT'S POINTERS ☞ Roses sure look lonely planted alone in a bed, all by themselves, but there's no law that says they have to be that way. My Grandma Putt always mixed her favorites in with other flowers to make gardens that were chock-full of blooms all summer long. Besides looking great, the roses she paired with other plants always seemed twice as healthy as those stuck off by themselves—maybe because those other bloomers attracted lots of beneficial insects to fight the bad bugs.

Robust Rose Food

Feed your established rosebushes initially in the spring with this fabulous fruity food. I guarantee that they'll go bananas over it!

INSTRUCTIONS: Mix these ingredients in a bucket, and sprinkle a handful or two around the base of each of your rosebushes. It has everything hungry roses need to spring into growth and prepare for a flower-filled summer!

INGREDIENTS:

5 lbs. of plant food (5-10-5 is fine)
2 cups of bonemeal
1 cup of Epsom salts
1 cup of sugar
4 dried banana peels (pulverized)

◆ WATCH OUT!

Don't be in a hurry to uncover your roses in spring. The covering will stop the buds from bursting too soon, so they won't get nipped by late frosts. But you *do* need to remove it as soon as new growth begins, so keep an eye on your bushes when the weather starts to warm up. Then be sure to get those covers off quick!

◆ PRUNING POINTERS

The best time to prune most roses? Late winter or early spring—just as some of the buds on the largest canes are beginning to swell. One exception is roses that bloom once in late spring to summer, which includes many old roses. Wait until after flowering to trim these beauties.

TERRIFIC TIME⏳SAVERS

Want to feed and water your roses at the same time? Cut the ends off a large, empty juice can, and push it all the way into the ground between two rosebushes. Then fill the can about halfway with pea-sized pebbles. Once a month during the growing season, add a small amount of rose food to the can. Pour directly into the can each time you water, and both you and your roses will enjoy the no-fuss feeding.

Rose Ambrosia

Dry fertilizers, like my Baker's Best Rose Chow (see **page 169**), are great for long-term rose feeding. But if you really want to get your roses off to a rousing start AND keep 'em full of flowers all summer long, follow up with this liquid lunch.

INSTRUCTIONS: Mix these ingredients in a bucket or watering can, then water each plant with 1 pint of the solution in the morning every three weeks. It'll keep those beautiful blooms comin'—GUARANTEED!

INGREDIENTS:

1 cup of beer
2 tsp. of instant tea granules
1 tsp. of 5-10-5 plant food
1 tsp. of fish emulsion
1 tsp. of hydrogen peroxide
1 tsp. of dishwashing liquid
2 gal. of warm water

◆ GET FRUITY

Roses aren't just for summer color anymore! When you choose roses that have showy fruits (called hips), you can enjoy them practically year-round. Plus, they've got lots of health benefits, too: Use 'em to tone up your lungs, boost your immune system, and even ease the aches of painful hemorrhoids (see **page 346**).

ASK JERRY

Q *I've been feeding my roses with your Rose Ambrosia and they look better now than they have in years, except for one thing—circles of leaf that are gone from otherwise healthy leaves. What could it be?*

A Leaf-cutter bees, that's what! They move so fast that you'll almost never see them at work, which consists of gathering bits of leaf that they use to build their nests. Don't chase them if you do see them: Scientists have a hunch that those holes stimulate your plants' immune systems, making them hold up better to other, much worse pests and diseases.

Rose Aphid-Fighter Tonic

Sick of having aphids suck the sap right out of your roses? Fight back with this citrusy spray to send them away for good!

INSTRUCTIONS: Put these ingredients into a blender, and blend on high for 10 to 15 seconds. Use a coffee filter to strain out the pulp. Pour the liquid into a hand-held sprayer. Before applying the tonic, get out your hose, attach a high-pressure spray nozzle, and blast your plants with water to dislodge some of the aphids. About 10 minutes later, thoroughly spray buds and young stems with this tonic. Repeat after four days, and your aphids should be history.

INGREDIENTS:

1 lemon or orange peel, coarsely chopped
1 tbsp. of baby shampoo
2 cups of water

◆ MINI MAGIC

When it comes to roses, bigger isn't always better! Miniature roses can be anywhere from 6 inches to 6 feet tall, but most fall into the 1- to 2-foot-tall category—just right for planting near the front of a flower garden among annuals, perennials, and bulbs. Monthly feedings, plus a heavy pruning in spring and a light shearing in midsummer, are the secret to keeping your minis making more blooms all season long. These little charmers get the same pests as their bigger cousins, so keep an eye out for the bad guys and give 'em a shot of my Rose Aphid-Fighter Tonic (above) if needed!

GRANDMA PUTT'S POINTERS ☞ Just a spoonful of sugar makes the rosebuds...open wide? That's right! If you have cut rosebuds that are slow to open, just pop a lump of sugar in their water, and they'll be fully open before you know it.

Rose Clean-Up Tonic

Fall is the best time to set back the insects and diseases that plague roses. So, after your plants have shed their leaves, but before you mulch them, treat them with this clean-up tonic.

INSTRUCTIONS: Mix these ingredients in a 20 gallon hose-end sprayer, and spray your plants well from top to bottom. That'll get your bushes squeaky clean for the winter and let them get off to a healthy start next spring.

INGREDIENTS:

1 cup of Murphy's Oil Soap®
1 cup of antiseptic mouthwash
1 cup of tobacco tea*
½ cup of hot, hot, hot sauce
½ cup of urine

To make tobacco tea, place half a handful of chewing tobacco in an old nylon stocking and soak it in a gallon of hot water until the mixture is dark brown.

◆ WINTER PREP TIPS

To get your roses ready for a long winter's nap, stop removing spent flowers in late summer or early fall, three to five weeks before the first frost in your area. Also, stop fertilizing after midsummer, but keep on watering, so your plants don't go to bed thirsty.

◆ ROSES UNDER COVER

If you live where winter temperatures sometimes dip below 0°F (Zone 6 and north), it's a good idea to protect Hybrid Teas, Grandifloras, Floribundas, and most English roses. Once the ground has frozen, pile shredded bark, soil, or compost over the base of the stems in an 8- to 12-inch-tall mound. Remove the mound in early spring.

MAKING CENTS

If you live in the North, where frigid winters freeze most roses to the quick, don't waste your money on tender roses! Canadian rose breeders have developed beautiful, super-hardy roses that are disease-resistant, too. Some of these super-tough roses include 'Champlain', 'Henry Hudson', 'John Cabot', 'Morden Fireglow', and 'William Baffin'.

Rose Revival Tonic

This one-two punch will get your bare-root roses off and growing like champs. First, wash your newly purchased bare-root bushes, roots and all, in a bucket of warm water with 1 tablespoon of dishwashing liquid and $\frac{1}{4}$ teaspoon of liquid bleach mixed in. Then, before planting, soak your bare-root rose-bushes in my Rose Revival Tonic.

INGREDIENTS:

2 tbsp. of clear corn syrup
1 tsp. of dishwashing liquid
1 tsp. of ammonia
1 gal. of warm water

<u>INSTRUCTIONS:</u> Mix these ingredients in a clean bucket, and let the roots soak for about half an hour before planting. This will help lessen the transplant shock and encourage healthy new roots to form.

◆ TRY 'EM—YOU'LL LIKE 'EM!

In late winter and very early spring, garden centers sell bare-root roses—dormant plants with their roots wrapped tightly in plastic. Although they don't look like much, good-quality bare-root roses are excellent buys. They're easy to plant and seldom need pruning to get off to a good start. For even better results, be sure to give them a good soak in my Rose Revival Tonic (above) before planting.

TERRIFIC TIME✕SAVERS

The only downside to choosing bare-root roses is having to plant them when the weather's pretty chilly—usually late winter or very early spring. But I've found an easy way to get around that: Prepare the beds well in advance! Pick a nice day in early fall, and decide where you're going to plant. Then dig the holes and get the soil all ready for your roses. When they finally arrive, it'll take just a few minutes to get 'em snug in their beds, and they'll be rarin' to grow when the warm weather finally returns!

Rose Transplant Tonic

The best time to move roses is when the bushes are dormant—that is, when the leaves have dropped and scales have formed over the growth buds for next year. Late fall is okay, but many professional rose growers prefer to move roses in early spring, before new growth starts. Whenever you transplant roses, ease the transition to their new homes with this terrific tonic.

INSTRUCTIONS: Mix these ingredients together in a bucket or watering can, and add 1 cup of the solution to each hole at transplant time. It'll help soothe the shock and get them settled in again in a flash.

INGREDIENTS:

1 can of beer
1 tbsp. of ammonia
1 tbsp. of instant tea granules
1 tbsp. of baby shampoo
1 gal. of water

◆ DO NOT DISTURB

When transplanting container-grown roses, you want to disturb the root ball as little as possible. So before planting, use a sharp knife to cut out the bottom of the container. Then set the container in the hole (use your fingertips to keep the root ball from slipping out of the pot). Cut away the sides of the container, and ease the pieces out before backfilling with soil. If you're careful and you handle the plant gently, your rose will hardly know it's been moved—so it'll settle in without missing a beat!

MAKING CENTS

If you're like me, you've misplaced a few gardening tools in your time, only to find them damaged or covered with rust weeks or months later. Well, here's a secret that'll save you a bundle in the long run: When you buy replacement tools, paint the handles bright yellow or orange. That way, you'll be sure to find them after you've set them down in the grass!

So Long, Suckers! Spray

Using bad bugs to kill other bugs is the basis behind my popular Dead Bug Brew (see **page 175**). But if you're dealing with tiny insects, like thrips and aphids, that are too small to handpick and whirl in a blender all by themselves, give this tonic a try.

INSTRUCTIONS: Put the plant parts in an old blender (don't use it again for either human or pet food—EVER), and whirl 'em with 2 cups of warm water (tiny bugs and all). Strain the goop through cheesecloth, dilute with 1 gallon of water, and pour the juice into a hand-held sprayer. Then spray your plants from top to bottom, on both sides of the leaves and stems. Repeat the treatment after each rain.

> **INGREDIENTS:**
>
> **2 cups of pest-infested flowers or leaves**
> **Water**

◆ SAVE THE EXTRAS

If you have any leftover So Long, Suckers! Spray (above), freeze it right away before bacteria can get a toehold. And be sure to label it clearly—believe you me, you don't want to have any of this stuff for dinner!

◆ DO THE ROSE SHIMMY

Open rose blooms tend to rot if they catch and hold water. To keep them in perfect condition, give them a little shake or two to dislodge some of the water drops from the petals after a heavy rain.

GREAT IDEA!

Does your yard tend to get whipped by wild winter winds?

Then it's smart to give your roses a little extra TLC in late fall. Cut back extra-long canes to keep them from blowing around, then tie the remaining canes together with an old nylon stocking, about three-quarters of the way up the bush.

Super Start-Up Tonic

Dry fertilizers are great for long-term feeding, but when your roses need to eat right away, liquids are where it's at. Here's the perfect meal to get newly planted rosebushes off to a quick start in spring.

INSTRUCTIONS: Mix these ingredients in a bucket or watering can, then pour the liquid all around the root zone of each of your prize rosebushes for a nice nutrient boost.

INGREDIENTS:
1 tbsp. of dishwashing liquid
1 tbsp. of hydrogen peroxide
1 tsp. of whiskey
1 tsp. of vitamin B_1 plant starter
$\frac{1}{2}$ gal. of warm brewed tea

◆ PERFECT PARTNERS

Stumped about what to plant with your roses? Think about the flowers you like to combine for indoor arrangements, then plant them together in your garden. Some spectacular annual companions for roses—both in and out of the vase—include cosmos, dahlias, larkspur, mealycup sage, statice, and zinnias.

Perennials pair well with roses, too: Lavender, summer-blooming phlox, pincushion flowers, Shasta daisies, and veronicas are just a few super perennial partners. And don't forget summer bulbs—gladiolus and lilies look absolutely elegant with roses.

GRANDMA PUTT'S POINTERS ☞ When you're almost finished planting a new rose—just before you water it in well with my Super Start-Up Tonic (above) and add mulch—sprinkle a tablespoon of Epsom salts over the soil's surface. Roses love the stuff, so take Grandma Putt's advice and give your established roses a spring feeding of Epsom salts, too. Simply rake off the old mulch in spring, sprinkle a tablespoon of Epsom salts over the soil around each bush, then add fresh, new mulch to set your roses up right for the growing season.

CHAPTER 5

A BOUNTY OF BULBS

FLOWERS THAT BLOOM from bulbs are a low-maintenance gardener's dream. They come equipped with their own stored food supply, and they know exactly what to do to replenish it each year. Best of all, bulbs produce incredibly showy flowers that are great for cutting, and many of them are easy to grow in containers, too!

While bulbs do a bang-up job looking after themselves, they'll grow even better with a little extra attention from you. Jump-start their growth in spring with a power-packed elixir or two, and next year's blooms will be better than you've ever dreamed! And if any bad bugs, dastardly diseases, or gate-crashing critters threaten to spoil the show, just use one of my magical mixers to fix the problem quick! Whatever your bulbs need, there's a ter-rific tonic to help them stay happy and healthy, year after year.

AROUND the YEAR

Bulbs may not need much care, but to get the best results, it's important to give them WHAT they need, WHEN they need it! So whether it's feeding established bulbs in spring, setting out tender bulbs for summer color, or planting new bulbs in fall, my step-by-step system will take all the guesswork out of the game and keep your bulbs bouncing all year-round!

 ## Spring

◆ **Step 1:** Once early spring rolls around, it's time to mix up a batch of my Out-to-Lunch Mix (see **page 206**) and give your bulb beds a beneficial boost:

10 lbs. of compost
5 lbs. of bonemeal
1 lb. of Epsom salts

Mix all of these ingredients in a bucket, stirring them together with a shovel. Top-dress established bulb beds with the mixture in early spring when the foliage starts to emerge from the ground. (This recipe makes enough for 100 sq. ft. of soil.) For an extra treat, add up to 5 pounds of wood ashes to the mix.

◆ **Step 2:** When it's time to plant gladiolus, cannas, and other tender bulbs, give them a soak in my Bug-Off Bulb Bath (see **page 199**) to discourage diseases and say bye-bye to bugs:

2 tsp. of baby shampoo
1 tsp. of antiseptic mouthwash
¼ tsp. of instant tea granules
2 gal. of hot water

Mix these ingredients in a bucket, then carefully place your bulbs into the mixture. Stir gently, then remove the bulbs one at a time and plant them. When you're done, don't throw the bath water out with the babies! Your trees, shrubs, and evergreens would love to have a little taste, so don't let it go to waste.

◆ **Step 3:** Are marauding deer destroying your hopes for a beautiful show of bulbs this year? Those brown-eyed bruisers will head for the hills when they get a whiff of my Fishy Deer Detergent (see **page 204**):

l cup of fish emulsion
3 tbsp. of liquid kelp
3 tbsp. of dishwashing liquid
Water

Mix the fish emulsion, kelp, and dishwashing liquid in a 3 gallon pump sprayer, and add water up to the fill line. Apply to plants to the point of run-off. Reapply every 7 to 10 days or following any heavy rain that washes the mixture off of plant leaves.

◆ **Step 4:** To discourage insects and diseases, apply my All-Season Clean-Up Tonic (see **page 197**) in the evening every two weeks throughout the growing season:

l cup of baby shampoo
l cup of antiseptic mouthwash
l cup of tobacco tea*

Mix these ingredients in a 20 gallon hose-end sprayer, and give everything in your yard a good shower in the early evening. You'll have the healthiest bulbs in town—GUARANTEED!

To make tobacco tea, place half a handful of chewing tobacco in an old nylon stocking and soak it in a gallon of hot water until the mixture is dark brown.

 Summer

◆ **Step 5:** Used regularly, my All-Season Green-Up Tonic (see **page 198**) will help all of your bulbs stay happy and healthy throughout the growing season:

l can of beer
l cup of ammonia
$1/2$ cup of dishwashing liquid
$1/2$ cup of liquid lawn food
$1/2$ cup of molasses or clear corn syrup

Mix these ingredients in a large bucket, pour into a 20 gallon hose-end sprayer, and spray everything in sight— not just your bulbs, but also your trees, shrubs, flower beds, lawn, and even vegetables. Apply this tonic every three weeks right up through the first hard frost, and your bulbs are sure to come through the hot summer months with flying colors!

 *Fall*

◆ **Step 6:** Get your new bulbs fresh-ened up before you plant them with a short, but sweet bath in my Bulb Soak (see **page 202**):

1 can of beer
2 tbsp. of dishwashing liquid
$1/4$ tsp. of instant tea granules
2 gal. of water

Mix these ingredients in a large bucket. Let your bulbs soak for a few minutes, then get busy planting!

◆ **Step 7:** Bulbs get by best with a slow and steady source of nutrients, so my Bulb Breakfast of Champions (see **page 200**) perfectly fits the bill at fall planting time:

10 lbs. of compost
5 lbs. of bonemeal
2 lbs. of bloodmeal
1 lb. of Epsom salts

Mix these ingredients in a wheelbarrow. Before setting out your bulbs, work this hearty meal into every 100 sq. ft. of soil in your bulb-planting beds. Or, if you're planting bulbs among other plants, work a handful of this mix into the soil in each hole before setting in the bulb.

◆ **Step 8:** When Jack Frost makes a return appearance, it's time to dig up your tender bulbs, and bring them indoors for the winter. AFTER you dig them up and brush off any loose soil, but BEFORE you store them away for the winter, dip them in my Bulb Cleaning Tonic (see **page 201**) to get rid of any lingering bugs or diseases:

2 tbsp. of baby shampoo
1 tsp. of hydrogen peroxide
1 qt. of warm water

Mix these ingredients in a bucket and then gently drop in your bulbs. Let them soak for a minute or so, then remove and set on a wire rack to drain. Be sure to let them dry thor-oughly before you put them away; otherwise, they'll rot.

TERRIFIC TIME⧗SAVERS

Where winters are cold, grow eye-catching cannas in large containers, and bring the pots into an unheated, but frost-free garage for the winter. Then all you have to do in spring is move them back to the great out-doors. No more digging and replanting!

All-Season Clean-Up Tonic

This is the one tonic that you ABSOLUTELY need to use religiously throughout the growing season. The shampoo cleans the plants and helps the other ingredients stick better; the mouthwash kills bad bacteria and discourages insects; and the tobacco tea contains nicotine, which does a double whammy on those pesky pests.

INGREDIENTS:

1 cup of baby shampoo
1 cup of antiseptic mouthwash
1 cup of tobacco tea*

INSTRUCTIONS: Mix these ingredients in a 20 gallon hose-end sprayer, and give everything in your yard a good shower in the early evening every two weeks throughout the growing season. You'll have the healthiest bulbs in town—GUARANTEED!

To make tobacco tea, place half a handful of chewing tobacco in an old nylon stocking and soak it in a gallon of hot water until the mixture is dark brown.

◆ NO MUSH FOR ME, THANKS!

When buying bulbs, steer clear of any with mushy gray spots on them. They're not worth carting home because they won't recover. But don't worry if the bulb's papery skin is loose; this is completely normal. And don't be concerned about a few nicks—they won't affect the development of otherwise healthy bulbs.

MAKING CENTS

No doubt about it: Cannas are some of the best bulbs for summer flowers and foliage. But buying new ones each year can really break the bank! Fortunately, there's no need to buy your favorite cannas more than once. In early spring, chop each rhizome into pieces with at least two growing points on each, then pot them up and grow them indoors until the weather warms up. With this trick, you can get three, four, or even more new cannas from just one rhizome!

All-Season Green-Up Tonic

If your bulbs are looking a bit peaked, give them a taste of this super-sweet snack. It's rich in nutrients and packed with energizers, too: just what your plants need to stay in tip-top form.

INSTRUCTIONS: Mix these ingredients in a large bucket, pour into a 20 gallon hose-end sprayer, and spray everything in sight—not just your bulbs, but also your trees, shrubs, flower beds, lawn, and even vegetables. Apply this tonic every three weeks right up through the first hard frost, and your bulbs will come through the hot summer months with flying colors!

INGREDIENTS:

1 can of beer
1 cup of ammonia
$1/2$ cup of dishwashing liquid
$1/2$ cup of liquid lawn food
$1/2$ cup of molasses or clear corn syrup

◆ DIVIDE TO CONQUER

After a few years, you'll probably notice that your daffodil, hyacinth, and tulip blooms just aren't as big and beautiful as they used to be. Chances are, the bulbs are overcrowded and need dividing. Dig 'em up as soon as their leaves have died back after bloom. Break the bulbs apart with your hands (be sure to wear gloves if you're handling hyacinths), then replant the separated bulbs at the proper depth. It doesn't get much easier than that!

GRANDMA PUTT'S POINTERS ☞

Everyone loves the fabulous flowers of daffodils, tulips, and other spring bulbs, but the yellowing foliage that follows in early summer is another matter. Don't even *think* of cutting off the leaves before they're completely yellow—they need to make food for next year's flowers! Instead, do what Grandma Putt did: Scatter some annual seeds around the declining bulb foliage. They'll fill in the empty space in no time at all.

Bug-Off Bulb Bath

Used BEFORE planting, this super spa treatment will help gladiolus, cannas, and other summer-blooming bulbs laugh at disease and pesky pests. What, you've never seen laughing flowers?

INSTRUCTIONS: Mix these ingredients in a bucket, then carefully place your bulbs into the mixture. Stir gently, then remove the bulbs one at a time and plant them. When you're done, don't throw the bath water out with the babies! Your trees, shrubs, and evergreens would love a little taste (and grow better for it), so don't let it go to waste.

INGREDIENTS:

2 tsp. of baby shampoo
1 tsp. of antiseptic mouthwash
$\frac{1}{4}$ tsp. of instant tea granules
2 gal. of hot water

◆ BEAUTIFUL BULB BEDMATES

Few of us have garden space to spare, so it just makes sense to get the most out of every square inch we've got. Well, here's a great way to get double the bloom without digging more beds—simply pair early spring bulbs with later-rising perennials! Daylilies are one of my top picks for partnering with bulbs in sunny spots, while hostas are super in sites that'll get summer shade. Besides providing summer and fall interest, the perennials will cover up the yellowing bulb foliage in late spring—which is another big plus!

GREAT IDEA!

No garden can have too many lilies, but it can get pretty pricey to buy a lot of these beauties all at once.

Why bother, when you can grow your own? Most lilies produce small, baby bulbs right above the main bulb, just below the soil surface. Loosen the soil carefully with a hand fork, pick off the babies, and then plant them in a holding bed or a corner of your vegetable garden. After a year or two, move them back to the garden for a great show!

Bulb Breakfast of Champions

Give your newly planted bulbs a big boost with a taste of this terrific tonic. It's packed with nutrients and organic matter to provide a small, but steady supply of food— just what's needed for balanced bulb growth.

INSTRUCTIONS: Mix these ingredients in a wheelbarrow. Before setting out your bulbs, work this hearty meal into every 100 sq. ft. of soil in your bulb-planting beds. Or, if you're planting bulbs among other plants, work a handful of this mix into the soil in each hole before setting in the bulb.

◆ BABY BULBS GO NEAR THE BACK

When it comes to planting small bulbs, I want you to break the rules: Plant them near the back of the border, rather than the front. Sounds odd, I know, but here's why—by the time your perennials come up, those little bulbs'll be done for the season, and big, bushy perennials will do a bang-up job of hiding the yucky bulb foliage.

ASK JERRY

Q *It's not even wintertime yet, and some of my bulbs are starting to poke their little noses out of the soil! What should I do?*

A Don't worry about it; this is common with a few hardy bulbs. Their leaf tips might get a little tattered, but the flowers will be just fine next year.

Bulb Cleaning Tonic

Instead of spending your hard-earned money on new dahlias, cannas, or other tender bulbs each year, why not simply keep the ones you already have? As soon as their leaves start to turn color in fall, dig 'em up and wash them in this tonic before storing them away in a frost-free place for the winter.

INSTRUCTIONS: Mix these ingredients in a bucket, and then gently drop in your bulbs. Let them soak for a minute or so, then remove and set on a wire rack to drain. Be sure to let them dry thoroughly before you put them away; otherwise, they'll rot.

> **INGREDIENTS:**
>
> 2 tbsp. of baby shampoo
> 1 tsp. of hydrogen peroxide
> 1 qt. of warm water

◆ NIP THRIPS IN THE BUD

The major pests of gladiolus are tiny insects called thrips, which cause off-color streaking on petals and leaves. If your glads have been bothered by thrips in the past, give them some extra TLC in the fall. After you dig 'em up and knock off the loose soil, place 'em in paper bags along with 2 tablespoons of moth crystals for every 100 corms. Fold over and clip the top of each bag, then keep 'em at about 70°F for three to four weeks. Remove the corms, dust them with powdered sulfur to stop funky fungi and bad bacteria from getting started during storage, and store them in a cool (40° to 50°F), dry place for the winter.

TERRIFIC TIME⧗SAVERS

Instead of struggling to grow grass under mature trees and shrubs, plant bulbs—they're made to order! They'll give you a great show of spring color year after year, then go dormant by the time the shrubs leaf out for summer.

Bulb Soak

After sitting around in a garden center for a few weeks, hardy bulbs can get pretty dried out by the time you get them home. To get them pumped full of life again, dip them in this super solution just before planting.

INSTRUCTIONS: Mix these ingredients in a large bucket. Let your bulbs soak for a few minutes, then get busy planting!

INGREDIENTS:
1 can of beer
2 tbsp. of dishwashing liquid
1/4 tsp. of instant tea granules
2 gal. of water

◆ PILE 'EM ON

Want to get twice—or even three times—the number of blooms in the same amount of space? Try my fantastic layering trick! Dig one hole about 8 inches deep, then plant several layers of bulbs in the same spot. Here's how:

- ◆ **Step 1:** Set the bulbs of the latest bloomers you've chosen (usually late tulips or lilies) in the bottom of the hole.

- ◆ **Step 2:** Replace enough soil to barely cover the bulb tips, then set in the next layer (try early and midseason tulips, or daffodils).

- ◆ **Step 3:** Add more soil, then set in the top layer of smaller bulbs (like snow crocuses).

- ◆ **Step 4:** Finish by covering with a mulch of leaves, shredded bark, or wood chips, plus a scattering of moth crystals over the top to keep critters away. It's that easy!

GRANDMA PUTT'S POINTERS ☞

After a day spent grubbing around in the garden planting bulbs, your fingernails can get pretty grimy. When I was a youngster, Grandma Putt had me try this trick: Before heading out to the garden, I lightly scratched my fingernails over a bar of soap. Come clean-up time, the dirt and soap would wash right out!

Elephant's Ears Elixir

The heart-shaped leaves of elephant's ears can grow to gigantic proportions—especially if you feed them with this magical mixer!

INSTRUCTIONS: Mix the beer, plant food, and ammonia in a 20 gallon hose-end sprayer, filling the balance of the jar with water. Then every three weeks, spray the plants to the point of run-off to keep them at their best and growing strong.

INGREDIENTS:

1 can of beer
1 cup of all-purpose plant food
1/4 cup of ammonia
Water

◆ PUT YOUR BEST FACE FORWARD, DAHLING!

Most dahlia flowers will face the sun—that means south and west. With a little planning, you can use this trick to your advantage! On the north and east sides of your house, plant dahlias on the edge of your property, so the blooms will face toward you. On the south and west sides, keep them next to the house, so they face into your yard.

◆ QUICK-START BEGONIAS

Want to enjoy tuberous begonia blooms before everyone else? Start them indoors, 8 to 10 weeks before your last spring frost date. Fill a shallow tray with barely moist potting mix, set the tubers on top, then almost cover them with mix. Put them in a bright area out of direct sun, and keep them barely moist. When the shoots are about 2 inches long, move each tuber to its own 4- or 5-inch pot. Plant outside after all danger of frost has passed.

TERRIFIC TIME⧗SAVERS

When buying cannas, look for the term "self-cleaning." No, this doesn't mean they'll do your laundry for you; it means the old flowers drop off the plants all by themselves—and that translates into time savings for you!

Fishy Deer Detergent

Once deer develop a taste for your garden, they're likely to come back again and again. So BEFORE they make your beautiful bulbs part of their breakfast buffet, give my Fishy Deer Detergent a try.

INSTRUCTIONS: Mix the fish emulsion, kelp, and dishwashing liquid in a 3 gallon pump sprayer, and add water up to the fill line. Apply to plants to the point of run-off. Reapply every 7 to 10 days, or following any heavy rain that washes the mixture off of plant leaves.

INGREDIENTS:

1 cup of fish emulsion
3 tbsp. of liquid kelp
3 tbsp. of dishwashing liquid
Water

◆ Bunny Barriers

Are rascally rabbits snacking on your bulb shoots as fast as they appear? To protect those tender shoots, cut the bottoms out of the black plastic nursery pots you buy perennials in, and slip one ring over each group of shoots. Push the bottom inch or so of each ring into the soil to secure it in place.

◆ Be Happy About Glads

For the most gorgeous glads on the block, give 'em a dose of dry 5-10-5 plant food (1 cup per 25 feet of row) as soon as they peek through the soil, then water them thoroughly. When the shoots are about a foot high, either stake 'em or mound up 4 to 6 inches of soil around the base of each stem to keep those beautiful blooms standing tall.

GREAT IDEA!

Aiming to get the biggest dahlia blooms possible?

Give your plants a good pinch now and then! Look for the largest bud on each stalk, then pinch out (or snip off) the buds that appear on either side of it. Pinch out any side shoots that come off the main stalk, too.

Gopher-Go Tonic

One look at the long front teeth of gophers and other chewing rodents, and you know that these are critters you don't want in your garden. I've had amazing results with this tonic, and so have a lot of other folks who have tried it!

INSTRUCTIONS: Mix the castor oil, dishwashing liquid, urine, and $1/2$ cup of warm water. Then stir the mixture into 2 gallons of warm water in a large watering can. Pour it over gopher-infested areas to send these vile varmints packin'.

INGREDIENTS:

4 tbsp. of castor oil
4 tbsp. of dishwashing liquid
4 tbsp. of urine
$1/2$ cup plus 2 gal. of warm water

◆ RODENT-PROOF TULIPS

If you don't even see leaves where your tulips are supposed to be, the usual suspects include voles, mice, or gophers, all of which consider tulips a tasty treat. So the next time you plant bulbs, surround your tulips with sharp, crushed gravel, line planting beds with $1/2$-inch hardware cloth, or plant groups of bulbs in wire mesh baskets. Sure, it's extra work—but believe me, it'll all be worthwhile when you see those beauties strut their stuff in spring!

ASK JERRY

Q *Hey, Jer—how come I have luck with some bulbs and not others in my Deep South garden?*

A Some bulbs—notably tulips and hyacinths—need a period of chilling to grow and bloom properly, and they don't get that if your soil stays warm in winter. But don't waste your hard-earned money buying "precooled" bulbs—do the job yourself! When you buy new bulbs in early fall, simply pop them in the vegetable drawer of your refrigerator for five to six weeks. Plant them in December, and they'll brighten your beds right on schedule in spring!

Out-to-Lunch Mix

Every spring, serve up this hearty lunch to your hardy bulbs. It'll give them all the nutrition they need to put on a really big show!

INSTRUCTIONS: Mix these ingredients in a bucket, stirring them together with a shovel. Top-dress established bulb beds with the mixture in early spring when the foliage starts to emerge from the ground. (This recipe makes enough for 100 sq. ft. of soil.) For an extra treat, add up to 5 pounds of wood ashes to the mix.

INGREDIENTS:

10 lbs. of compost
5 lbs. of bonemeal
1 lb. of Epsom salts

◆ ONIONS FOR EVERYONE

Ornamental onions (*Allium*) aren't just pretty—they're downright handy to have around! Here's why:

- ◆ Break up chive blossoms into salads, or mix them with softened butter for a touch of color and a burst of flavor.

- ◆ Let the seedheads of large alliums dry right in the garden, then use them in dried arrangements. Spray-paint them for extra color!

- ◆ Pour enough boiling water over 1 cup of packed chive leaves to cover them; let cool, strain, and use this mix to repel flower pests. This also helps prevent scab on apple trees.

MAKING CENTS

Lilies make top-notch cut flowers, but they cost a bundle if you buy them from a florist. So save yourself some dough, and grow your own! Here's a little trick that'll save you a lot of clean-up time and effort: Make sure you pick off the anthers—those pollen-covered bits that dangle on long stalks from the center of each flower. Otherwise, the pollen will drop off, and it can permanently stain fabric and furniture.

Rhubarb Bug Repellent

Here's a potent spray that'll say "Scram!" to just about any bug—and you probably have the key ingredient growing right around the corner in your vegetable garden!

INSTRUCTIONS: Chop up the rhubarb leaves, put the pieces in the water, and bring to a boil. Let the mixture cool, then strain it through cheesecloth to filter out the leaf bits. Mix in the dishwashing liquid. Apply this terrific tonic to your plants with a small hand-held sprayer, and kiss your pest problems good-bye! Just remember, rhubarb leaves are highly poisonous, so never use this spray on edible plants.

INGREDIENTS:

3 medium-size rhubarb leaves
$\frac{1}{4}$ cup of dishwashing liquid
1 gal. of water

◆ THE COMBACK KIDS

If you're buying new tulip bulbs every year because the old ones never seem to bloom well after the first year, it's probably because you're buying the wrong bulbs. It's easy to have the same tulips come back spring after spring—*if* you choose the right ones! Your best bets are Kaufmanniana, Fosteriana, and Greigii tulips, along with Darwin Hybrid or Triumph tulips. Species tulips are good choices, too—especially *Tulipa saxatilis, T. batalinii*, and *T. tarda*.

GREAT IDEA!

Want to make your cut daffodils last longer?

First, pick daffodils when they're about half open. Make a 1-inch-long slit up through the base of each stem, then stand the flowers in water up to their necks for several hours before putting them with other flowers in an arrangement. Daffodil stems are full of sap that clogs the stems of other flowers, so this prevents the problem and lengthens the vase life of ALL the flowers in your bouquet.

Scat-Cat Solution

Are prowling pussycats traipsing through your tulips or chewing on your crocuses? Surround your prized plants with this pungent potion, and the kitties are sure to go elsewhere for their munchies.

INGREDIENTS:

5 tbsp. of flour
4 tbsp. of dry mustard
3 tbsp. of cayenne pepper
2 tbsp. of chili powder
2 qts. of warm water

INSTRUCTIONS: Mix these ingredients in a large watering can, then sprinkle the solution around your bulbs to keep cats from sleeping in (or snacking on) them.

◆ TWICE AS NICE

If you're as penny-wise as I am, you'll love this little trick I use each year to double, or even triple my dahlia display! Start the tubers in pots indoors in early spring, and keep them warm and moist. When the shoots are about 6 inches tall, cut them off 1 inch above the soil line, then stick them halfway into a mixture of half sand and half compost. After watering lightly, cover the potted cuttings with a clear glass jar, and set them in a place with bright, but indirect light. In four to six weeks, they'll be rooted and ready for the garden.

ASK JERRY

Q *When I'm planting bulbs, can I just drop them in the hole, or do I have to plant them in any special way?*

A With some bulbs, it's anyone's guess as to which is the top and which is the bottom. But for most, there's an obvious difference: The top of the bulb comes to a point, while at the base there is usually a flat part from which roots will grow later on. So remember—look for the nose, not the toes, and plant your bulbs "heads up"!

Slug-It-Out Tonic

Slugs can do a real number on tender bulb shoots, chewing through buds, chomping off leaves, and generally destroying your chances for a bountiful bulb display. To fight back, take steps to trap these dastardly destroyers BEFORE they get busy.

INSTRUCTIONS: Mix these ingredients in a bowl, and let 'em sit for 24 hours. Then pour the mixture into shallow aluminum pie pans, and set the pans so that the rims are just at ground level in various areas of your garden. You'll catch lots and lots of slugs, and you'll know that they died happy!

> **INGREDIENTS:**
> 1 can of beer
> 1 tbsp. of sugar
> 1 tsp. of baker's yeast

◆ DID YOU KNOW?

Boys are the boss when it comes to growing gorgeous begonias! Most tuberous begonias produce clusters of three flowers: one male flower flanked by two females. The female flowers have a swollen seed capsule right behind the petals, while the male doesn't. So, when the blooms are still small buds, pinch off the two female flowers. All the growing energy in that stem will go into making one huge bloom!

MAKING CENTS

Believe it or not, you can grow the world's costliest spice right in your backyard! I'm talking about saffron crocus (*Crocus sativus*). The small red parts (called stigmata) in the center of each bloom are the source of saffron—a spice used to add yellow coloring and delicate flavoring to foods.

Plant the corms as soon as you get them in late summer for blooms in fall. When they flower, pick the red stigmata, dry them, and store in an airtight glass jar for later use.

Spicy Squirrel Stopper

You carefully planted a bunch of bulbs yesterday, and today, they're scattered all over your yard! Don't blame your dogs, or the kids down the street—squirrels are probably the culprits. It's not the bulbs themselves that these pesky critters are after; it's the loose, fluffy soil that seems to draw them like a magnet. To discourage them from digging, try this spicy solution.

INSTRUCTIONS: Mix these ingredients in a bowl, and pour the mixture into a squirt bottle (such as an old ketchup bottle).

INGREDIENTS:

1 teaspoon of Tabasco® sauce
1 teaspoon of chili powder
½ teaspoon of dishwashing liquid
1 pint of water

After planting your bulbs in late summer or fall, squirt the mixture on the soil where you planted. Come spring, mix a new batch and spray it around the edges of your bulb beds.

◆ GET WIRED

For extra protection from squirrelly scallywags, lay chicken wire over the area immediately after planting, and cover it with mulch. Remove the wire any time the following year.

◆ PLANT BULBS IN BULK

The biggest mistake people make when planting bulbs? Trying to spread them out too much! You'll get the biggest bang for your gardening buck by planting them in groups of five or more, with bulbs no more than 6 inches apart.

GRANDMA PUTT'S POINTERS ☞ Grandma Putt loved all kinds of daffodils, but when she wanted an especially spectacular show, she'd always choose multiflowered (or cluster-flowered) types, such as 'Geranium' and 'Thalia'. These bodacious beauties will produce anywhere from 2 to 20 flowers on each and every stem!

Super Spider Mite Mix

Spider mites are tiny, all right, but they can get up to mite-y BIG mischief in your garden! When they show up, send 'em scurryin' with this floury remedy.

INSTRUCTIONS: Mix these ingredients in a large bucket, and pour some into a hand-held sprayer. Shake well, and apply to affected plants to the point of run-off. This mix will suffocate the little buggers, without harming any of your flowers.

> **INGREDIENTS:**
> 4 cups of wheat flour
> $1/2$ cup of buttermilk
> 5 gal. of water

◆ THE NOSE KNOWS

When you're shopping for daffodils, use bulb size for an easy price comparison. "Landscape-size" or "single-nose" bulbs produce one flower stem the first year. They're inexpensive and usually a good buy. "Bedding-size" or "double-nose" bulbs produce two flower stems. "Exhibition-size" or "triple-nose" bulbs are the most expensive, but each bulb will produce three or more flower stems—that's three times the flower power of a "single-nose"!

◆ TULIPS CAN'T TAKE THE HEAT

All leaves and no flowers make tulips mighty dull, indeed! So what happened? It's likely that the bulbs you bought weren't stored or handled properly. Tulips exposed to temperatures above 70°F in storage don't bloom well (if at all). In any event, just be patient; you should have flowers the following year.

TERRIFIC TIME⊠SAVERS

Have more than a handful of bulbs to plant? Instead of digging dozens of individual holes, things will go a whole lot quicker if you dig one larger hole that can hold several bulbs. If you place the soil you dig out onto a sheet of plastic, it'll be easy to dump the dirt back in the hole when it comes time for refilling!

CHAPTER 6

DIVINE VINES & GROUNDCOVERS

WHAT'S THE SIGN of a true green thumb? A yard where every bit of available space is put to good use! Low-growing groundcovers are perfect for carpeting the ground beneath trees, under shrubs, and along walkways—wherever a tidy, well-groomed look is important. But these beauties are more than just pretty faces. They'll grow in tough sites where lawn grass would turn up its toes and die, and they'll work hard all year long with barely any care from you. So what's not to love?

And while we're talking about no-fuss plants, let's remember to deck the walls with vines, too! These climbers can work miracles in even the smallest of spaces, livening up boring fences and buildings with loads of easy-care color. So whether you're adding new vines and ground-covers to your yard or perking up existing plantings, I've got a great bunch of tonics for feedin', weedin', and keepin' them in the pink of health!

AROUND *the* YEAR

Both vines and groundcovers can get by with hardly any care, but if you really want to see these garden gems shine, a tonic here and there will really set 'em right! Just follow these few simple steps to keep 'em hearty and healthy all year-round.

 ## Spring

◆ **Step 1:** Ready to get your vines and groundcovers off to a rousing start? My terrific Breath-of-Fresh-Air Tonic (see **page 220**) is just what the doctor ordered to get 'em growing:

1 cup of 3% hydrogen peroxide
$1/4$ cup of clear corn syrup
2 tbsp. of whiskey
2 tbsp. of baby shampoo
$1 1/2$ cups of warm water

Mix these ingredients in a 20 gallon hose-end sprayer. Apply liberally to everything in your yard just as new growth begins, then stand back and admire the amazing results!

◆ **Step 2:** Spring is a super time to get new groundcovers going in your garden. Treat 'em to a taste of my Groundcover Starter Chow (see **page 228**) when you set 'em out:

3 parts bonemeal
1 part Epsom salts
1 part gypsum

Mix these ingredients in a bucket. Place $1/2$ cup in each planting hole and spread $1/2$ cup on the soil surface when planting your groundcovers.

◆ **Step 3:** Happy, healthy groundcovers are your very best defense against pesky weeds, so keep 'em growin' strong with a taste of my Terrific Top-dressing (see **page 239**):

20 parts Milorganite®
10 parts earthworm castings
5 parts ground-up fresh apples
$1/2$ bushel of peat moss

Mix these ingredients in a wheel-barrow, and scatter the mixture generously over the top of your ground-covers in spring. Then mix 1 can of beer and 4 teaspoons of instant tea granules in 2 gallons of water in a large watering can, and water the whole area.

◆ **Step 4:** My All-Season Clean-Up Tonic (see **page 217**) is one tonic that you ABSOLUTELY need to use religiously throughout the growing season to keep pests and diseases at bay:

1 cup of baby shampoo
1 cup of antiseptic mouthwash
1 cup of tobacco tea*

Mix these ingredients in a 20 gallon hose-end sprayer, and give everything in your yard a good shower in the early evening every two weeks throughout the growing season.

*To make tobacco tea, place half a handful of chewing tobacco in an old nylon stocking and soak it in a gallon of hot water until the mixture is dark brown.

# Summer

◆ **Step 5:** Keep your green scene in tip-top shape by treating all your plants to my nutrient-packed All-Season Green-Up Tonic (see **page 218**):

1 can of beer
1 cup of ammonia
$\frac{1}{2}$ cup of dishwashing liquid
$\frac{1}{2}$ cup of liquid lawn food
$\frac{1}{2}$ cup of molasses or clear corn syrup

Mix these ingredients in a large bucket, pour into a 20 gallon hose-end sprayer, and spray everything in sight— not just your vines and groundcovers, but also your trees, shrubs, lawn, flowers, and even vegetables. Apply this tonic every three weeks right up through the first hard frost, and your plants will survive the hot summer months with flying colors!

◆ **Step 6:** If pesky pests get out of hand, knock 'em for a loop with my super-spicy Garden Cure-All Tonic (see **page 226**):

4 cloves of garlic
1 small onion
1 small jalapeño pepper
1 tsp. of Murphy's Oil Soap®
1 tsp. of vegetable oil
Warm water

Purée the garlic, onion, and pepper in an old blender, and let the mix steep in a quart of warm water for 2 hours. Strain the mixture, and further dilute the liquid with three parts of warm water. Add the Murphy's Oil Soap and vegetable oil. Pour into a hand-held sprayer, and apply to your plants several times a week until pests disappear.

◆ **Step 7:** Even with regular feeding, vines and groundcovers can start looking a little tired by midsummer. But you can perk 'em up in a flash—just treat 'em to a taste of my Just Desserts Tonic (see **page 229**):

4 tbsp. of hydrogen peroxide
l tbsp. of Epsom salts
l tbsp. of baking powder
l tbsp. of ammonia
½ tsp. of unflavored gelatin
½ tsp. of dishwashing liquid
4 One-a-Day® multivitamins
    with iron, dissolved in 1 cup
    of hot water
1 gal. of rainwater or filtered water

Mix the peroxide, Epsom salts, baking powder, ammonia, gelatin, dishwashing liquid, and dissoved vitamins in a bucket. Mix l cup of this liquid with the rainwater or filtered water, and treat your plants liberally with the mixture.

 *Fall*

◆ **Step 8:** Don't let wicked weeds get the better of your beautiful vines and groundcover plantings! My Easy Weed Killer (see **page 222**) is just the ticket for zapping those ugly weeds into oblivion:

1 gal. of vinegar
l cup of table salt
l tbsp. of dishwashing
    liquid

Mix these ingredients in a hand-held sprayer, and apply liberally to weeds. Just make sure you don't get it on plants you want to keep!

 **GRANDMA PUTT'S POINTERS** ☞ Treating vine and groundcover cuttings with a rooting hormone is a great way to get new roots in a hurry. But you don't have to shell out your hard-earned dough to buy this wonderful stuff at your local garden center. If you have access to any kind of willow tree, you can make your own, just like Grandma Putt did! Simply snip off a few twigs, cut 'em into 1-inch pieces, and soak 'em in a quart of water for a few days. Take out the twigs, and use the brew to water your cuttings. They'll be growin' fine on their own in a flash!

All-Purpose Weed Killer

This potent solution will rout weeds from wherever they're growing, whether it's the middle of your groundcovers or up through cracks in the sidewalk

INSTRUCTIONS: Bring the water to a boil, then add the vinegar and salt. While the mixture is still hot, pour it directly on the weeds, and then wave good-bye. (Be sure not to get it on plants you want to keep!)

INGREDIENTS:
5 tbsp. of vinegar
2 tbsp. of table salt
1 qt. of water

◆ CORRAL THOSE CREEPERS

Need a surefire way to keep groundcovers from creeping where you don't want 'em? Plant 'em where existing barriers do most of the controlling for you! For example, plant groundcovers between the sidewalk and the street, and you've got 'em trapped. All you need to do is trim along the edges once in a while. Or plant 'em in a bed surrounded by lawn, so when you mow the grass, you'll trim off any wandering groundcover shoots, too.

ASK JERRY

Q *What can I use to kill poison ivy seedlings that are in my groundcovers?*

A If there are only one or two small seedlings, stick your hand in an empty plastic bread bag, and pull up the seedlings with your covered hand. Keeping hold of them with that hand, use your other hand to pull the top of the bag down your arm and over the plants. Now you've got those bad boys neatly bagged for the garbage! If there are too many plants to hand-pull, wash them down with soap and water (2 tablespoons of dishwashing liquid per gallon of warm water applied with a hand-held sprayer). Then spray with any of the commercial poison ivy killers available at garden centers.

All-Season Clean-Up Tonic

This is the one tonic that you ABSOLUTELY need to use religiously throughout the growing season. The shampoo cleans the plants and helps the other ingredients stick better; the mouthwash kills bad bacteria and discourages insects; and the tobacco tea contains nicotine, which does a double whammy on those pesky pests.

INSTRUCTIONS: Mix these ingredients in a 20 gallon hose-end sprayer, and give everything in your yard a good shower in the early evening every two weeks throughout the growing season. You'll have the healthiest vines and groundcovers in town!

> **INGREDIENTS:**
>
> 1 cup of baby shampoo
> 1 cup of antiseptic mouthwash
> 1 cup of tobacco tea*

*To make tobacco tea, place half a handful of chewing tobacco in an old nylon stocking and soak it in a gallon of hot water until the mixture is dark brown.

◆ HERBAL RENEWAL

Sure, everyone loves herbs in their gardens, but here's a way to surprise your visitors: Plant herbs as groundcovers! Catmints, lavenders, oregano, and thymes are all tough, no-nonsense plants that can cover the ground with ease. Just give them full sun and well-drained soil, then sit back and enjoy!

TERRIFIC TIME◪SAVERS

Want to transform a barren slope into a great-looking groundcover planting? Try this compost-as-you-go trick! In spring, mark off a strip across a slope that's about 3 feet wide by 4 or 5 feet long. Lightly loosen the soil, then spread leaves, grass clippings, manure, and some topsoil there, too. Add your kitchen scraps and garden trimmings all summer long, and dig 'em in. The following spring, plant groundcovers in the strip of compost, then start a new strip above or below it. In just a few seasons, you can transform an entire slope, one strip at a time!

All-Season Green-Up Tonic

If your vines and groundcovers are looking a bit peaked, give them a taste of this sweet snack. It's rich in nutrients and packed with energizers, too: just what your plants need to look and grow their very best. They'll green up in a jiffy!

INSTRUCTIONS: Mix these ingredients in a large bucket, pour into a 20 gallon hose-end sprayer, and spray everything in sight—not just your vines and groundcovers, but also your trees, shrubs, lawn, flowers, and even vegetables. Apply this tonic every three weeks right up through the first hard frost, and your plants will survive the hot summer months with flying colors!

INGREDIENTS:

1 can of beer
1 cup of ammonia
$\frac{1}{2}$ cup of dishwashing liquid
$\frac{1}{2}$ cup of liquid lawn food
$\frac{1}{2}$ cup of molasses or clear corn syrup

◆ THIS IDEA STINKS!

To rid your groundcovers of moles, open up their tunnels in different locations, and drop in freshly cut-up garlic bulbs. Then cover up the holes you've made. The moles will take one whiff, and run in the opposite direction!

There are two smart shopping strategies when it comes to buying groundcovers. One option is to buy a bunch of small potted plants or a tray of rooted cuttings. These tend to be pretty cheap, but the small plants will take a while to fill in. Your other option is to look for midsummer or fall sales, then buy pots of overgrown groundcovers at bargain-basement prices. Divide the crowded clumps when you get 'em home, and you'll have lots of good-sized starts for just a few bucks!

Basic Oil Spray

Scale insects (and a whole lot of other pests, too) go belly-up when they strike oil—or rather, when oil strikes them! Here's how to hit pay dirt.

INSTRUCTIONS: Pour the oil and Murphy's Oil Soap into a plastic squeeze bottle, and store at room temperature. To use, put 1 table-spoon of the mixture in 2 cups of water in a hand-held sprayer, and spray your pest-ridden plants thoroughly from top to bottom. (Shake the bottle now and then while you're spraying to make sure the oil and water stay mixed.)

INGREDIENTS:

1 cup of vegetable oil
1 tbsp. of Murphy's Oil Soap®
Water

◆ THE TIES THAT BIND

Whenever you need to tie vines to their supports, always use strips of soft cloth, old pantyhose, or some other material that won't chafe against tender stems as they rustle in the wind. And remember: A bruised or cut stem leaves any plant wide open to pests and diseases!

GREAT IDEA!

Your hand-held, rechargeable vacuum cleaner is a perfect pest control tool in disguise!

When you find a bunch of bugs bugging your blooms, run the vacuum lightly over the infested plants. With your other hand, brush the leaves and stems gently to encourage the pests to fly up and be caught in the suction. When you're done, simply dump the pests into a bucket of soapy water, away from your plants—then say "So long, suckers!"

Breath-of-Fresh-Air Tonic

Are your vines and groundcovers looking a little limp and tired? This tonic is like a breath of fresh air for your plants.

INSTRUCTIONS: Mix these ingredients in a 20 gallon hose-end sprayer. Apply liberally to everything in your yard just as new growth begins, then stand back and admire the amazing results!

INGREDIENTS:

1 cup of 3% hydrogen peroxide
¼ cup of clear corn syrup
2 tbsp. of whiskey
2 tbsp. of baby shampoo
1 ½ cups of warm water

◆ USE THESE CLUES

Not sure when it's time to water? Your plants will tell you! Here is what to look for:

- ◆ Leaves droop slightly during the heat of the day, but recover in the evening once the sun goes down.

- ◆ Leaves are duller or grayer than normal.

- ◆ The foliage of fleshy-leaved plants shrivels slightly or feels soft to the touch.

One word of warning: Before you water, always take a look at the soil to make sure the ground isn't actually waterlogged. Plants that have *too much* moisture can show the same symptoms as those that don't have enough.

ASK JERRY

Q *How can I figure out how much water my sprinkler is putting out?*

A It's easy! Place several low, straight-sided cans (like tuna or cat food cans) in the area you're trying to irrigate. Turn the water on, wait 15 minutes, turn off the water, and see how much you've caught. Multiply that figure by 2 to find out how much water your plants will get in 30 minutes. If it's a little over an inch, you're right on target.

Clematis Chow

Grandma Putt grew truly magnificent clematis, thanks to the Clematis Chow she developed especially for it. This mixture helps keep clematis roots moist, well-fed, and luxuriating in soil that always has a near-neutral pH.

INSTRUCTIONS: Mix these ingredients in a wheelbarrow. (You may want to leave out the lime if your soil is already on the alkaline side.) Spread the mixture over the root zone of your clematis first thing in the spring. Then add a rich mulch of half-rotted compost to make sure the soil stays cool and moist. Follow up with my Royal Clematis Cocktail (see **page 235**) for a real royal boost to your blooming beauties!

INGREDIENTS:

5 gal. of well-cured horse or cow manure

$1/2$ cup of lime

$1/2$ cup of bonemeal

◆ A SOCIAL CLIMBER

Clematis have a different climbing strategy than most vines. Instead of twining their stems around a structure, like wisteria does, they wrap their leaf stems around something that's about finger thickness or smaller. Plastic netting around a post or downspout, or a string hanging down from a wall will help them clamber up quickly. Want the vines to cover a trellis or a sheet of lattice? Make sure those structures are made from wood or metal pieces less than an inch across.

GRANDMA PUTT'S POINTERS

Grandma Putt had a no-fail way to figure out where to set out a new clematis clump. She always looked for a site where the vines could have their "heads in the sun and feet in the shade." You see, clematis like cool soil, but bloom best with plenty of sun, so give 'em a site where low-growing shrubs or bushy perennials will shade their roots.

Easy Weed Killer

Are weeds trying to take over your gorgeous groundcover patch? Give those pesky plants a shot of this heavy-duty spray to send them to that great weed patch in the sky.

INSTRUCTIONS: Mix these ingredients in a hand-held sprayer, and apply liberally to weeds. Just make sure you don't get it on plants you want to keep!

INGREDIENTS:
1 gal. of vinegar
1 cup of table salt
1 tbsp. of dishwashing liquid

◆ SUPER-SPEEDY GARDEN STARTING

Do weeds and grass stand between you and the garden of your dreams? Try one of these tricks to get your vines and groundcovers flourishing quick!

◆ Cut weeds and grass as close to the soil surface as possible, then cover the site with a thick layer of newspaper (8 to 10 sheets). Spread several inches of topsoil over the paper, top with an inch of mulch, and then plant.

◆ Use a sharp spade to slice off lawn grass about an inch below the surface, then dig a 1- to 2-inch layer of compost into the soil. It's hard work, but you'll have a great garden in no time!

◆ Till the site, grass and all. Wait two weeks, then till under the new crop of weeds that have sprouted. Repeat until the weeds are discouraged, then till one more time to work a 1- to 2-inch layer of compost into the soil.

GREAT IDEA!

Are people and/or pets making a pathway through your groundcover plantings?

You'll know for sure if you see smashed plants, compacted soil, and yellowed leaves. What's the solution? Make that pathway official! Simply widen the existing path and spread a layer of mulch over it, or install stepping stones.

Fabulous Fern Food

Are ferns delicate and hard-to-grow? Hardly! Many ferns make terrific groundcovers for a shady site. To keep your outdoor ferns looking lush, give them a dose of this milky brew.

INSTRUCTIONS: Combine these ingredients in a 20 gallon hose-end sprayer, and give your ferns a generous drink by applying the mixture to the point of run-off.

INGREDIENTS:
2 cups of milk
2 tbsp. of Epsom salts

◆ A FACELIFT FOR TIRED GROUNDCOVERS

There's no getting around it—the best groundcovers like to spread their wings. Once your plantings have filled in, watch for signs that they're overgrown. Fewer flowers and fewer leaves are both common signs of crowding; look for very congested, twiggy growth, too. What's the solution? Dig out some of the plants, divide 'em, and use 'em to start new patches in other parts of your yard. Back at the original patch, add some fresh soil to the bare spots. The remaining plants will fill in again before you know it!

◆ ADD A FEW DUTCH DANDIES

Here's a bright idea for adding extra color to your groundcover beds—think *bulbs*! Taller daffodils work great with almost any groundcover. Shorter bulbs, like snowdrops, will show up only on the edges of plantings, or in groundcovers that die back to the ground each winter. And don't overlook later-blooming bulbs like fall-flowering crocuses— you just can't beat 'em for an extra shot of groundcover color!

When you need a little something to drape over the edges of your pots, planters, and windowboxes, there's no need to buy more plants—simply dig up a few sprigs of periwinkle or ivy from your groundcover patches. These gorgeous greens look great with cut flowers, too!

Far-Away Feline Spray

It's no secret that cats are territorial creatures with minds of their own. They don't see any problem with digging or rolling in freshly turned dirt—even if it's where you've just spent hours setting out a new groundcover planting! So when your cats—or somebody else's—are getting up to no good in your garden, safeguard your plants with this potent mixture.

INGREDIENTS:

4 tbsp. of dry mustard
3 tbsp. of cayenne pepper
2 tbsp. of chili powder
5 tbsp. of flour
2 qts. of warm water

INSTRUCTIONS: Mix these ingredients in a bucket or watering can, and sprinkle or spray the solution anyplace you want to set out the "Cats Unwelcome" mat.

◆ MORE MEOW-VA-LOUS TONICS

Looking for more options to keep kitties at bay? You can make them turn their noses and head elsewhere by overspraying the perimeter of your yard with either of these two tonics:

◆ **Tonic #1:** Mix ½ cup of tobacco tea and ¼ cup of dishwashing liquid in 2 gallons of warm water. (To make tobacco tea, place half a handful of chewing tobacco in an old nylon stocking and soak it in a gallon of hot water until the mixture is dark brown.)

◆ **Tonic #2:** Add 1 clove of garlic (crushed), 1 tbsp. of cayenne pepper, and 1 tsp. of dishwashing liquid to 1 qt. of warm water, and purée the heck out of it.

GRANDMA PUTT'S POINTERS ☞

Grandma Putt's way of heading off problems with frisky felines was to grow a big patch of catnip just for them. They'd be so busy romping and rolling in their own "garden" that they wouldn't even bother coming over to visit Grandma's groundcovers!

Flower Surge Tonic

Here's a powerful prep mix that'll get all your flowering vines and groundcovers off to an extra-vigorous start.

INSTRUCTIONS: Mix these ingredients in a wheelbarrow, and work the mixture well into the soil where you plan to plant flowering vines or groundcovers. (One batch makes enough to cover about 100 sq. ft. of soil area.)

INGREDIENTS:

50 lbs. of peat moss
25 lbs. of gypsum
10 lbs. of organic plant food
4 bushels of compost

◆ FOLLOW-UP FEEDING

Ample moisture and fertilizer will speed up the growth of new groundcover plantings, so the plants will fill in the space *before* weeds can get a foothold. Use an organic or controlled-release fertilizer at planting time, like my Flower Surge Tonic (above), and follow up six weeks later with my All-Season Green-Up Tonic (see **page 218**).

◆ MULCH MAGIC

To keep watering chores to a minimum, make friends with mulch! A 2- to 3-inch-deep layer of this magic material shields the ground from sun and wind, so any water that's already in the soil *stays* there. One tip: If your soil is already dry, water thoroughly *before* you mulch. Otherwise, you'll have to water twice as much because the mulch will absorb a lot before the moisture makes its way down to the soil.

TERRIFIC TIME⊠SAVERS

Don't break your back trying to dig holes for your new groundcover patch in hard, dry soil. Water the area thoroughly, then try again the next day. You'll be done digging lickety-split—and save yourself a bunch of blisters, too!

Garden Cure-All Tonic

Don't let bad bugs get the best of your beautiful vines and ground-covers! Fight back with my Garden Cure-All Tonic.

INSTRUCTIONS: Purée the garlic, onion, and pepper in an old blender, and let the mix steep in a quart of warm water for 2 hours. Strain the mixture, and further dilute the liquid with three parts of warm water. Add the Murphy's Oil Soap and vegetable oil. Pour into a hand-held sprayer, and apply to your plants several times a week until pests disappear.

INGREDIENTS:

4 cloves of garlic
1 small onion
1 small jalapeño pepper
1 tsp. of Murphy's Oil Soap®
1 tsp. of vegetable oil
Warm water

◆ ANTI-PEST POINTERS

Mulch is great for your garden—it holds in soil moisture, keeps roots cool, and prevents soil from splashing on leaves. But these cool, damp conditions are also perfect for soil-dwelling pests, like slugs, snails, and cutworms. So if you have problems with these creepy-crawlies, take all the mulch off for a few weeks, then replace it once you've got the pest problem under control.

GREAT IDEA!

Want to keep soil from running off slopes during rainstorms?

The secret to saving precious soil on slopes—especially steep ones—is slowing down the water, so it has time to soak in. For a super-simple solution, spread natural burlap over your slope, and fasten it down with wooden pegs. Cut holes in the burlap, and plant right through it. By the time the burlap rots away, your groundcovers will be well established and able to provide plenty of protection against erosion.

Great-Guns Garlic Spray

A few aphids aren't a serious problem, but when they start congregating on shoots and damaging tender leaves, it's time to take action. This garlicky spray will halt an aphid invasion faster than you can say "Hold it right there!"

INSTRUCTIONS: Mix these ingredients in a blender, and pour the solution into a hand-held sprayer. Then take aim and fire on infested plants. Within seconds, those aphids'll be history!

INGREDIENTS:

1 tbsp. of garlic oil*
3 drops of dishwashing liquid
1 qt. of water

To make garlic oil, mince 1 whole bulb of garlic and mix it in 1 cup of vegetable oil. Put the garlic oil in a glass jar with a tight lid and place it in the refrigerator to steep for a day or two. Then strain out the solids, and pour the oil into a fresh jar. Keep it in the fridge and use it in any tonic that calls for garlic oil.

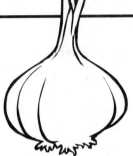

◆ SAY GOOD-BYE, BUGS!

Here's another good use for garlic: Whip up a pungent pest repellent for your potted plants. It's simple; just cut up 6 cloves of garlic, and mix them with 1 tablespoon of baby shampoo and 1 quart of water. Apply this mix to your plants with a hand-held sprayer, and bugs will stay away!

GRANDMA PUTT'S POINTERS ☞ If you want to give your kids or grandkids a real treat, do what Grandma Putt did for me: Make a bamboo tepee and show the youngsters how to plant morning glories or other annual vines around it. They'll love hiding inside of it at playtime—and they just might discover that gardening is a whole lot of fun!

Groundcover Starter Chow

When you plant them in well-prepared soil, you can expect groundcovers to form a solid carpet in two to three years. Just make sure you give them a good, healthy dose of my Groundcover Starter Chow at planting time!

INSTRUCTIONS: Mix these ingredients in a bucket. Place ½ cup in each planting hole and spread ½ cup on the soil surface when planting your groundcovers.

INGREDIENTS:
3 parts bonemeal
1 part Epsom salts
1 part gypsum

◆ DRAWING THE LINE

Once you've figured out where you want a new groundcover bed to be, try "drawing" it right on the lawn just like my Grandma Putt did—with garden hoses! Arrange hoses in the shape you're planning, fine-tune the size and shape until you're happy with the result, then dig in!

◆ SMOTHERING INSTINCT

Before planting groundcovers on a new site, you'll need to get rid of anything that's already growing there. If you choose to use a chemical weed killer, make sure you follow the label directions carefully. Prefer a chemical-free option? Cover the area with black plastic in early summer, and fasten down the edges of the plastic with U-shaped wire pins. Wait two months, then till the smothered grass under, and add compost to the soil before planting.

TERRIFIC TIME❖SAVERS

Here's a neat way to kill two birds with one stone—turn your gardening tools into handy measuring devices! Simply use a file to mark your long-handled tools, inch by inch, from the top to the bottom. Then use stain or ink to fill in the file marks. Voilà! Now you've got an easy way to measure between plants when you're tooling around the old garden.

Just Desserts Tonic

Want to give your garden favorites a special midsummer boost? Treat all of your vines and groundcovers to a dose of this tasty Just Desserts Tonic—and you'll have beautiful blooms and fantastic foliage on into the fall.

INSTRUCTIONS: Mix the peroxide, Epsom salts, baking powder, ammonia, gelatin, dishwashing liquid, and dissolved vitamins in a bucket. Mix 1 cup of this liquid with the rainwater or filtered water, and treat your plants liberally with the mixture.

INGREDIENTS:

4 tbsp. of hydrogen peroxide
1 tbsp. of Epsom salts
1 tbsp. of baking powder
1 tbsp. of ammonia
$1/2$ tsp. of unflavored gelatin
$1/2$ tsp. of dishwashing liquid
4 One-a-Day® multivitamins with iron, dissolved in 1 cup of hot water
1 gal. of rainwater or filtered water

◆ CONSIDER THE LILIES

Need a whole bunch of daylilies to cover a slope or fill an empty spot in your yard? Instead of buying individual plants, check mail-order nursery catalogs for daylily collections, which are often great bargains. For the best bloomers on the block, stick to collections of top-notch named or labeled plants, and stay away from inexpensive "hybridizers' mixes," which often consist of rejected seedlings that only have ho-hum flowers.

GREAT ✳IDEA!

Want a groundcover that tastes as good as it looks?

Believe it or not, daylily flowers are edible! Toss a few buds into a Chinese- or Thai-style stir-fry, or add them fresh from the garden to salads and soups. They taste just like green beans!

Lethal Leaf-Eater Spray

Vines and groundcovers are generally pretty tough, but once in a while, pests can get out of hand. This potent potion will bid adieu to all kinds of leaf-eating bugs.

INSTRUCTIONS: Put the garlic, peppers, onion, and water in an old blender and liquefy. Let the mixture sit overnight, strain out the solids, and add the baby shampoo. Pour into a hand-held sprayer, and when the enemy comes into view, let 'em have it!

INGREDIENTS:

4 to 6 cloves of garlic
2 hot peppers or 1 tsp. of
    cayenne pepper
1 small onion
3 drops of baby shampoo
1 qt. of water

◆ GIVE 'EM SOME SPACE

Always keep vines pruned away from the woodwork of your house because they can cause wood to rot. I like to keep mine on a lattice trellis that's positioned about 6 inches away from the exterior wall of my house. This way, the wall stays clean and dry, and the vines benefit from good air circulation.

ASK JERRY

Q *I'm totally confused about when to prune my clematis. Is there a right and wrong time to get the job done?*

A The trick is to know what kind you have. Early-blooming clematis, like alpine clematis, flower in early spring to early summer. They get along fine without annual pruning, but you can trim them right after they flower.

Early large-flowered hybrids, such as 'Niobe', bloom from late spring into early summer. Cut out any dead or damaged growth, and trim off the vine tips, just above any pair of plump buds, in spring.

Late-flowering clematis, like 'Jackmanii', bloom from summer to early fall. Cut 'em back each year in early spring, to 8 to 12 inches above the ground.

Mighty-Mite Rhubarb Spray

This potion will make mites—and other pests, too—mighty sorry they ganged up on your plants!

INSTRUCTIONS: Boil the rhubarb leaves in the water for about half an hour. Then strain out the solids, and pour the liquid into a hand-held sprayer. Add the dishwashing liquid, shake well, and spray away! When you're done, bury the soggy rhubarb leaves near your cabbage-family plants to fend off clubroot. Just one caution: Rhubarb leaves are highly poisonous, so never use this spray on edible plants.

INGREDIENTS:

1 lb. of rhubarb leaves, chopped
2 tsp. of dishwashing liquid
1 qt. of warm water

◆ MULTIPLY YOUR VINES

Have a favorite vine you'd like to make more of? Then layering's the way to go! Here's how:

◆ **Step 1:** In spring or early summer, gently bend a flexible stem to the ground, and bury it in loosened soil. Leave the last few inches of shoot tip exposed.

◆ **Step 2:** Hold the stem in place with a wire pin or a rock if it won't stay down. Water regularly through the summer.

◆ **Step 3:** In late summer or early fall, scratch away some of the soil to check for roots. If they're still small, rebury the stem. Once the new roots are a few inches long, snip off the stem where it's still attached to the original plant, and transplant it wherever you want it to grow.

GREAT IDEA!

Vines show off best when they can rise up high.

But many can do double duty as groundcovers if you let 'em sprawl. Sweet potato vine is one of my favorites: It's especially nice cascading down slopes, and it'll smother weeds like a pro!

Natural Bug-Busting Juice

Who'd have guessed that the makings for a super pest repellent are as close as your flower garden? Toss in some garlic, and you've got yourself a dandy spray that's sure to keep all kinds of pests away!

INSTRUCTIONS: Chop the flower tops finely, and mix them with the garlic and the warm water in a large bucket. Let the mixture sit overnight. The next day, add it to your watering can, and sprinkle it over any area of your garden that needs protection.

INGREDIENTS:

¼ cup of marigold flower tops
¼ cup of geranium flower tops
¼ cup of garlic cloves, minced
5 gal. of warm water

◆ TWO FOR TEA

Here's a super time-saver—an excellent elixir that lets you water and feed your plants at the same time! To make this power-packed brew, toss a shovelful of compost into a 5-gallon bucket. Add two heaping handfuls of salt-free alfalfa pellets (available from animal feed stores), then fill the bucket with water. Let the mixture sit for at least two days, stirring once or twice a day. Dilute it with water until the tea is light brown before using it to water/feed your garden.

ASK JERRY

Q *I'm looking for some especially nice flowering ground-covers for a dry, sunny site. What do you recommend?*

A Catmints are just about the easiest-care groundcovers you'll ever find! Forget watering and feeding, and don't worry about dividing 'em unless they slow down on flowering. The one bit of attention they do appreciate is a simple summer haircut. Once the first flush of flowers has faded, cut each clump back by one-half to two-thirds. They'll bounce right back and bloom 'til frost!

Ornamental Grass Chow

Get ornamental grasses started just like you would any other groundcover, by setting them out in early spring into well-prepared planting holes. But don't worry about fertilizer right now—just give them a good helping of my Ornamental Grass Chow to get them growing in the right direction.

INSTRUCTIONS: Mix these ingredients in a bucket. Toss a handful of this mixture into each planting hole, and work it into the soil. Set in the plants, backfill with soil, then scatter any leftover chow on top of the soil. That's all there is to it!

> ### INGREDIENTS:
> 2 lbs. of dry oatmeal
> 2 lbs. of crushed dry dog food
> 1 handful of human hair

◆ TRIM WITH TWINE

Most grasses benefit from a yearly trim to stay neat and tidy. To make clean-up a snap, wrap some twine around the tops before you cut 'em down in spring. That way, you'll have one tidy bundle to take to the compost pile, instead of a mess of stems falling all over to rake and pick up!

◆ GET CENTERED

Here's a super-simple way to spruce up a large grass clump that has died out in the center: Cut the foliage back so you can see what you're doing, then use a post-hole digger to clean out the dead center of the clump. Fill the hole with fresh soil, and the grass'll be back to growing on the right root in no time!

MAKING CENTS

When you're planting groundcovers, pruning ornamental grasses, or doing some other chore that requires you to spend a while on your knees, a kneeling pad can really come in handy! But don't bother buying one—simply stuff an old hot-water bottle with rags, handkerchiefs, or pantyhose, then say good-bye to cold, damp, muddy knees!

Quack-Up Slug Cookies

Slugs can be real nuisances in shady groundcover beds. But don't let the slimeballs get you down—just whip up a batch of my deadly cookies. Slugs will think it's time to party when they get a yeasty whiff of these tasty treats. But after a couple of bites, they're sure to have a killer hangover!

INSTRUCTIONS: Mix the quackgrass and bran in a bowl, then slowly add the beer, stirring until the mixture has the consistency of cookie dough. Run the dough through a meat grinder, or chop it into small bits (roughly $\frac{1}{8}$ to $\frac{1}{4}$ inch thick). Let the "cookies" air-dry overnight, then sprinkle them on the ground among your plants, and let the good times roll!

> **INGREDIENTS:**
> 1 part dried quackgrass blades, finely chopped
> 1 part wheat bran*
> 1 can of beer

Available in supermarkets and health food stores.

◆ It's No Angel

Spotted deadnettle (*Lamium maculatum*) makes a gorgeous groundcover for shade, but watch out for its close cousin, yellow archangel (*L. galeobdolon*). It looks great in a pot at the garden center, with trailing stems clad in handsome silver-and-green leaves. But in your yard, this thug'll quickly take over, sending stems out in all directions—including into your lawn and flower beds!

TERRIFIC TIME✖SAVERS

Are you planning to support your annual vines with string? Whatever you do, *don't* use the plastic kind; otherwise, you could spend hours unwinding the dead vines come fall clean-up time. Instead, use biodegradable cotton string or uncoated jute. Then, at the end of the season, simply cut down the whole mass of withered stems and string, and chuck it onto your compost pile.

Royal Clematis Cocktail

Clematis is often called "queen of the climbers" because it's such a royally fine vine. Your clematis will surely put on a regal show if you feed it this excellent elixir.

INSTRUCTIONS: Mix the beer, ammonia, fish emulsion, and shampoo in a 2-gallon watering can, filling the balance of the can with warm water. Pour the solution around the roots of your clematis every three weeks throughout the growing season, and it'll grow like gangbusters!

INGREDIENTS:

1 can of beer
4 tbsp. of ammonia
2 tbsp. of fish emulsion
2 tbsp. of baby shampoo
Warm water

◆ THANKS FOR YOUR SUPPORT

My number one rule for success with vines? Always, always, *always* put the support in place *before* you plant! If you're planting against an existing wall or fence, you're already good to go. But don't even think about putting up a trellis after your vine's in the ground. Inevitably, you'll end up stepping on and compacting the soil—or worse yet, cutting the roots when you set in the trellis. You might even trample the vine itself! So remember: Get a support system in place first, then stand back and let your vine do its thing.

ASK JERRY

Q *I love the look of vines, but do they need any special care after planting?*

A It's smart to check on them every few days to see if they need any help. Sometimes, you may need to twirl the stem tips around the support to get them growing onward and upward. If a little extra assistance is in order, tie the stems to the trellis with soft yarn or strips of old pantyhose. Once they grab hold, an occasional pinch or snip should be enough to keep wayward stems growing in the right direction!

Rust Relief Tonic

Old cars aren't the only things that get rusty—plants can, too! Ornamental grasses, in particular, can be bothered by funky fungi that produce rusty orange streaks on leaves and stems. To prevent problems, try this terrific tonic; it'll keep rust-prone plants green all summer long.

INSTRUCTIONS: Mix these ingredients in a bucket, and pour the solution into a hand-held sprayer. Then give your grasses a weekly morning shower throughout the growing season.

INGREDIENTS:
6 tbsp. of vegetable oil
2 tbsp. of baking soda
2 tbsp. of liquid kelp
1 gal. of water

◆ TRIMMING TIME

Good old hand-held hedge clippers that work like giant scissors are my favorite tools for trimming back the tops of ornamental grasses in spring. Cut the plants down to where new blades will emerge—usually 6 to 12 inches above the ground (or higher for really big grasses, like pampas grass), and they'll be off to a flying start.

◆ TRY A GREEN SCREEN

If you (or your neighbors) get tired of looking at your compost pile, don't give it up—simply camouflage it! Place a trellis around it, then plant gourds, morning glories, sweet peas, or other ornamental vines alongside and train them to grow up the support. Or, you can surround it with a screen of great-looking ornamental grasses.

You don't have to bust your budget—or your back—to get growing with groundcovers. Instead, start with just a half-dozen or so plants, and set them out in a corner of the area you want to fill in. After that, take cuttings two or three times each summer, or divide the plants each year, and use the new plants to fill in more of the space. You'll have a handsome patch of groundcover in no time at all!

Soil Energizer Elixir

No matter which vines or groundcovers you're planning to grow, you'll always get great results if you perk up the soil before planting with this power-packed potion.

INSTRUCTIONS: Mix these ingredients in a bucket, and pour into a 20 gallon hose-end sprayer. Over-spray the soil in your garden to the point of run-off (or just until small puddles start to form), then let the area sit for at least two weeks to give it a chance to do its stuff. This recipe makes enough to cover 100 sq. ft. of groundcover bed.

INGREDIENTS:
1 can of beer
1 cup of regular cola (not diet)
1 cup of dishwashing liquid
1 cup of antiseptic mouthwash
$\frac{1}{4}$ tsp. of instant tea granules

◆ GIVE 'EM A JUMP START

Newly planted groundcover patches need a little help to get off to a great start. Here's a quick list of three things you can do to speed them along:

- ◆ Water thoroughly after planting, then spread a 1- to 2-inch-deep layer of mulch between the plants.

- ◆ Plan on a regular weeding session once a week for the first year.

- ◆ To fill in bare patches, loosen the soil, then move wandering stems into that area, and fasten them down with U-shaped pieces of wire.

GREAT IDEA!

Don't settle on just one groundcover in your garden.

Instead, fill an area with patches of two or more different kinds. First, they'll likely bloom at different times, so you'll get a longer season of color. And second, if a disease or other problem strikes one type of plant, the others will still be there, ready to fill in!

Super Dry Food Mix

If your soil tends to be on the poor or sandy side, give my Super Dry Food Mix a try. It'll provide a super jump-start for your new vine and groundcover beds—GUARANTEED!

INSTRUCTIONS: Mix these ingredients in a wheelbarrow, and add ½ cup of the mixture to each planting hole. If there's any left, scatter it on top of the soil and scratch it in lightly with a hand fork. You'll be AMAZED at the results!

INGREDIENTS:

2 parts all-purpose
   (dry) plant food
1 part bonemeal
1 part gypsum
1 part garden soil
½ part Epsom salts

◆ Isn't That Sweet?

If you need a cheap, nearly instant groundcover to fill in around tulips, hyacinths, or other spring bulbs, think sweet alyssum! Start with seeds or pick up plants from the garden center, and pop 'em in anywhere. They'll fill the space in a flash and crowd out weeds in the process.

◆ Just Say No!

There's a lot to love about flowering vines, but beware—there are a few bad apples in the bunch, so don't go planting just any vine before you do your homework. Here are three real thugs that are no bargain at *any* price:

- ◆ Japanese honeysuckle (*Lonicera japonica*)
- ◆ Oriental bittersweet (*Celastrus orbiculatus*)
- ◆ Silver lace vine (*Polygonum aubertii*)

TERRIFIC TIME⧗SAVERS

Here's a simple step that can save you hours of aggravation! Before settling on a final shape for your groundcover beds, think about how you'll mow around them. Beds with scalloped or zigzag edges take lots of extra time to trim, since you have to keep backing up the mower and going forward again. Gentle curves, though, are a breeze to mow around!

Terrific Topdressing

Groundcovers are often neglected because they look great without a lot of fuss—unless wicked weeds sneak their way in. But I've found that my Terrific Topdressing, watered in with a mix of 1 can of beer and 4 teaspoons of instant tea granules in 2 gallons of water, makes groundcover thick enough to stop just about any weed!

INGREDIENTS:

20 parts Milorganite®
10 parts earthworm castings
5 parts ground-up fresh apples
$\frac{1}{2}$ bushel of peat moss

INSTRUCTIONS: Mix these ingredients in a wheelbarrow, and scatter the mixture generously over the top of your groundcovers in spring. Then follow up with the liquid topdressing to really get things cooking!

◆ SPRING SPRUCE-UP

Ugh! Dead growth on groundcovers sure isn't pretty! But here's a fast, easy way to get overgrown groundcovers looking great again: Give 'em a quick trim with your lawn mower in late winter or early spring. Simply set your mower blade as high as it will go, run it over the area you want to spruce up, then rake off the trimmings, and toss 'em in your compost pile. To make the area look really nice, spread a 1-inch layer of my Terrific Topdressing (above) over the soil, too.

GREAT IDEA!

Do you love the "please-touch-me," furry foliage of lamb's ears, but cut off the unattractive flowers as they appear?

To save yourself this step, do what I do, and plant cultivars that produce few or no bloom spikes! 'Silver Carpet' and 'Countess Helene von Stein' (also sold as 'Big Ears') are both great, easy-care choices.

CHAPTER 7

INCREDIBLE EDIBLES

GROWING VEGGIES and other edibles is a lot like playing baseball, except you're not one of the players—you're the coach! It's your job to make sure each crop on your team performs at its peak. Almost all edibles need plenty of sun and plenty of deep, rich soil, too. So start with the best site you can find in your yard, and give your soil a good going-over with a shovel or garden fork in spring. After planting, keep your team growing strong with plenty of fertilizer, and be prepared to take action against bad bugs and dastardly diseases that want a share of your harvest. Pretty soon, you'll have more produce than you'll know what to do with—and your friends and family will be enjoying the fruits of your labor. All it takes is some commonsense gardening know-how—and my surefire super-tonics—to give your team the most successful growing season ever!

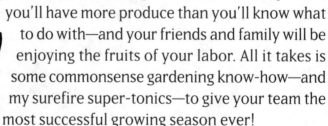

Not sure where to start? Just follow this step-by-step guide to growing through the year, and before you know it, you'll be enjoying a bounty of excellent edibles!

 *Spring*

◆ **Step 1:** Ready to get your soil rarin' to grow? Fortify it each year with my Vegetable Power Powder (see **page 302**):

25 lbs. of organic plant food
5 lbs. of gypsum
2 lbs. of diatomaceous earth
1 lb. of sugar

Mix these ingredients in a wheelbarrow, and put them into a broadcast spreader. Set the spreader on medium, and apply the mixture over the top of your garden in early spring. Work it into your soil to provide an ample supply of nutrients for all of your hungry veggies!

◆ **Step 2:** Follow up immediately by overspraying the area with my Spring Soil Energizer (see **page 294**):

1 can of beer
½ cup of regular cola (not diet)
½ cup of dishwashing liquid
½ cup of antiseptic mouthwash
¼ tsp. of instant tea granules

Mix these ingredients in a 20 gallon hose-end sprayer, and saturate the soil. Wait two weeks before you start planting. (This recipe makes enough to cover 100 sq. ft. of garden area.) By the time you're ready to plant, your soil will be rich and mellow, and begging to be filled with great things to eat!

◆ **Step 3:** Once you've sown your veggie or herb seeds, indoors or out, give them an energy boost with my Seed and Soil Energizer (see **page 289**):

1 tsp. of whiskey
1 tsp. of ammonia
1 tsp. of dishwashing liquid
1 qt. of weak tea water*

Mix these ingredients in a bucket, and pour the solution into a hand-held sprayer. Shake it gently, and apply a good misting to the surface of newly planted seedbeds or plant containers.

Soak a used tea bag and 1 teaspoon of dishwashing liquid in a gallon of warm water until the mix is light brown.

◆ **Step 4:** Give your veggie and herb transplants a break on moving day by serving them a sip of my Seedling Transplant Recovery Tonic (see **page 292**):

l tbsp. of fish emulsion
l tbsp. of ammonia
l tbsp. of Murphy's Oil Soap®
l tsp. of instant tea granules
l qt. of warm water

Mix these ingredients in a bucket and pour into a hand-held sprayer. Mist your little plants several times a day until they're off and growing again.

◆ **Step 5:** To get your edibles off to a super spring start and keep the harvest comin' all summer long, treat them to regular doses of my All-Season Green-Up Tonic (see **page 247**):

l can of beer
l cup of ammonia
$\frac{1}{2}$ cup of dishwashing liquid
$\frac{1}{2}$ cup of liquid lawn food
$\frac{1}{2}$ cup of molasses or clear
    corn syrup

Mix these ingredients in a large bucket, pour into a 20 gallon hose-end sprayer, and spray everything in sight—not just your vegetables, but also your trees, shrubs, lawn, and flowers, too. Apply this tonic every three weeks right up through the first hard frost, and your crops will come through the hot summer months with flying colors!

Summer

◆ **Step 6:** My All-Season Clean-Up Tonic (see **page 246**) is one tonic that you ABSOLUTELY need to use religiously to keep pests and diseases away:

l cup of baby shampoo
l cup of antiseptic mouthwash
l cup of tobacco tea*

Mix these ingredients in a 20 gallon hose-end sprayer, and give everything in your yard a good shower in the early evening every two weeks throughout the growing season. You'll have the healthiest vegetables in town—GUARANTEED!

To make tobacco tea, place half a handful of chewing tobacco in an old nylon stocking and soak it in a gallon of hot water until the mixture is dark brown.

◆ **Step 7:** Lots of bugs love to hide in broccoli florets and other nooks and crannies in vegetables. Here's a surefire way to make your harvest bug-free—give it a good soak in my Veggie Harvest Bath (see **page 303**):

Fresh-picked broccoli (or other
    veggies)
¼ cup of salt
1 tbsp. of vinegar
Cold water

Pour the salt and vinegar into a sinkful of cold water, and submerge the veggies for 15 minutes or so. The bugs will float up to the surface, where they can be easily picked off. Rinse the veggies with fresh water, and they're ready to eat.

◆ **Step 8:** When you've got weeds that won't take no for an answer, knock 'em flat on their backs with my Wild Weed Wipeout Tonic (see **page 308**):

1 tbsp. of vinegar
1 tbsp. of baby shampoo
1 tbsp. of gin
1 qt. of warm water

Mix these ingredients in a bucket, and then pour into a hand-held sprayer. Drench each weed to the point of run-off, taking care not to get any spray on the surrounding plants.

◆ **Step 9:** Tired of rabbits, deer, and other four-legged marauders spoiling your veggies? My Hit-the-Trail Mix (see **page 272**) will make any critter hightail it away from your garden:

4 tbsp. of dry mustard
3 tbsp. of cayenne pepper
2 tbsp. of chili powder
2 tbsp. of cloves
1 tbsp. of Tabasco® sauce
2 qts. of warm water

Mix these ingredients in a watering can, and sprinkle the solution around the perimeter of your vegetable beds.

 GRANDMA PUTT'S POINTERS ☞ Need a quick-and-easy solution for all kinds of bad bugs? Grandma Putt came up with this winner: Simply put 1 tablespoon of mustard (the hotter the better) in 1 quart of warm water, and mix it thoroughly. Pour it into a hand-held sprayer, and lightly spray your vegetable plants at the first sign of trouble.

Fall

◆ **Step 10:** When I know Old Man Winter is waiting in the wings and my plants are still chock-full of unripe veggies, I give my garden a big drink of my Hurry-Up-the-Harvest Tonic (see **page 273**):

1 cup of apple juice
1/2 cup of ammonia
1/2 cup of baby shampoo
Warm water

Mix the apple juice, ammonia, and shampoo in a 20 gallon hose-end sprayer, filling the balance of the jar with warm water. Then spray the tonic on your garden to the point of run-off to speed up the ripening process.

◆ **Step 11:** Once Jack Frost has called a halt to the growing season, cover your vegetable garden beds with a mixture of shredded leaves and grass clippings, and treat them to a taste of my Fall Vegetable Garden Tonic (see **page 260**):

1 can of regular cola (not diet)
1 cup of dishwashing liquid
1/4 cup of ammonia
Warm water

Mix the cola, dishwashing liquid, and ammonia in a 20 gallon hose-end sprayer, filling the balance of the jar with warm water. Saturate the layer of mulch that's on top of the soil to give your garden a good bedtime snack.

GREAT IDEA!

Is cloudy, drizzly weather moving in?

Then it's the perfect time for moving seedlings to the garden, so get out your rain gear! Your youngsters will settle in quickly without being baked by the sun, and you won't have to worry so much about watering when you're done planting.

All-Purpose Critter Control

No doubt about it: There are lots of crafty veggie-gulpers just waiting to sink their sharp teeth into your harvest. But gophers, skunks, and just about any other critter will turn tail and run when they get a whiff of this powerful tonic!

INSTRUCTIONS: Mix these ingredients in a bucket, then let the mixture sit for three or four days. Paint it on fences, trellises, and wherever else unwanted varmints are venturing.

INGREDIENTS:
2 eggs
2 cloves of garlic
2 tbsp. of hot chili pepper
2 tbsp. of ammonia
2 cups of hot water

◆ DRINKS, ANYONE?

Believe it or not, squirrels and other varmints that take big chunks out of your tomatoes are often doing so to quench their thirst. So before you arm yourself with all kinds of pest controls, install a birdbath or other water source in your yard. If you give the thirsty critters an easy drink, they just might leave your tomatoes alone!

◆ A LITTLE DAB'LL DO YA

Here's a neat trick that'll drive raccoons and birds crazy—and save your corn crop in the process. Place the toe of a nylon stocking over each ear of corn after the pollen drops. Then just touch the top of the stocking with a dab of perfume. One whiff, and the thieves will steer clear of your crop!

GRANDMA PUTT'S POINTERS ☞ If you can't beat 'em, fool 'em! Grandma Putt used to paint small rocks red, then scatter them around her strawberry patch before her berries ripened. The birds got so disgusted pecking at the rocks that they soon took their act elsewhere. Try it—it works!

All-Season Clean-Up Tonic

This is the one tonic that you ABSOLUTELY need to use religiously throughout the growing season. The shampoo cleans the plants and helps the other ingredients stick better; the mouthwash kills bad bacteria and discourages insects; and the tobacco tea contains nicotine, which does a double whammy on those pesky pests.

INGREDIENTS:

1 cup of baby shampoo
1 cup of antiseptic mouthwash
1 cup of tobacco tea*

INSTRUCTIONS: Mix these ingredients in a 20 gallon hose-end sprayer, and give everything in your yard a good shower in the early evening every two weeks throughout the growing season. You'll have the healthiest vegetables in town—GUARANTEED!

*To make tobacco tea, place half a handful of chewing tobacco in an old nylon stocking and soak it in a gallon of hot water until the mixture is dark brown.

◆ BE KIND TO THESE CATERPILLARS

If you see some black-striped green caterpillars munching on your carrots, don't call out the hit squad. Instead, pick them up very gently and move them to a clump of Queen Anne's lace, parsley, or dill. You'll be glad you did: In a few weeks, those caterpillars will turn into swallowtail butterflies.

◆ STAY AWAY, SPOT!

There's nothing more frustrating than having neighborhood pets tramping through your carefully planted veggies! Keep dogs and cats away from your crops by dusting cayenne powder in and around the beds.

MAKING CENTS

Roll out the red carpet...or any other color carpet, for that matter! Cut your old carpeting and rugs into strips, and lay them down in your vegetable garden between the rows. They'll keep weeds down and act as a mulch around your veggies.

All-Season Green-Up Tonic

If your veggies are looking a bit peaked (and even if they're not), give them a taste of this sweet snack. It's rich in nutrients and packed with energizers, too: just what your plants need to keep the harvest comin' along all summer long.

INGREDIENTS:

1 can of beer
1 cup of ammonia
$\frac{1}{2}$ cup of dishwashing liquid
$\frac{1}{2}$ cup of liquid lawn food
$\frac{1}{2}$ cup of molasses or clear
    corn syrup

INSTRUCTIONS: Mix these ingredients in a large bucket, pour into a 20 gallon hose-end sprayer, and spray everything in sight—not just your vegetables, but also your trees, shrubs, lawn, and flowers, too. Apply this tonic every three weeks right up through the first hard frost, and your crops will come through the hot summer months with flying colors!

◆ KEEP OUT

Here's a simple secret that'll save you a lot of heartache—don't handle, spray, prune, or pick vegetables from plants that are stressed out because of drought. If your garden is very dry, water it, let the water soak for a few hours, and *then* go to work.

ASK JERRY

Q *I just don't have the energy to dig a vegetable garden like I used to. Any suggestions?*

A Try planting your crops in a bale of straw! Place the bale on a sheet of plastic or a cut-open trash can liner, and soak it thoroughly with water. Then make small holes in the bale, fill them with rich topsoil or compost, and plant your seeds or seedlings in the topsoil. Keep the soil moist, and every three weeks, apply my All-Season Green-Up Tonic (above).

Asparagus Soak

Don't take a chance that diseases will claim your asparagus crop before you can! Always disinfect newly purchased asparagus roots before planting by soaking them briefly in this simple solution.

INSTRUCTIONS: Mix these ingredients in a bucket, and drop in your asparagus roots. Let them soak for an hour or so, then plant them right away.

INGREDIENTS:

1 cup of bleach
¼ cup of dishwashing liquid
1 gal. of warm water

◆ A STANDING ORDER

Be sure to allow asparagus tops to stand over the winter to catch and hold snow. This may help prevent deep freezing and sudden changes in soil temperature. The added moisture provided by the melting snow is also important for the shoots that will be produced the following spring. Once spring returns, you can lop off the dead tops and toss 'em onto your compost pile.

◆ NIGHTTIME'S THE RIGHT TIME

Plan to harvest your leafy vegetables by the light of the moon, or at least in the early evening—and *not* during the day. That's because during the day, the sun burns up a lot of the vitamins and minerals stored in the plant leaves. But as soon as ol' Sol starts to set, the plants begin to replenish and fortify themselves. So if you wait until evening, you'll be picking your vegetables when their vitamin content is at its peak.

Need a quick-fix trellis for your veggies? Here's something you may not have thought of: Use a net! An old tennis or badminton net, that is. Simply string small sections of the net between two poles, and voilà—you have a sturdy, *free* trellis!

Baking Soda Spray

Powdery mildew and its kissin' cousin, downy mildew, can spell the end for plenty of veggies. But you can fight these funky fungi and keep your garden growing great guns by spraying your plants every week with my special Baking Soda Spray.

INSTRUCTIONS: Mix these ingredients in a bucket, and pour into a hand-held sprayer. Spray plants thoroughly at the first sign of mildew.

INGREDIENTS:

$\frac{1}{2}$ cup of baking soda
2 drops of dishwashing liquid
1 qt. of water

◆ Wash Diseases Away

Protect your currants and gooseberries from blight and mildew in spring with an alkaline wash of diluted lime water. Mix $\frac{1}{2}$ cup of lime in 1 gallon of warm water, stir, and sprinkle over your plants, trying to get both the tops and the bottoms of the leaves. This should help keep those dastardly diseases at bay!

◆ Making Your Bed

The soil in raised beds warms up faster and stays warm longer than it does in traditional garden rows. That's great if you live in the cool-as-a-cucumber North. But in places with sweltering summers, a veggie's roots will fry if you leave too much soil exposed to the sun. So, if you live in hot climates, don't build free-standing beds that are more than 4 inches above the ground.

GREAT IDEA!

Need a tasty snack that's a low-calorie, low-fat treat?

Cut off the ends of two pickling cucumbers, slice them lengthwise into quarters, and put them in a plastic bag with 1 tablespoon of salt and two peeled garlic cloves. Seal tightly and refrigerate for a few hours, then enjoy!

Berry Booster

No room for fruit trees? You can still enjoy growing bush fruits, like blueberries and elderberries. These plants take up about the same amount of space as typical landscape shrubs, but they're a whole lot more productive! To keep them bursting with tasty berries, treat them to this nutritious tonic.

INSTRUCTIONS: Mix these ingredients in a 20 gallon hose-end sprayer, and apply every three weeks during the growing season to keep those luscious berries coming.

INGREDIENTS:

1 can of beer
¼ cup of fish emulsion
2 tbsp. of instant tea granules

◆ SOOTHE THE STING

Sooner or later, you're probably going to run into some bees when you're out harvesting your ripe fruits and berries. If you get stung, make a paste with baking soda and water or rubbing alcohol. Apply this paste directly to the sting to ease the pain.

◆ THE DIRT ON BERRIES

If your berries are dirty, don't wash them immediately after picking. Instead, put them in a plastic food-storage bag, and pop them into the refrigerator for a few hours. The cold air will firm them up, and then you can wash them without losing a lot of the juice.

GRANDMA PUTT'S POINTERS ☞ Don't throw out those old, worn-out cotton socks—they come in "berry" handy for berry picking! Grandma Putt would take a pair and cut two holes in the foot of each; one hole for my thumb to slip through and the other one large enough for my four fingers. Then I'd pull one sock over each hand and arm to protect my skin from thorns—and go get those berries!

Blight-Buster Veggie Tonic

At the first sign of blight on potatoes, tomatoes, or celery, haul out this powerful weapon and fight back!

INSTRUCTIONS: Mix these ingredients in a bucket, pour into a hand-held sprayer, and spray your plants to the point of run-off to keep them in tip-top shape.

INGREDIENTS:
1 tbsp. of light horticultural oil
1 tbsp. of baking soda
1 gal. of water

◆ THE BIG FRAME-UP

Want to harvest fresh celery all winter long? Simply dig up your plants with a fair amount of roots attached to them before the freezing weather sets in, and then replant them in a deep cold frame. They'll be easy to reach even when the ground is covered in deep snow!

◆ FINE RINDS

Citrus peels don't have to be banished to the compost pile—use them as super indoor plant starters instead! Simply clean out each half-rind, and poke several holes in it to provide drainage. Fill with potting soil, then plant your veggie seeds inside. After the seeds sprout, set the seedlings out in your garden, rinds and all!

ASK JERRY

Q *My carrots were a real disappointment this year; they were stunted and deformed, and didn't grow very big. What happened?*

A Sounds like you have a nematode problem (they're tiny microorganisms that live in the soil). To get rid of them, spread 5 pounds of sugar over every 50 square feet of garden area, and work it well into the soil. Then next spring, overspray the area with a mix of 1 can of beer and 1 cup of molasses in a 20 gallon hose-end sprayer. That should do the trick!

Blueberry Potting Mix

You couldn't ask for an easier-to-grow plant than a blueberry bush. Just give it a pot or a raised bed filled with this root-pleasing mix, and get ready for a fine, fruitful feast.

INSTRUCTIONS: Mix these ingredients in a wheelbarrow, and use the mixture to fill your containers or raised beds. Then plant whenever you're ready!

*Don't use beach or sandbox sand; it's too fine and can be alkaline, which blueberries hate.

INGREDIENTS:

2 parts garden soil
2 parts chopped, composted leaves
2 parts coarse builder's sand*
1 part compost

◆ Java Jive

Don't you dare throw out those old coffee grounds! Give 'em to your blueberries instead, and they'll be as pleased as punch. You see, coffee grounds help keep soil on the acidic side—and that's exactly what keeps blueberries in the pink! Not a coffee drinker? Then tuck your used tea bags into the soil; they'll serve the same purpose.

◆ Handle with Care

Handpick ripe apples; don't shake them off or allow them to drop on the ground. Otherwise, you'll end up with bruised fruits that rot quickly in storage.

TERRIFIC TIME⊠SAVERS

No time or space to tend to a full-scale compost pile? Try this trick: Save your table scraps—peels, shredded vegetables, eggshells, and the like (just no meat or fat). Every few days, place the scraps in a food processor or blender and cover them with water. Add a tablespoon of Epsom salts to the mix, and liquefy. Pour this compost cocktail onto the soil in your garden, lightly hoe it in, and your plants will jump for joy!

Brussels Sprouts Weed Brush-Off

Brussels sprouts are one of the healthiest veggies we can eat, but they're definitely NOT healthy for weeds. Serve up this marvelous mix in early spring, before the seeds germinate, and it'll deliver a real knockout punch to those wicked weeds!

INSTRUCTIONS: In a blender, combine the Brussels sprouts with just enough water to make a thick mush. Then add the dishwashing liquid, and pour the mixture into cracks in your sidewalk and driveway, or any place you want to stop weeds before they pop up. Just don't use it in places where you want flower, herb, or veggie seeds to grow.

> **INGREDIENTS:**
>
> 1 cup of Brussels sprouts
>   (or cabbage leaves)
> $\frac{1}{2}$ tsp. of dishwashing liquid
> Water

◆ A PINCH IN TIME

Here's a little secret that'll help you grow bigger, stronger cucumbers this year: Once the vines are off and running, leave only four fruits on the plant at any one time. Pinch or cut off other small cukes as they form, and you'll be rewarded with a much better, all-around harvest.

◆ STEP ON IT!

To grow the biggest onions on the block, you don't need to use your head—use your feet instead! When your onions are about the size of your thumb, simply step on them, pressing them back down deeper into the soil. That's all there is to it!

ASK JERRY

Q *My neighbor told me that I can use lawn fertilizer to feed my cabbage plants. Is this true?*

A Sure is. You can use lawn food for just about anything that grows above the ground, except for tomatoes.

Cabbageworm Wipeout

Don't you hate cutting into a cabbage head, only to find cabbage-worms hidden inside? To make this problem a thing of the past, use this simple remedy as soon as your plants begin to head. In addition to killing cabbageworms that eat the stuff, the powdery residue on the plants makes wanderers easy to spot and pluck off.

INSTRUCTIONS: Mix these ingredients in a bucket and sprinkle over your cabbage, broccoli, and cauliflower plants. The flour swells up inside the worms and bursts their insides, while the hot pepper keeps other critters away.

INGREDIENTS:

1 cup of flour
2 tbsp. of cayenne pepper

◆ Here, Birdie!

Sparrows and other birds will help you out by pecking up pesky caterpillars. So I like to push 4-foot-long branches into the soil in my cabbage patch to give birds a place to perch. I figure if the birds pause there for a second, they might spy a cabbageworm or two that will make a tasty snack.

◆ Double Your Harvest

Here's a great space-saving trick: When Brussels sprouts, cabbage, and broccoli seedlings are just a few inches tall, sow lettuce seeds all around them. By the time the other crops start needing the elbow room, all of the lettuce will be long gone to the salad bowl.

MAKING CENTS

Whenever you need to sprinkle Cabbageworm Wipeout (above) or any other nonpoisonous powder over your plants, don't spend money on a fancy-schmancy duster. Simply place the mixture in a small paper bag with about five small holes punched in the bottom. Blow up the bag with air (be careful not to inhale the powder), twist the neck tightly, and shake away.

Chive Tea

With so many dastardly diseases ready to attack, growing apples and peaches can be a real challenge. So, try this super-simple solution to foil foul fungi before they can get a foothold on your fruit!

INSTRUCTIONS: Put the chive leaves and water in a pan, and bring the water to a boil. Then remove the pan from the heat, let the tea cool, and strain out the leaves. Pour the remaining liquid into a hand-held sprayer. Spray your fruit trees every seven days, and say "Farewell, fungus!"

INGREDIENTS:

1 part chive leaves (horse-radish leaves work, too)
4 parts water

◆ THE GREAT GARLIC CURE

Garlic's not only a great insect repellent—it's also an *amazing* antibiotic for sickly plants. Mince several large cloves, and soak them overnight in mineral oil. The next day, strain the mixture, and then mix 2 teaspoons of the oil and 2 teaspoons of dishwashing liquid in 1 pint of warm water. Put this in a 20 gallon hose-end sprayer, and fill the balance of the jar with warm water. Spray every two weeks in the evening to keep your crops growin' strong!

GREAT IDEA!

Take this tip from professional apple growers: Dislodge insects with plain old water!

Yep, just use good ol' H_2O. Apple growers use a water spray in the spring to dislodge loose bark, which helps to control codling moths. The most effective way to do this is with a standard orchard sprayer held 2 to 3 feet away from the tree and directed against the trunk. Also spray large branches where the bark is rough or loose, and don't forget the crotch of the tree.

Compost Booster

Whether you use it as a mulch or dig it into the soil, you can never have too much compost! To keep your pile really cookin', and the compost comin', try the following formula.

INSTRUCTIONS: Mix these ingredients in a 20 gallon hose-end sprayer, and saturate your compost pile every time you add a new layer of ingredients to it. This'll really get things goin'!

INGREDIENTS:

1 can of beer
1 can of regular cola (not diet)
1 cup of ammonia
$\frac{1}{2}$ cup of weak tea water*
2 tbsp. of baby shampoo

*Soak a used tea bag and 1 teaspoon of dishwashing liquid in a gallon of warm water until the mix is light brown.

◆ HOLD THE MEAT, PLEASE

Go vegetarian—at least as far as your compost is concerned! Never, and I mean *never*, use meat, fish scraps, or cooking fats in your compost pile. They'll attract varmints and insects, cause bad odors, and slow down decomposition of the pile.

◆ A HAIRY HINT

Whether it comes from a human or any other kind of animal, hair is full of iron, manganese, and sulfur—good stuff for your garden. Work it into the soil or toss it onto the compost pile, and watch your plants eat it up!

TERRIFIC TIME⧗SAVERS

To make sure your compost pile gets the air it needs for speedy decomposition, drill holes along the length of a large PVC pipe. Then place the pipe upright in the center of the pile, and add your compost materials around it. Believe you me, it's a whole lot easier than turning the pile with a pitchfork every few weeks!

Container Garden Booster Mix

When it's time to plant your container veggies, add this miracle food to a half-and-half mixture of good commercial potting soil and compost. I guarantee, you'll get a harvest that will put many an in-ground plot to shame!

INSTRUCTIONS: Combine these ingredients in a bucket, then work the mixture thoroughly into your planting mix. Fill your containers, and get busy planting!

INGREDIENTS:

4 eggshells (dried and crushed to powder) per bushel of soil

$\frac{1}{2}$ cup of Epsom salts

$\frac{1}{4}$ cup of coffee grounds

1 tbsp. of instant tea granules

◆ BOOST THE BLOOMS

Potted peppers and tomatoes will develop faster if you provide them with magnesium in a form they can use quickly. To do this, mix 2 tablespoons of Epsom salts in 1 gallon of water. Apply 1 pint of this mixture to each plant just as the blooms appear.

GREAT IDEA!

Have an abundance of ripe tomatoes, but not the time to can them?

Try this super-simple recipe for making great-tasting tomato juice! Simply wash and core the tomatoes (work in batches of six or so, depending on their size), and cut away any bad spots. Put the tomatoes in a blender, and blend on high speed or purée until smooth. Then can or freeze the vitamin-packed juice. It's that easy!

Energizing Earthworm Elixir

To grow the sweetest, juiciest tomatoes and melons in town, mix up a batch of this soil-energizing mix before planting.

INSTRUCTIONS: Mix these ingredients in a bucket, and put 1 cup in the bottom of each hole as you plant. Your tomatoes and melons will grow beyond your wildest dreams!

INGREDIENTS:

5 lbs. of earthworm castings
1/2 lb. of Epsom salts
1/4 cup of instant tea granules

◆ A Shady Solution

Are the tips of your lettuce plants brown and burnt-looking? It's not a disease you're dealing with: It's a condition called tip burn, caused by a combination of heat and an irregular water supply. To prevent it, keep the soil evenly moist, and put up a barrier between your tender plants and the brutal sun—a piece of lattice or a heat-loving crop growing on a trellis is just the ticket!

◆ So Long, Suckers!

If you want to grow whopper tomatoes (and who doesn't?), pinch off all of the suckers that develop in the crook between the branches and the main stem. This will make the plant stronger and the fruit much bigger.

GRANDMA PUTT'S POINTERS ☞ When a storm knocks a lot of blossoms off your tomato plants, don't panic: You can still get a good crop. Just pollinate the remaining flowers yourself with an old trick Grandma Putt taught me. Rub an old nylon woman's slip to build up static electricity, and lay it on the blossoms of one plant. Then take it off and shake the pollen onto another plant. You'll get 100 percent pollination every time!

Fall Berry Bed Prep Mix

Well-tended berries will reward you with a tasty harvest for many years, so it makes sense to get them off to a great start. Here's a super soil energizer that Grandma Putt used to grow the biggest berries in town.

INGREDIENTS:

50 lbs. of manure
50 lbs. of shredded leaves

INSTRUCTIONS: Mix these ingredients in a wheelbarrow, and work them deep into every 100 sq. ft. of garden soil. Afterwards, top-dress the bed with 25 lbs. of gypsum, and let it sit for the winter.

◆ FOILING OUR FEATHERED FRIENDS

Most of us enjoy the company of birds in our yards—until they start snapping up our sprouts, seeds, and berries, that is! If your bird population is high, it's worth spending a few dollars to buy some polyester bird netting. This lightweight mesh will keep birds away from anything you cover with it. If you handle it gently, you can switch the netting around as needed to protect young corn sprouts in spring, ripening tomatoes in summer, and berries, grapes, and tree fruits whenever they need it.

If birds cause aggravation on just a few plants, like a little cherry tree or a pair of blueberry bushes, you probably can do without the netting. Instead, discourage feeding by spritzing the plants with my Bye-Bye, Birdie Tonic (see **page 69**) between rains.

ASK JERRY

Q *Rabbits and mice are making mincemeat out of the bark on my fruit trees! How can I stop them?*

A Wrap the bark with tree wrap all the way down to the soil. Then place a ring of medium-sized stones right around the base of the tree.

Fall Vegetable Garden Tonic

Once Jack Frost has called a halt to the growing season, cover your vegetable garden beds with a mixture of shredded leaves and grass clippings, and treat them to a taste of this tonic.

INSTRUCTIONS: Mix the cola, dishwashing liquid, and ammonia in a 20 gallon hose-end sprayer, filling the balance of the jar with warm water. Saturate the layer of mulch that's on top of the soil to give your garden a good bedtime snack.

INGREDIENTS:
1 can of regular cola (not diet)
1 cup of dishwashing liquid
¼ cup of ammonia
Warm water

◆ THE MANURE CURE

To my mind, there's nothing like good old barnyard manure to keep veggie garden soil in super shape. But fresh manure can burn tender roots, so you should always cure it before you add it to your soil. Here's how I make mine cool, weed-free, and—believe it or not—almost odor-free!

◆ **Step 1:** Spread a big tarpaulin on the ground, and dump the manure on top. Fold up the edges of the tarp around the pile of manure.

◆ **Step 2:** Lay another tarp across the top, and add a few rocks, so that it stays put. Cut three or four slits in that tarp, so the heat can get out.

◆ **Step 3:** Let it sit for six months or so, and—presto!—you've got the best food a garden could ever ask for.

Don't go to great expense buying frost protectors for you veggies—old lamp shades will do the trick. Just remove the fabric, set the wire frame over a plant, and drape a piece of old sheet or a plastic garbage bag over it. Voilà!

Fruit Defender Traps

Are bad bugs bugging your fruit trees and spoiling your harvest? Here's a sweet trick for trapping those pesky pests.

INSTRUCTIONS: Mix the sugar, vinegar, and banana peel in a clean, 1-gallon milk jug, filling the balance of the jug with water to about 2 inches from the top. Hang one jug in each fruit tree or set them among your raspberry bushes, and leave them in place all summer.

INGREDIENTS:

1 cup of sugar
$\frac{1}{2}$ cup of vinegar
1 banana peel
Water

◆ FRUITY FIX-UPS

It's a good idea to remove any mummified fruit and cankered branches from your fruit trees in February, before they spread disease spores to healthy branches. While you're out there, take a minute to tamp down any snow around the trunks, so that mice don't make runs to the trunks or feed on the bark.

ASK JERRY

Q *I just moved into an old house with a small orchard. The trees have been neglected for years and are in bad shape. Is it worth attempting to save them?*

A I would sure give it a try! First, remove all the dead and broken limbs. Then poke holes 3 feet apart and 8 inches deep in a circle out at the drip line (below the tips of the farthest branches of each tree). Use these holes to feed each tree with 15 pounds of low-nitrogen plant food. Then apply half a pound of moth crystals to the soil beneath each tree within 3 feet of the trunk to help control borers. With this TLC, your trees should sprout healthy new growth and bear fruit again.

Fruit Tree Planting Tonic

Here's a terrific old-time tonic that still works wonders for giving new fruit trees a root-boosting jump start!

INSTRUCTIONS: Mix these ingredients in a large bucket, then soak the young plants in the solution for an hour or so before planting. Dribble any leftover mix over the soil after you're all done planting.

INGREDIENTS:

$^1/_2$ cup of Fels Naptha® soap solution*
$^1/_2$ cup of Epsom salts
$^1/_2$ cup of brewed tea
5 gal. of water

To make this solution, shave ¼ bar of Fels Naptha or Octagon® Soap into 1 quart of boiling water. When the soap is completely dissolved, add ¼ cup of dishwashing liquid. Let the mixture cool, then store it in a suitable container until it's needed.

◆ PINT-SIZE STRAWBERRIES

Think you don't have the time or space to grow fruit? You need to try alpine strawberries (*Fragaria vesca*)! These little cuties produce tidy, 6- to 8-inch-tall clumps of bright green leaves dotted with tiny white flowers and small, but succulent fruits from late spring to frost. Unlike hybrid strawberries, alpines don't send out runners, so they make great edging plants for all kinds of beds and borders.

GREAT IDEA!

Need an easy way to pick apples?

Make a handy apple picker with an old broomstick, a nail, and an empty, gallon-size plastic milk jug. Turn the jug upside down, and shove the neck onto the end of the broomstick. Then drive a small nail into the neck of the jug and through the broomstick to secure it in place. In the bottom of the jug, cut a hole just big enough for the fruit to fit through, and you're ready to start picking!

Fruit Tree Soil-Builder Mix

It takes LOTS of energy to produce awesome apples, top-notch cherries, and perfect peaches. This power-packed mix is just the ticket for feeding the soil so it can feed your fruit trees—and they can feed you!

INSTRUCTIONS: Mix these ingredients in a wheelbarrow, then work this tonic thoroughly into every 100 sq. ft. of soil area. Your fruit trees will thank you for it!

INGREDIENTS:

3 bushels of compost
5 lbs. of bonemeal
2 ½ lbs. of gypsum
1 lb. of Epsom salts

◆ LEAF MOLD IS BLACK GOLD

There's nothing I know of that makes a better all-around plant food than leaf mold—and nothing could be easier to make. Simply shred fall leaves with your lawn mower (smaller pieces will decompose faster), and scoop the shreds into large, black plastic garbage bags. Add some water, close the bags up tight, and forget about 'em for about six months. Then come spring, you'll have a great supply of super-chow to feed your vegetable garden.

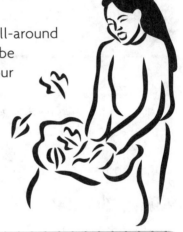

GRANDMA PUTT'S POINTERS ☞

If you have a fruit tree that isn't bearing fruit, do what Grandma Putt did—give it a few scratches to encourage it to begin bearing. When a tree is slightly damaged, it concentrates its energy in order to heal its wounds. Sometimes, this burst of energy is just what is needed to stimulate the tree to bear fruit. Use a utility or carpet knife to scar the tree on the trunk and some of the main branches. Don't overdo it, though, and be sure that you don't cut completely around the trunk or any of the branches.

Fungus-Fighter Soil Drench

When foul fungi are fussin' around in your soil, they can cause your veggies to produce poorly, wilt, or worse! Polish 'em off with this potent potion.

INSTRUCTIONS: Mix these ingredients in a big pot and bring to a boil. Then turn off the heat, and let the mixture cool to room temperature. Strain the liquid into a watering can, and soak the ground around fungus-prone plants. Go VERY slowly, so the elixir penetrates deep into the soil. Then dump the strained-out garlic bits onto the soil, and work them in gently, so as not to disturb any plant roots.

INGREDIENTS:

4 garlic bulbs, crushed
½ cup of baking soda
1 gal. of water

◆ BAG IT!

If you choose to leave root vegetables in the ground for the winter, toss leaf-filled bags on top to insulate them from freezing temperatures. You'll be able to enjoy your carrots, rutabagas, and parsnips all winter long!

◆ SHAPE 'EM UP

Whatever shape you make your vegetable garden beds, keep them narrow enough so that you can reach into the center comfortably without stepping on the planting area. Why? Because stepping on cultivated soil compacts it, which can damage the roots of even big trees. So just imagine what it will do to your tender young seedlings!

TERRIFIC TIME⌛SAVERS

When you've tilled your garden plot in spring, don't be in a hurry to sow seeds right away. Instead, sit back and wait for the first rain. Within a few days, your garden beds will be chock-full of baby weeds, and you can hoe 'em right up. You'll save a whole lot of weeding time in the long run!

Garlic-and-Onion Juice

Aphids, caterpillars, whiteflies, and whatever other pesky pests are bugging your crops will head for the hills when they get a whiff of this aromatic elixir!

INSTRUCTIONS: Put these ingredients in a blender, and whirl them up. Strain out the solids, pour the remaining liquid into a hand-held sprayer, and use it whenever your plants need potent relief from soft-bodied insects. Bury the leftover solids in your garden to keep pests from coming back.

INGREDIENTS:

3 medium onions
2 cloves of garlic
3 cups of water

◆ Don't Delay

If you've had trouble with maggots in your radishes, early planting is the cure. The key is to plant early enough to get a mature radish crop by June 1. Do this, and your radishes will be practically maggot-free!

◆ Keep Alert for Cutworms

Adult cutworm moths lay their eggs around the bases of weeds and grasses, so you can expect serious cutworm problems when growing edibles in new beds that were previously lawn areas. To minimize the risk, prepare the bed in fall or in early spring. That'll move the cutworms up close to the soil surface, where birds can spot them, zero in, and eat the pesky pests for lunch.

ASK JERRY

Q I need some serious help growing garlic! All I've gotten so far is small bulbs in the ground, with tops like golf balls on the stems.

A For your next crop, dig a hole about a foot across and a foot deep, and fill it with a mixture of ⅓ topsoil, ⅓ professional potting soil, and ⅓ builder's sand. Plant your garlic in it, and that should do the trick!

Happy Herb Tonic

Herbs generally don't like a whole lot of food, but they do appreciate a mild feeding every now and again. This tonic is one I swear by for keeping all kinds of herbs happy and high-yielding.

INSTRUCTIONS: Mix these ingredients in a watering can, and sprinkle the solution over your herbs every six weeks during the growing season.

INGREDIENTS:

$\frac{1}{4}$ cup of brewed tea
$\frac{1}{2}$ tbsp. of bourbon
$\frac{1}{2}$ tbsp. of ammonia
$\frac{1}{2}$ tbsp. of hydrogen peroxide
$\frac{1}{2}$ tsp. of dishwashing liquid
1 gal. of warm water

◆ A Tasty Tip

It stands to reason that herbs with edible leaves have edible flowers, too! Toss fresh herb flowers into salads, float 'em in soups, or mix 'em in with herb leaves in pesto. Herbs with especially flavorful flowers include basil, borage, chives, dill, mint, oregano, parsley, rosemary, sage, and thyme.

◆ Pinch an Inch

To keep your herb plants looking great and producing generously, pinch off the growing tips periodically. Begin pinching when the plants are 6 inches tall, and repeat after every 4 to 6 inches of new growth. By the way, you can enjoy these tender trimmings as salad toppers!

There's no need to spend a bundle buying herbal teas—you can harvest the ingredients for a tasty cup of tea right from your own garden. Some flavorful flowers for tea include bee balm, chamomile, lemon balm, lemon verbena, and mints. Add a few rose hips, too; they're a terrific source of vitamin C. Just remember—**never spray pesticides on or around any herbs or roses you plan to pick, either for cooking or for brewing!**

Healthy Container Herb Tonic

Potted herbs don't have much soil to support them, so they depend on you for a steady supply of food. This mild, but nutritious tonic fits the bill perfectly!

INGREDIENTS:

1 tbsp. of dishwashing liquid
1 tbsp. of antiseptic mouthwash
1 tbsp. of ammonia
$\frac{1}{4}$ cup of brewed tea
1 qt. of warm water

INSTRUCTIONS: Mix these ingredients in a watering can, and water your potted herbs with the solution once a week. Besides giving your herbs a gentle nutrient boost, it'll help fight insects and diseases, too!

◆ HIGH AND DRY

To dry herbs at home, just bundle a few stems of fresh herbs together with a rubber band, and hang 'em upside down in a warm, dark, airy place until the leaves are crispy. To keep dust off them, cut a hole in the bottom of a brown paper bag and a few flaps in the sides for ventilation. Turn the bag over, slip it over the stems of an herb bundle so they poke through the hole in the bottom, and hang up the covered bundle.

GREAT IDEA!

Do you yearn for a taste of summer even when there's snow on the ground?

Then grow some herbs on a sunny windowsill. In early fall, divide and pot up perennial herbs (oregano, tarragon, thyme, and mints are good candidates) or take cuttings (easy with lemon balm, marjoram, and mints). You can also start many annual herbs from seed; try this with basil, dill, fennel, marjoram, parsley, and cilantro.

Hello Jell-O® Seed Starter

To get your veggie seeds off to a disease-free start, try this tasty trick. (**Note:** Any flavor will work, but lemon is the best choice because it repels some bugs.)

INSTRUCTIONS: Pour these ingredients into an empty salt shaker, and sprinkle the mix lightly over newly planted seeds. Gently press down the powder, cover lightly with soil, and keep the soil evenly moist. Your seedlings will be stronger and healthier than you ever imagined!

INGREDIENTS:

1 package of Jell-O powder
Powdered skim milk, an
   amount equal to the
   Jell-O powder

◆ A SWEET TREAT

Here's a fun summertime activity that's so simple, even kids can do it—making bee balm sugar! Take a clean, pint-size glass jar and fill it about a third full with granulated sugar. Add a handful of bee balm petals, then more sugar until the jar is half full. Add more petals and more sugar, until the jar is almost full. Put the lid on tight and shake the jar. Set it in a cool, dark place for at least two weeks before sifting out the flowers and storing the flavored sugar for later use in tea or baking.

GRANDMA PUTT'S POINTERS ☞

When she was looking for something extra-special to decorate desserts, Grandma Putt and I would make candied flowers! It's a snap: Simply beat egg whites until they are slightly frothy, then use a small, clean brush to paint them on both sides of each edible flower or petal. Use tweezers to dip the flowers or petals into very fine granulated sugar. Place the sugared parts on waxed paper to dry, and presto— perfect candied flowers!

Herb Booster Tonic

Just like people, herbs enjoy a nice, cool drink when the going gets hot. Quench their thirst with this simple summertime pick-me-up.

INSTRUCTIONS: Mix these ingredients in a 20 gallon hose-end sprayer, then give your herbs a good dousing every six weeks during the growing season to keep them as cool as cucumbers!

INGREDIENTS:

1 can of beer
1 cup of ammonia
$\frac{1}{2}$ cup of Murphy's Oil Soap®
$\frac{1}{2}$ cup of clear corn syrup

◆ THE KINDEST CUT

The key to a healthy harvest—for your herbs, that is—is using a sharp pair of scissors or garden shears to clip off leaves and stem tips. Otherwise, you're likely to damage your plants when you tug on shoots as you try to pinch or snap them off. At best, the plants may just grow a little more slowly as they recover; at the worst, you might pull a whole plant out of the ground! Believe me, making a clean cut with sharp shears is a much better way to go.

MAKING CENTS

With a little advance planning, there's no need to waste your money on fresh herbs from the store during the winter! When your summer harvest is in full swing, spread freshly picked herb leaves on cookie sheets, and stick 'em in the freezer. When they're frozen to a crisp, place the leaves in plastic bags for space-saving storage, then keep them in the freezer until you need 'em. Or, pack fresh herb leaves into a food processor, top with a bit of olive oil, and chop away. Pack the mix into ice-cube trays, freeze, then store the cubes in plastic bags. Drop them into soups and sauces as needed.

Herb Garden Helper Tonic

Herbs do more than just smell and taste great—they can also help keep bad bugs away from your veggies. To get 'em off to a rip-roarin' start, treat them to my Herb Garden Helper Tonic at planting time.

INSTRUCTIONS: Work this mix into each 50 sq. ft. of herb garden area to a depth of 12 to 18 inches, and then let it sit for 7 to 10 days before planting.

INGREDIENTS:
5 lbs. of lime
5 lbs. of gypsum
1 lb. of 5-10-5 plant food
$\frac{1}{2}$ cup of Epsom salts

◆ THE LADDER TO SUCCESS

Believe it or not, an old wooden ladder makes a great quick-and-easy herb garden. Simply lay the ladder down on a flat area, fill in between the rungs with soil, and plant a different herb in each section.

◆ TAKE A WHIFF

Watch out—not all herbs are created equal! Seed-grown plants of tarragon and oregano may or may not smell or taste the way they're supposed to. (Some don't have any flavor at all!) So when you go to buy herb plants, make sure you're getting what you want—always rub and sniff a leaf before you buy it. If it doesn't smell the way it should, walk on by.

ASK JERRY

Q *I love growing mint, but I hate the way it spreads all over my garden. Do I have to give it up altogether?*

A A simple solution is to plant it in a bottomless bucket sunk in the garden. Then cut off any roots that creep out over the edge of the bucket. Or plant 'em in an out-of-the-way spot, and just let 'em go wild! When the plants go too far, cut them down with your lawn mower.

Herbal Soap Spray

Aromatic herbs appeal to people, but bugs sure can't stand the smell of 'em! When you combine these fragrant plants with soap to make this tonic, you'll end up with a spray that kills the bad bugs already around AND keeps them from coming back, too.

INGREDIENTS:

1 cup of wormwood or tansy
1 cup of lavender
1 cup of sage
1 tsp. of Murphy's Oil Soap®
Water

INSTRUCTIONS: Put the herbs in a canning jar, and fill the jar with boiling water. Let it cool, then strain out the herbs. Mix $\frac{1}{8}$ cup of the liquid with 2 cups of water and the Murphy's Oil Soap, pour into a hand-held sprayer, and apply to bug-bothered plants to send pests packin'.

◆ HERE'S A SHOCKING IDEA!

Some trellises and supports can actually supercharge your vegetable garden! It has to do with an old-time kind of gardening called electroculture. Have you ever noticed how your lawn suddenly greens up after a thunderstorm? That's electroculture at work: Electricity flying around in the air joins oxygen and nitrogen to form nitric oxide, and that's great for plants!

To create the same conditions in your garden, use metal supports and trellises—especially copper ones—to attract static electricity. Tying up plants with strips of old pantyhose can help, too. (If you don't know how that could attract electricity, just ask any woman about "static cling.") Try it for yourself, and you'll be *amazed* at the results!

GREAT IDEA!

Always plant basil, bee balm, and borage near your tomatoes.

These aromatic herbs are the best neighbors your tomatoes will ever have, and they'll boost your plants to new heights!

Hit-the-Trail Mix

Tired of rabbits, deer, and other four-legged marauders spoiling your veggies? This spicy concoction will make any critter hightail it away from your garden.

INSTRUCTIONS: Mix these ingredients in a watering can, and sprinkle the solution around the perimeter of your vegetable beds.

INGREDIENTS:
4 tbsp. of dry mustard
3 tbsp. of cayenne pepper
2 tbsp. of chili powder
2 tbsp. of cloves
1 tbsp. of Tabasco® sauce
2 qts. of warm water

◆ RODENT REPELLERS

Are mice, voles, and other rascally rodents ruining your harvest? Gather up six or eight empty glass soda or beer bottles and half-bury them, top ends up, in a line near the critters' hangouts. When the wind passes over, it'll make a scary sound that tells these varmints to vamoose!

◆ FOIL 'EM WITH OIL

Believe it or not, plain old mineral oil can really help protect your corn crop from worm damage. How? It's simple—just apply a drop of oil to the tip of each ear when the silks begin to brown. Reapply every five or six days, for a total of three applications per season, to keep thoses wicked worms away.

GRANDMA PUTT'S POINTERS ☞ If Grandma Putt noticed a lot of little flies buzzing around her onions, she'd head right for the fireplace to get some wood ashes. Why? When sprinkled around onions (cabbage, too), wood ashes discourage the flies whose babies are pesky root maggots.

Hurry-Up-the-Harvest Tonic

When I know Old Man Winter is waiting in the wings and my plants are still chock-full of unripe veggies, I give my garden a big drink of this tonic.

INSTRUCTIONS: Mix the apple juice, ammonia, and shampoo in a 20 gallon hose-end sprayer, filling the balance of the jar with warm water. Then spray the tonic on your garden to the point of run-off to speed up the ripening process.

INGREDIENTS:
1 cup of apple juice
$\frac{1}{2}$ cup of ammonia
$\frac{1}{2}$ cup of baby shampoo
Warm water

◆ GIVE 'EM A LEG UP

Abundant onions? Grab some hose—pantyhose, that is—and tie them up. Put an onion in the toe, tie a knot above it, add another onion, tie a knot above it, and so on, until the leg is filled. Hang this leggin' in a cool, dry place. Then when you need an onion, simply cut below the knot.

◆ WATER AWAY FROST

If Jack Frost snuck up on your plants before you had a chance to cover them, don't worry. You may be able to revive hardy crops like chard, collards, and mustard. Simply sprinkle them gently with water from your garden hose *before* the sun shines on them. That may be enough to prevent damage, so you can keep on harvesting a while longer.

TERRIFIC TIME⬦SAVERS

Need a quick and easy way to protect your crops from frost? Drive a stake into the ground at each end of the garden, and stretch a rope or wire between the stakes. Then toss an old sheet over the rope to make a tent. This'll protect your plants from getting frostbite at night.

Jerry's Lime Rickey

Back in my Uncle Art's day, lime soda pop rickeys were all the rage. Well, this rickey isn't made with soda pop, but it WILL make cabbage maggots rage!

INSTRUCTIONS: Stir the lime into the water, and let it sit overnight. Then pour the solution around the root ball of each maggot-plagued plant. Before you can say "Put a nickel in the jukebox," those maggots'll be history!

> ### INGREDIENTS:
> 1 cup of lime
> 1 qt. of water

◆ ANOTHER TIME FOR LIME

Are flea beetles making Swiss cheese of your eggplant leaves? Dust the plants with lime to keep these little menaces away. For best results, dust lightly in the early morning, when plants are still wet with dew, so the powder clings better.

◆ THE NET RESULT

To keep cabbage butterflies off of your veggies, use bird netting. Make a frame out of wood or PVC that stands several inches above the plants, and double up the netting for safety's sake. Tack it to the ground with rocks, sticks, or earth staples. It's easy to lift up to get to your veggies and won't take up much space when stored. And it sure beats picking the pesky larvae off your plants by hand!

MAKING CENTS

Want to get twice the return from a single planting of cabbage? At harvest time, instead of pulling cabbages up by their roots, just cut the heads off, leaving as much stalk behind as possible. Usually, a cluster of small heads will grow out of the stalk that's left behind. Clip these off when they're small and enjoy their mild, tender leaves in a tossed salad.

Knock-'Em-Dead Insect Tonic

This potent mixture will deal a death blow to squash bugs, bean beetles, and any other foul felons that are after your veggies.

INSTRUCTIONS: Mix these ingredients in a bucket, and let the mixture sit overnight. Strain out the solids, pour the liquid into a hand-held sprayer, and knock those buggy pests for a loop!

INGREDIENTS:

6 cloves of garlic, finely chopped

1 small onion, finely chopped

1 tbsp. of cayenne pepper

1 tbsp. of dishwashing liquid

1 qt. of warm water

◆ FLEA BEETLE BEATERS

If the leaves of your eggplants are so full of holes that they look like lace, flea beetles are the likely culprits. In the cool of the morning, hit 'em with my Knock-'Em-Dead Insect Tonic (above). Then for long-term protection, make yellow sticky traps: Paint 1- by 6-inch boards yellow, tack them to sticks, and coat the surfaces with a sticky substance such as honey or Tangle-trap®. Poke the sticks into the soil among troubled plants to trap flea beetles.

◆ BRING ON THE BORON

Like its brother the beet, Swiss chard needs boron in its soil to grow well. If it doesn't get enough, its stems will crack. To make sure your crops have all the boron they need, sprinkle a little borax in and among the rows at planting time to keep 'em growing strong.

✳ IDEA!

GREAT

Are root maggots polishing off your carrot crop faster than you can say "Bugs Bunny"?

To keep the vile villains where they belong—far, far away—sprinkle coffee grounds or wood ashes over your whole carrot patch.

Lethal Weapon Tonic

Garlic and onions are definitely double-duty crops—besides tasting great, they provide the key ingredients for a perfect pest-fighting spray!

INSTRUCTIONS: Mix these ingredients together in a bucket, and pour into a 20 gallon hose-end sprayer. Spray on your vegetables every 10 days to prevent damage from aphids and many other pests.

INGREDIENTS:

3 tbsp. of garlic-and-onion juice*
3 tbsp. of skim milk
2 tbsp. of baby shampoo
1 tsp. of Tabasco® sauce
1 gal. of water

Make garlic-and-onion juice by chopping 2 cloves of garlic and 2 medium onions. Combine in a blender with 3 cups of water, then strain and use the remaining liquid.

◆ TREAT THESE LADIES RIGHT!

If aphids are tormenting your turnips (or any other crop), plant some hairy vetch next to your veggies, and your troubles will be over. To a ladybug, a big patch of hairy vetch is palatial living quarters, and a ladybug's idea of a four-star restaurant is a plantful of aphids. It's a simple equation: More ladybugs = fewer aphids!

ASK JERRY

Q *No matter what I do, cucumber beetles just won't leave my cukes alone. Help!*

A Cucumber beetles are drawn to cukes by a bitter compound that most varieties have in their skin. These bad beetles tend to steer clear of kinds like 'Aria', 'Holland', 'Jazzer', and 'Lemon', which don't have that chemical attraction. But you won't want to steer clear of them—they turn out some of the tastiest harvests you'll find!

Marvelous Melon Soil Mix

Melons are mighty particular about the ground they call home, so it's worth putting some extra effort into making their bed. This mixture suits 'em to a "T."

INSTRUCTIONS: Mix these ingredients in a bucket or wheelbarrow. Use the mixture to fill each of your melon planting holes, then get ready to modestly accept your town's Most Mouthwatering Melon Award!

To make Mouthwatering Melon Mix, combine 5 pounds of earthworm castings (available in catalogs), ½ pound of Epsom salts, and ¼ cup of instant tea granules.

INGREDIENTS:
2 parts coarse builder's sand (not beach or "sandbox" sand)
1 part compost
1 part professional planting mix
1 cup of Mouthwatering Melon Mix*

◆ MAKE A MELON CRADLE

One of my favorite tricks for recycling plastic milk jugs is using them in the melon patch to prevent the fruit from rotting. Simply cut a jug in half lengthwise, lay one half on the ground, and set the ripening melon inside. Not only will this plastic perch prevent rot, but it will also discourage critters from nibbling on your melons!

◆ THE BRICK TRICK

If you just can't wait to slice into a ripe, juicy melon, try fast-forwarding their ripening time. Place your young melons on bricks while they're still attached to the vine, and the heat that the bricks absorb will speed up the ripening process. Works every time!

GRANDMA PUTT'S POINTERS ☞ Here's a little secret I learned from Grandma Putt back when I was a boy: To grow the absolute biggest pumpkins in town, remove all but the two biggest fruits from each vine.

Mighty Mouse Control

Here I come to save the day! To keep mice and other small varmints from nibbling your young fruit trees and shrubs to nubs, give 'em a taste of this highly effective repellent.

INSTRUCTIONS: Mix these ingredients together in a bucket, then pour into a hand-held sprayer. Drench all young tree and shrub trunks with it in late fall, and repeat every few weeks, if the weather is rainy, to keep the scent fresh.

INGREDIENTS:

2 tbsp. of Tabasco® sauce

2 tbsp. of cayenne pepper

2 tbsp. of Murphy's Oil Soap®

1 qt. of warm water

◆ COON CONFUSERS

Nothing starts a raccoon's heart pitter-patterin' faster than a big patch of sweet corn. Keeping these rascals out can take some doing, but here are some of my better ideas:

- ◆ Prop old screens or bushel baskets against the cornstalks.

- ◆ Cover the silks with pantyhose toes dabbed with perfume.

- ◆ Drape strings of blinking Christmas-tree lights in and among the stalks.

- ◆ Lay crumpled newspaper on the ground between the rows.

ASK JERRY

Q *I'm never quite sure when to harvest my sweet corn. How can I tell when it's ready for picking?*

A Pop 'em, then pick 'em! What do I mean? Start testing your corn about 15 days after the silk appears. Peel back the husk a couple of inches, and press on a kernel with your fingernail until it pops open. If the juice is milky, the corn is perfect for picking. If it's watery, then give it a few more days. If it's pasty, then you're late, so you'd better get picking right away!

Mite-Free Fruit Tree Mix

Mites may be teeny, but they can do BIG damage to fruit trees. When these pests attack, protect your crop with this easy recipe.

INSTRUCTIONS: Mix these ingredients together, and keep the potion in a tightly closed garbage can. Stir before adding to a 6 gallon pump sprayer, and spray weekly until the mites are history.

INGREDIENTS:

5 lbs. of white flour
1 pt. of buttermilk
25 gal. of water

◆ BRIGHTEN YOUR DAY WITH BORAGE

Anytime I was down in the dumps, Grandma Putt would make me a big dish of potato salad made special with bright blue borage flowers. Nowadays, I add these beautiful herb blooms to tossed salads, sprinkle them on cottage cheese, or blend them with cream cheese for a colorful sandwich spread. Besides being a real taste treat, borage packs a good supply of calcium and potassium, too!

◆ SAFETY FIRST

A little common sense goes a long way where edible flowers are concerned. First, harvest only those that you know are safe to eat, and only those that you know have not been sprayed with chemicals. Use them sparingly at first, until you get used to their flavors. Be especially cautious if you have asthma or hay fever; if your allergies are severe, in fact, you might want to avoid edible flowers altogether.

GREAT IDEA!

Need some advice on using edible flowers?

Here are some fun ways to add excitement to meals:

◆ Use 'em as a garnish for dips or prepared food.

◆ Enjoy 'em as colorful additions to scrambled eggs.

◆ Freeze small flowers or petals in ice cubes to perk up a punch.

◆ Make candied flowers (see "Grandma Putt's Pointers" on **page 268**).

Nettle Tea

Stinging nettles pack a load of nitrogen that's as potent as manure, and they give off pest-repelling chemicals, too. So what are you waiting for? Brew a pot of this powerful tea, and double your firepower!

INSTRUCTIONS: Put the nettles in a bucket, pour in the water, and let the mixture steep for at least a week. Strain out the leaves, and water your plants with the brew. Then toss the leaves on the compost pile, or bury them in the garden to give your plants an extra nutrient boost.

INGREDIENTS:

1 lb. of stinging nettle
leaves
1 gal. of water

◆ BROCCOLI BOOSTER

Some folks like to spread out their broccoli plants 18 to 24 inches apart, and that's fine if your objective is big central heads. When you set them just 8 inches apart, however, you get smaller central heads, but the side-shoot population will explode, giving you a *much* bigger harvest overall.

◆ DON'T OVER N-DULGE

Leaf crops like lettuce and spinach need plenty of nitrogen, but for other veggies, go easy on the Big N (nitrogen). If they get too much, they'll lose interest in setting fruit (like squash or melons) or producing big, plump, tasty roots and tubers (like potatoes, turnips, and carrots).

GRANDMA PUTT'S POINTERS ☞

Here's an old-time secret that Grandma Putt showed me for getting radishes off to a super-speedy start. Before planting, she'd soak her seeds in water for 24 hours. Then she put them in a brown paper bag and set it in the sun. Within a day, the seeds sprouted, and she'd get 'em right in the ground to start growin'!

Nut Tree Booster

Before planting nut trees, Grandma Putt always made up a batch of this marvelous mix to enrich the soil and really give 'em something extra special to grow on.

INSTRUCTIONS: Mix these ingredients in a bucket. Work the mixture into the bottom and sides of the planting hole, and sprinkle some on top of the soil after you're done planting.

INGREDIENTS:

5 parts bonemeal
2 parts gypsum
1 part Epsom salts

◆ STAY AWAY FROM WALNUTS

Whatever you do, keep your vegetable garden far, far away from walnut trees—both black and English kinds. They produce a chemical called juglone that's toxic to many plants, including potatoes and tomatoes.

◆ A BALANCING TRICK

There's nothing better for building up your soil than organic matter, but keep in mind that it can "tie up" lots of nitrogen while it's in the process of breaking down. When you add large amounts of fresh leaves, straw, or clippings to your garden all at once, it can take a month or so for the imbalance to right itself. To correct the temporary nitrogen shortage quickly, simply add 1 pound of nitrate of soda, ¾ pound of ammonium sulfate, or ½ pound of ammonium nitrate to each bushel of material you add to the soil.

Black walnuts give off a sticky black juice that can be the devil to remove from skin and clothing. To keep your clothes from getting ruined, spread plastic drop cloths on the ground before you start beating the branches at harvest time. Once all the nuts have fallen, simply gather up the drop cloths (and your crop). That way, you'll stay as clean as a whistle!

Orange Aid Elixir

You'll love the aroma of this citrusy spray—but caterpillars HATE it! Whether it's cabbageworms on your broccoli or armyworms on your tomatoes, my Orange Aid Elixir will solve all of your caterpillar problems.

INSTRUCTIONS: Put the orange peels in a blender or food processor, and pour $1/4$ cup of boiling water over them. Liquefy, then let the mixture sit overnight at room temperature. Strain through cheesecloth, and pour the liquid into a hand-held sprayer. Fill the balance of the jar with water, and spray your plants from top to bottom.

INGREDIENTS:

1 cup of chopped orange peels (lemon, lime, or grapefruit peels work, too)

Water

◆ GARDEN GOLD

If soil insects have been bugging your crops this year, try this trick: Collect as many marigold plants as you can in fall, lay them in a row on your lawn, then run your lawn mower over them with the catcher bag attached to it. When you're done, sprinkle them over your freshly turned vegetable garden soil, then fill your 20 gallon hose-end sprayer with a can of beer, and drench the soil. By spring, the beds will be in great shape for planting, and pests should be a thing of the past!

ASK JERRY

Q *Do you have any suggestions for making lettuce last longer after picking? Mine goes brown and mushy within a week.*

A You bet! Simply pull up the whole plant, roots and all, and put it into a glass full of water, just as you would with a cut flower. Then put a big plastic bag over the whole thing and set it in the fridge for a truly handy harvest!

Paralyzing Pest Salsa

Here's a super-spicy, south-of-the-border surprise that'll sock it to any pest that is pestering your vegetable garden!

INSTRUCTIONS: Chop the tomatoes, chili peppers, onion, and garlic, then liquefy them in an old blender. Add the vinegar and pepper to the mixture, then strain out the solids. Pour the liquid into a hand-held sprayer, and apply directly onto any pests that you see in your garden.

INGREDIENTS:

2 lbs. of ripe tomatoes
1 lb. of chili peppers
1 large onion
2 cloves of garlic
1 cup of vinegar
$1/2$ tsp. of pepper

◆ THE BIG COVER-UP

Melon and squash vines need to stay toasty-warm to grow fast and produce their tasty fruits. So keep some floating row covers handy and toss them over your seedlings if the temperature dips below 65°F at night. If you want, you can leave the covers on all the time throughout the early growth stages; they help keep bad-guy bugs at bay, too. But be sure to whisk them off the minute flowers appear on the plants; otherwise, the good-guy bugs won't be able to pollinate them, and you won't have anything to harvest!

GRANDMA PUTT'S POINTERS ☞ Grandma Putt always waited until the apple trees bloomed before she planted her carrot-family crops. She knew that by then, the carrot flies had laid all their eggs elsewhere and her veggies wouldn't be bothered by the pesky larvae!

Peach Protection Tonic

What could be worse than biting into a sweet, juicy peach and finding a nasty old worm? Finding HALF a worm! Here's one way to keep all your peaches worm-free by trapping the adults before they can lay their eggs in your fruits.

INSTRUCTIONS: Mix these ingredients in a 2-quart jar, and hang it from your peach tree when it's in full bloom to lure the adult moths to their doom.

INGREDIENTS:

1 cup of sugar
1 cup of vinegar
1 qt. of water

◆ AUTUMN ORCHARD CHORES

Fall garden cleaning is a lot like housecleaning—you get such a smug, virtuous feeling when the job is well done! But there's a more serious reason to keep your garden clean—to keep insects and diseases at bay. Here's a quick rundown for the backyard fruit grower:

◆ Rake and burn all fallen fruits that are rotting on the ground to control a wide range of pests and diseases.

◆ Cut away and burn any apple and pear branches that were killed by bacterial fire blight. Make sure you cut them off several inches below the visibly infected portion.

◆ Fight peach tree borers with a ring of moth crystals sprinkled about 1 inch away from the trunk and mounded over with soil.

◆ Break off and dispose of tent caterpillar egg clusters on peach or apple twigs.

✳ IDEA!

GREAT

Want to keep artichokes at just-picked freshness?

Place them in a vase—just as you would flowers—with their heads sticking out and their stems submerged in the water. This'll keep 'em ready-to-eat fresh until you're ready to eat them!

Pepper Boost Tonic

If you love peppers as much as I do, you know you can never get enough of 'em. But I do have a great trick for at least getting MORE of 'em—this magical Pepper Boost Tonic!

INSTRUCTIONS: Mix these ingredients in a watering can, then soak the soil around your peppers as they start to flower to stimulate fruit development.

INGREDIENTS:

2 tbsp. of Epsom salts
1 tsp. of baby shampoo
1 gal. of water

◆ Bigger Is Better

Peppers and eggplants often produce a lot of little flowers, which will result in a lot of small vegetables. But if you remove some of the flowers, your plants will spend their energy developing a few high-quality fruits, rather than many little ones!

◆ Beat the Heat

Hot peppers don't just *taste* hot—they *feel* hot, too! The juices in the fruits and plants can burn your skin, and take it from me—it hurts. So always wear gloves when you're working with hot peppers, whether it's in the kitchen or in the garden—*and keep your hands away from your face!*

◆ Build the Burn with Water

Here's a little secret to help you get the hottest hot peppers in town. Just before you're ready to harvest, flood their bed with water. Yup, water! This stresses the roots and sends out a signal to "turn up the heat."

Have a bunch of old matchbooks cluttering up a drawer? Put 'em to work in your garden by burying two or three matches under each of your pepper plants at planting time. The sulfur in the matches will give the plants a boost and take your harvest to new heights!

Pest Pulverizer Potion

There's nothing more frustrating than putting a lot of time and energy into your vegetable garden, only to have it feasted upon by any and all bugs that walk, crawl, or fly by. Well, here's a surefire way to keep those pesky pests at the proper distance—treat 'em to a little heat!

INSTRUCTIONS: Purée these ingredients in a blender, then strain out the solids. Pour the liquid into a hand-held sprayer, then apply to pest-plagued plants to get rid of bad bugs and keep 'em from comin' back.

INGREDIENTS:

3 hot peppers
2 tbsp. of baby shampoo
1 qt. of water

◆ USE THE NEWS

Are earwigs making a mess of your corn or other crops? Set out sections of dampened, rolled-up newspaper in your garden at night. The next morning, they'll be filled with earwigs. Drown 'em or crush 'em—the choice is yours!

◆ THE CORN BOWL

If you live in a dry climate—or if your weather forecast predicts drought this summer—plant your corn in a bowl! Dig a flat-bottomed circle about 12 inches in diameter and 4 inches below the level of the bed. Then plant four seeds in the bottom. The bowl will collect every drop of water that falls and deliver it right to thirsty roots.

TERRIFIC TIME⬛SAVERS

Aluminum foil reflects light, which confuses aphids and lots of other pests, making it difficult for them to find your plants. To put this trick to work in your own garden, try using foil as a mulch around your squash, cucumbers, and corn. This simple secret works wonders to keep the local insect population away from your veggies!

Robust Rhubarb Tonic

Grandma Putt served this nutritious slop to her rhubarb plants twice a year, and she had the biggest and best rhubarb in town!

INSTRUCTIONS: Whip these ingredients together in a blender or food processor, then pour the mushy mix over the soil in your rhubarb bed. Serve up one meal in the spring, and another in the fall.

INGREDIENTS:

1 cup of brewed tea
1 tbsp. of Epsom salts
Vegetable table scraps (all that you have on hand—but no meat or fats)
1 qt. of water

◆ ATTENTION, RHUBARB LOVERS!

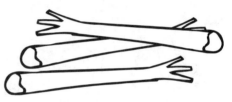

Believe it or not, you can harvest fresh rhubarb all winter long. Start by digging up a few crowns after the first frost, laying them on the ground, and covering them with a few inches of sand. After seven weeks, dig up the frozen clumps, plant them indoors in large buckets, baskets, or even plastic bags, and keep them lightly moist. The leaves will be yellowish, but the stems (the part you want) will be red and ready to harvest throughout the winter.

ASK JERRY

Q *How long does it take before rhubarb matures? Our rhubarb is very good, but the rhubarb stalks sold in the grocery store are much fatter.*

A Two-year-old plants should be ready to please your taste buds. To fatten up your stalks, give your plants an extra boost in the winter by taking all of your nonmeat table scraps, pulverizing them in a blender, and adding a little regular cola (not diet) and beer to liquefy the mixture. Then pour it over the rhubarb mound. Follow up with my Robust Rhubarb Tonic (above) in spring.

Rot-Go Tonic

Those dark patches on the tail ends of your tomatoes look like a disease, but they're not. Blossom end rot is really a nutritional disorder that develops when tomato plants are growing so fast that they just can't get enough calcium to the far end of the fruits. Fortunately, there's a simple way to prevent this pesky problem: my Rot-Go Tonic!

INSTRUCTIONS: Mix these ingredients in a bucket. Then when you plant your tomato seedlings, add a trowelful to each planting hole to get 'em off on the right root.

INGREDIENTS:

1 heaping shovelful of compost
1 tsp. of gypsum
1 tsp. of Epsom salts

◆ GET MILK!

Tobacco mosaic virus is best known for infecting tomatoes and their close relatives in the vegetable garden: eggplants, peppers, and potatoes. Symptoms include slow growth, greatly reduced fruit set, and thickened leaves mottled with various shades of green. If you suspect this virus is lurking somewhere in your garden, try this tactic: When you're working near a susceptible plant, keep a bowl handy that's filled with a half-and-half mixture of milk and water. Then every few minutes, dip your hands and tools into the liquid. It'll stop those vicious viruses dead in their tracks!

GRANDMA PUTT'S POINTERS ☞ I'll bet you didn't know that tomatoes go bananas over bananas! Grandma Putt always placed one skin in the bottom of each planting hole to get her young tomatoes off to a supercharged start. She'd add a few around the base of the plants through the growing season, too. Try it—you won't believe the difference it makes!

Seed and Soil Energizer

Once you've sown your veggie or herb seeds, indoors or out, give them an energizing boost with this excellent elixir.

INSTRUCTIONS: Mix these ingredients in a bucket, and pour the solution into a hand-held sprayer. Shake it gently, and apply a good misting to the surface of newly planted seedbeds or plant containers.

Soak a used tea bag and 1 teaspoon of dishwashing liquid in a gallon of warm water until the mix is light brown.

INGREDIENTS:

1 tsp. of whiskey
1 tsp. of ammonia
1 tsp. of dishwashing liquid
1 qt. of weak tea water*

◆ TRY THIS TRICK

If you've saved seeds from last year and aren't sure they're rarin' to grow this season, here's an easy way to tell if they'll live up to their potential. Simply pour them into a glass of water. The ones that sink have a good chance of growing up big and strong. The seeds that float to the top are losers, so throw them on your compost pile.

One word of warning, however: You'll have to sow the good seeds right away, because they'll have soaked up some water and will be on their way to sprouting.

GREAT ✷IDEA!

Want to know if that packet of seeds is still viable?

Fold a few seeds in a strip of blotting paper, and stick the paper in a pan of moist sand. Keep the sand warm and moist for a few days, and the best of the seeds will sprout. If about 75 percent of them sprout, go ahead and plant the rest as you normally would; otherwise, you're better off buying a whole new packet of seeds.

Seed Starter Solution

No matter what kind of seeds you're planting, this terrific tonic will get 'em off to a rip-roarin' start—GUARANTEED!

INSTRUCTIONS: Mix these ingredients in a bowl. Then bundle up your seeds in cheesecloth or an old pantyhose toe (one kind of seed per bundle). Drop the bundles into the liquid, and put the container in the fridge to soak for 24 hours. Your seeds will come out rarin' to grow!

> **INGREDIENTS:**
> 1 tsp. of baby shampoo
> 1 tsp. of Epsom salts
> 1 qt. of weak tea water*

Soak a used tea bag and 1 teaspoon of dishwashing liquid in a gallon of warm water until the mix is light brown.

◆ PEAS, PLEASE!

If you live in one of the hotter parts of the country, don't fret: Your home-grown peas can be just as tasty as anyone's up North. The secret is to plant your crop in December, instead of March. And for an extra-speedy start, soak the seeds in my Seed Starter Solution (above) before planting them.

GRANDMA PUTT'S POINTERS ☞ Melons and squash appreciate the extra warmth they get when you sow them indoors, but they don't take kindly to having their roots disturbed at transplanting time. Here's a terrific trick Grandma Putt came up with to get around this: Dig up a piece of turf that's about 3 inches deep, and cut it into 2-inch-square chunks. Turn the sod pieces upside down, and poke two or three seeds into each piece. When your seedlings are ready to head outdoors, simply transplant them as is—sod and all. They'll never know they've been moved!

Seedling-Saver Solution

The tender stems and soft leaves of veggie and herb seedlings are easy targets for dastardly diseases, so it's smart to be prepared ahead of time. Put out the "Not Welcome" mat with a batch of my Grandma Putt's special Seedling-Saver Solution.

INSTRUCTIONS: Mix these ingredients in a bowl, and let steep for at least an hour. Strain out the solids, and pour the liquid into a hand-held sprayer. Mist your seedlings as soon as their little green heads poke out of the soil to foil attacks by foul fungi.

INGREDIENTS:
4 tsp. of chamomile tea
1 tsp. of dishwashing liquid
1 qt. of boiling water

◆ WHAT A GRAPE IDEA!

If pesky birds pluck up your corn seeds as soon as you plant them, sprinkle the soil over the seeds with grape Kool-Aid®, straight from the packet. Birds dislike it so much that they'll go elsewhere for lunch!

◆ GIVE 'EM THE BRUSH-OFF

Here's a trick the pros use in commercial greenhouses: To get seedlings to grow hardier and sturdier, brush your hand across them several times a day.

◆ TOUGH LOVE FOR TRANSPLANTS

Just before you transplant your vegetable seedlings, water them with a solution of 2 ounces of salt or baking soda per gallon of water. This will temporarily stop their growth and increase their strength, so they can stand right up to the challenging conditions they'll face outdoors.

TERRIFIC TIME✖SAVERS

Tiny veggie and herb seeds can be the dickens to sow evenly. To keep them from clumping up, mix them with dried coffee grounds before you sow them. They'll be as easy to handle as the biggest of the big guys!

Seedling Transplant Recovery Tonic

Give your veggie and herb transplants a break on moving day by serving them a sip of this soothing drink. It'll help them recover more quickly from the shock of transplanting.

INSTRUCTIONS: Mix these ingredients in a bucket and pour into a hand-held sprayer. Mist your little plants several times a day until they're off and growing again.

INGREDIENTS:

1 tbsp. of fish emulsion
1 tbsp. of ammonia
1 tbsp. of Murphy's Oil Soap®
1 tsp. of instant tea granules
1 qt. of warm water

◆ A Sweet Idea

When you're transplanting sweet potato slips, dip the roots of each one into a pan of muddy water. This protects the roots with a coating that prevents them from drying out while being handled, and also ensures direct contact with the soil once they're planted.

◆ Wagons, Ho!

If you have a lot of seedlings that need to get used to the great outdoors, make the daily commute less of a grind by setting 'em on a couple of old children's wagons. Then just roll out the wagons, park them under a tree for the day, and roll 'em back in again at night!

MAKING CENTS

Don't spend a bundle buying frost protectors for your tender veggie seedlings! It's easy to create on-the-spot plant protectors with paper grocery bags. Dig your planting hole, then set the bag inside so that 10 inches or so sticks up above the surface. Fill the bottom of the bag with soil, roll the top down, and plant your seedling inside. If frost threatens, roll up the collar and fasten it with a clothespin or two.

Slugweiser

Beer is the classic bait for slug and snail traps. But what attracts the slimy thugs isn't the alcohol in the beer, or even the hops and malt—it's the yeast. So fill up your traps with this potion. After all, why waste a good brewski on the enemy?

INSTRUCTIONS: Mix the sugar and yeast in a 1-gallon jug, fill it with warm water, and let the mixture sit for two days, uncovered. Then pour it into your slug traps, and watch the culprits belly up to the bar!

INGREDIENTS:

1 lb. of brown sugar
1/2 package (1 1/2 tsp.) of active dry yeast
Warm water

◆ SUPER SLUG SPRAY

Need a way to zap slugs that aren't making it into your traps? Pour 1 1/2 cups of ammonia, 1 tablespoon of Murphy's Oil Soap®, and 1 1/2 cups of water into a hand-held sprayer. Shake well, then take aim, and fire!

◆ DON'T FENCE 'EM IN

It's easier than you might think to keep slugs out of your veggie beds: Just surround them with mini-fences! Thin copper sheeting works best, because it gives the rascals a jolt of electricity when they try to squirm over the top. Just make sure you get every last slug *out* of the bed before you put up the barrier. Otherwise, they'll have a field day inside the ballpark!

ASK JERRY

Q *My broccoli and cauliflower produce small heads that aren't very firm. Is there anything I can do to get bigger, firmer heads?*

A I want you to mix crushed eggshells into the soil around the plants to provide extra calcium, which these plants need to produce large, high-quality heads.

Spring Soil Energizer

After you dig, but before you plant your vegetable garden, fortify the soil with this potent potion. Take my word for it—it'll really get things cookin'!

INSTRUCTIONS: Mix these ingredients in a 20 gallon hose-end sprayer, and saturate the soil. Wait two weeks before you start planting. (This recipe makes enough to cover 100 sq. ft. of garden area.)

INGREDIENTS:

1 can of beer
$1/2$ cup of regular cola (not diet)
$1/2$ cup of dishwashing liquid
$1/2$ cup of antiseptic mouthwash
$1/4$ tsp. of instant tea granules

◆ BE A CHUNKY MONKEY

If you're trying to bring clay soil up to snuff, feed it with organic matter that's on the chunky side, like straw, pine needles, wood chips, or mature plant stalks. These materials take longer to break down than fine-textured stuff, like grass clippings or leaves. During that waiting period, they'll open up the soil so that water, nutrients, and worms all can navigate better.

◆ GET EDGY

Tired of spring rains washing away your newly planted veggie seeds? Snip some old mini-blinds into 6-inch pieces, then slip them into the soil between your rows of seeds to make little edgings. That'll keep the rain from washing the seeds from one part of the bed to another.

GRANDMA PUTT'S POINTERS ☞

Grandma Putt knew that a hand-held bulb planter is the *perfect* tool for planting potatoes! Use it to make the holes 8 inches deep and spaced about 12 inches apart. Plant a piece of potato in each one, and then backfill with the soil you removed. It doesn't get any easier than that!

Squirrel Beater Tonic

To keep pesky squirrels and chipmunks from stealing your crop, spray your fruit and nut trees with this spicy potion.

INSTRUCTIONS: Mix these ingredients in a bucket, then pour the mixture into a hand-held sprayer. Shake well, then coat all of your fruit- and nut-bearing trees and bushes from top to bottom to let bothersome critters know they're not welcome!

INGREDIENTS:

2 tbsp. of cayenne pepper
2 tbsp. of Tabasco® sauce
2 tbsp. of chili powder
1 tbsp. of Murphy's Oil Soap®
1 qt. of warm water

◆ A TRULY HANDY HARVEST

Here's a great way to enjoy fresh celery-flavored greens all winter long: In fall, plant a celeriac root in a big clay pot filled with sand, and put it in a sunny window. Keep the sand moist, and soon, the root will start sending up little stalks with frilly green tops. As long as you keep clipping the stalks for salads, the root will keep churning them out!

◆ CHILL OUT

If you find yourself with leftover veggie seeds after the spring planting season, don't throw them out! You can keep them for next year by sealing them in their original packets, putting them in small, airtight jars, and tucking them away in your refrigerator. Be sure the temperature stays between 36 and 45°F.

TERRIFIC TIME⌧SAVERS

Some herbs, like basil and parsley, are slow to air-dry, and they often lose their green color in the process. Use this trick to dry them: Put 'em in brown paper lunch bags, and shut the tops of the bags with clothespins. Write the name of the herb on each bag, and set them in the fridge. Check on them in a few days; they're ready when they're crispy to the touch. You can thank your fridge's dehumidifying action for this quick and easy miracle. Store the dried herbs—bags and all—in the fridge until you need 'em!

Strawberry Success Solution

Just before you plant your strawberries, give them a bath with this root-rousin' tonic. It'll do a bang-up job plumping up those dried-out roots and getting them ready, willing, and able to take off in a flash.

INSTRUCTIONS: Mix these ingredients in a bucket, and soak your berries' bare roots in the solution for about 10 minutes before you tuck them into their holes. When you're finished planting, dribble the leftover solution on the soil around your plants.

INGREDIENTS:

1 can of beer
$\frac{1}{2}$ cup of cold coffee
2 tbsp. of dishwashing liquid
2 gal. of water

◆ HASTE MAKES WASTE?

Not when it comes to planting strawberries! It's best to set out your strawberry plants as soon as they arrive. If you must hold them for a day or two, keep them wrapped in the same plastic in which they arrived, and put them in your refrigerator. Or keep them in as cool a place as you can find, like a root cellar or basement.

◆ A BERRY GOOD MULCH

Oak leaves are awesome for mulching strawberries, because their bitter taste deters slimy slugs and grazing grubs. They also won't pack down like softer leaves, such as maple.

GREAT IDEA!

Do you want to speed up production in your strawberry patch?

Then remove the blooms that appear six to seven weeks after planting by snapping them off at the stem. Why? Because this allows the plants to grow much faster and produce runners more readily. The result? A huge harvest the following year!

Super Seed-Starting Mix

Regular potting soil is way too rich for small seedlings, and it can foster a bunch of funky fungi that'll quickly wipe out a whole lot of baby plants. To get your seeds up and growing safely, I suggest blendin' up a batch of this mix.

INSTRUCTIONS: Mix the peat moss and perlite or vermiculite in a bag or bucket. The day before sowing seeds, moisten the mix by adding warm water—a few cups at a time—and working it in with your hands until the mix feels evenly moist to the touch.

INGREDIENTS:

2 parts peat moss
1 part perlite or vermiculite
Warm water

◆ SHAKE AND SOW

To get tiny seeds like carrot and lettuce evenly spaced in their beds, put them into an old salt shaker. Then just sprinkle them over the soil!

◆ GET SNIPPY

When thinning beet seedlings, always clip off the little greens at ground level with a pair of scissors. (Never pull them up, because that disturbs the other roots in the patch.) Then rush right inside with those tender little greens and toss 'em up in a salad. They're delish!

GRANDMA PUTT'S POINTERS ☞ Grandma Putt used to start her seeds in eggshells, and I still do. Here's how: When you break an egg, carefully remove and discard only the top third or so, then poke a hole in the remaining two-thirds of the shell. Rinse it out and set it back into an empty egg carton to dry. Come planting time, fill the shells with seed-starting medium, and plant your seeds. When it's time to transplant, gently crack the shell so the roots can get out easily, and plant the whole shebang.

Sweet Success Spray

This sugar-packed spray is sure to lure bees to your veggie plants and ensure pollination. What's more, it'll kill nasty nematodes in the soil. So with this one mixture, you get two benefits for the price of one!

INSTRUCTIONS: Pour the sugar into 2 cups of water and bring to a boil, stirring, until the sugar is completely dissolved. Let the mixture cool, dilute it with 1 gallon of water, and pour the solution into a hand-held sprayer. Then spritz your bloomin' plants to the point of run-off. Before you know it, willing winged workers will fly to your rescue!

INGREDIENTS:
$\frac{1}{2}$ **cup of sugar**
Water

◆ BRAMBLE RAMBLINGS

Grandma Putt always told me that we had to keep red raspberries and black raspberries apart by at least several hundred feet. This was because these plants are both susceptible to the same fungal and viral diseases. Also, she said to avoid planting them in soil where potatoes, tomatoes, eggplants, or melons had been grown in several years, or where any brambles (including roses) had grown in the last 20 years. Otherwise, there's a good chance that your patch will produce zip in the way of berries!

MAKING CENTS

If you grow peas in your vegetable garden, you'll love this great recycling trick: Use the branches you prune off your trees and shrubs to make perfect pea stakes. A good trellis branch is about 4 feet long and splits into several sturdy stems. Stick the branches into the pea row so they barely overlap. These super stakes are just the kind of support peas need—and they're *free!*

Tomato Blight Buster

To ward off many common tomato diseases, use this mix on your newly transplanted tomato seedlings.

INSTRUCTIONS: Mix these ingredients in a bucket, then sprinkle a handful of the mixture into each planting hole. For additional disease defense, sprinkle a little more powdered milk on top of the soil after planting, and repeat every few weeks throughout the growing season.

INGREDIENTS:

3 cups of compost
$^1/_2$ cup of powdered nonfat milk
$^1/_2$ cup of Epsom salts
1 tbsp. of baking soda

◆ TOMATO DISEASE FIGHTER

If you know that your tomatoes have been bothered in the past by deadly diseases, give them some extra protection by treating them to a mix of 1 part skim milk and 9 parts water. Apply with a hand-held sprayer to the point of run-off in the early part of the summer to discourage diseases from getting started.

ASK JERRY

Q *How can I keep blight from killing all of my tomato plants? I've tried many different fungicides, and even moved the plants to different parts of my garden, but I still keep losing them. Do you have any ideas?*

A Problems this serious calls for serious measures. I want you to spray your garden soil late in the fall and early next spring with a mixture of 2 tablespoons of bleach and 2 tablespoons of baby shampoo in a gallon of water. This will cover about 100 square feet of garden area. Then during the growing season, spray the plants every two weeks with an all-purpose liquid fruit tree spray at the recommended rate.

Tomato Booster Tonic

Want to get the best tomato crop on the block? Treat your plants with my Tomato Booster Tonic, then get prepared for a bumper harvest this year!

INSTRUCTIONS: Mix these ingredients in a watering can. Generously soak the soil around your tomato plants in early summer, just as they show a bunch of yellow flowers, to stimulate fruit set.

> **INGREDIENTS:**
> 2 tbsp. of Epsom salts
> 1 tsp. of baby shampoo
> 1 gal. of water

◆ ISN'T THAT SWEET?

For the sweetest, juiciest tomatoes in town, take a tip from Mary Poppins and me: Add a spoonful of sugar to each hole at planting time. Your tomatoes will be so lip-smacking good, the kids will be eating them right off the vine!

◆ GIVE THE GIFT OF HERBS

I like to surprise my special friends with gifts from my garden—my own homemade herbal vinegars. They're easy to make and wonderful to give. Simply place a few sprigs of thyme, chives, or tarragon into a sterilized jar or decorative bottle, and cover them with boiling vinegar. Leave the jar unsealed at room temperature until the vinegar has cooled. Then seal the jar and set it somewhere out of direct sunlight. The vinegar will be ready to use in about two weeks.

GRANDMA PUTT'S POINTERS ☞

Grandma Putt used to plant her tomato seedlings sideways—and so do I! First, strip off all the leaves except the top two sets, then lay the plants in a trench a few inches deep, covering all but the leafy tip with soil. The shoot will quickly straighten itself out, while the buried stem develops lots of life-giving roots to help boost the harvest!

Toodle-oo Terrors Tonic

Our ancestors thought tomatoes were poisonous, so they avoided them like the plague—and flea beetles still do. So if these little buggers are doing a number on your veggies this year, just spray 'em with this timely tonic, and kiss your flea-beetle battles good-bye!

INSTRUCTIONS: Put the leaves and water in a pan, and bring the water to a simmer. Then turn off the heat and let the mixture cool. Strain out the leaves, and add the dishwashing liquid to the water. Pour the solution into a hand-held sprayer, and spritz your plants from top to bottom. This potent potion also repels whiteflies, asparagus beetles, and cabbageworms. (As with all repellent sprays, though, you'll need to renew the supply after every rain to keep the scent fresh.)

> **INGREDIENTS:**
> 2 cups of tomato leaves, chopped
> ½ tsp. of dishwashing liquid
> 1 qt. of water

◆ THANKS FOR YOUR SUPPORT!

Here's a neat idea—to support tall veggies like peppers and Brussels sprouts, use a small extension-type curtain rod. Then as the plants grow, you can adjust the rod so that it is always at just the right height.

MAKING CENTS

Don't toss your grapefruit rinds onto the compost pile—they make fantastic (and *free*) traps for cutworms! Just scrape out the insides, and set the rinds around your garden in the evening. When you go back in the morning, the cutworms will be clustered inside and you can scoop them up. Then squash the creeps or dump them into hot, soapy water to get rid of 'em for good.

Vegetable Power Powder

I think of my Vegetable Power Powder as comfort food for your garden—kind of like mashed potatoes or macaroni and cheese—only for your soil and the plants that grow there!

INSTRUCTIONS: Mix these ingredients in a wheelbarrow, and put them into a broadcast spreader. Set the spreader on medium, and apply the mixture over the top of your garden in early spring. Work it into your soil, and then overspray the prepared beds and rows with my Spring Soil Energizer (see **page 294**). By the time your seeds and seedlings are ready to plant a couple of weeks later, your soil will be rich and mellow, and begging to be filled with great things to eat!

INGREDIENTS:
25 lbs. of organic plant food
5 lbs. of gypsum
2 lbs. of diatomaceous earth
1 lb. of sugar

◆ KEEP OUT!

Don't you dare pick beans when the plants are wet! Rust and other diseases are almost always present, and working around your beans when the foliage is wet is the best way to spread a disease through the entire planting. To be safe, pick these delectable delights only when the plants are completely dry.

ASK JERRY

Q *How often should I feed my corn? And when should I start—as soon as I plant it?*

A Never use fertilizer with newly planted seed, or it will rot. I use any lawn food to feed corn for the first time when it's a foot tall, and then again when its silk shows. There's no need to feed corn beyond that.

Veggie Harvest Bath

Lots of bugs love to hide in broccoli florets and other nooks and crannies in vegetables. Here's how to make sure your harvest is bug-free—give it a bath!

INSTRUCTIONS: Pour the salt and vinegar into a sinkful of cold water, and submerge the veggies for 15 minutes or so. The bugs will float up to the surface, where they can be easily picked off. Rinse the veggies with fresh water, and they're ready to eat.

INGREDIENTS:

Fresh-picked broccoli
  (or other veggies)
1/4 cup of salt
1 tbsp. of vinegar
Cold water

◆ MELON MAGIC

Not sure if your melons are ripe for picking? Check the blossom end (opposite the stem) by pressing on it. If it's ripe and ready for pickin', it should give way slightly and smell kind of sweet.

◆ ROOT AID

To encourage deep rooting—and cut down on your watering time—the trick is to water your veggies thoroughly, then not water again for a week or so. To make sure you've really delivered the goods, stick a finger down into the soil after you think you've watered enough. It should be wet several inches down. If not, continue watering, then check again.

When you bring your harvest inside, do you soon find yourself swatting at fruit flies hovering over your fruits and vegetables? You can make a free fruit fly trap out of a fast-food drink cup, a lid, and some regular cola. Fill the cup one-quarter full of cola, put on the lid, and insert a straw so that it doesn't touch the cola, leaving about 1 inch of the straw extending out of the lid. Then set it near your fruits or vegetables. The flies will fly down the straw into the cola, but they can't get out!

Veggie Tonic

Vegetable plants really work up an appetite churning out all that good food for us, and even the most well-balanced diet needs a little kick now and then. So every three weeks during the growing season, feed your garden with my All-Season Green-Up Tonic (see **page 247**). But for a change of pace, use my Veggie Tonic once in a while to keep things going.

INSTRUCTIONS: Mix these ingredients in a 20 gallon hose-end sprayer, and spray all of your veggies to the point of run-off. This tonic will turn them into lean, mean, growing machines!

INGREDIENTS:

1 can of beer
1 cup of ammonia
4 tbsp. of instant tea granules
2 tbsp. of baby shampoo

◆ ANOTHER OPTION

For even more variety in your feeding regimen, try this mixture in place of my All-Season Green-Up Tonic (see **page 247**) or my Veggie Tonic (above). Simply mix ½ cup of fish emulsion; 2 tablespoons each of whiskey, Epsom salts, and instant tea granules; and 1 tablespoon of baby shampoo in a 20 gallon hose-end sprayer. Then apply liberally to the point of run-off.

◆ GIVE 'EM A PUSH

To keep the greens from breaking off when you harvest carrots, push the carrots into the ground a little, then pull them up with a twisting motion.

TERRIFIC TIME✖SAVERS

Here's a timesaving trick for making sure water can get right down to the roots of your crops: Cut off both ends of big coffee cans. Then dig a hole every few feet in the garden, put a can in each hole, and fill it up with gravel. When you water, fill those cans to the brim. That way, your veggies' roots can drink their fill at their leisure!

Veggie Vitalizer

Here's a really out-of-the-ordinary tonic that packs a double punch: It'll get your plants up and growin' to new heights AND help repel nasty pests, too!

INSTRUCTIONS: Mix these ingredients in a 20 gallon hose-end sprayer, and apply liberally to your vegetable garden every three weeks during the growing season.

> **INGREDIENTS:**
> $\frac{1}{2}$ **can of beer**
> $\frac{1}{4}$ **cup of pepper-onion-mint juice***
> **3 tbsp. of fish emulsion**
> **2 tbsp. of dishwashing liquid**

To make this juice, finely mince 1 green pepper, 1 onion, and 2 tablespoons of mint leaves. Add to 1 quart of hot water, and combine in a blender. Strain, and use the remaining liquid in this tonic.

◆ A GREAT GARLIC TRICK

The strong smell of garlic offends as many bugs as it does people! To make a pungent pest repellent, cut up 6 cloves of garlic, and mix with 1 tablespoon of baby shampoo and 1 quart of warm water. Spray it on your plants, and bugs will stay away.

◆ GROW YOUR OWN TRELLIS

Thinking of growing pole beans this year? Save yourself the trouble of putting up a trellis by planting them right next to your sunflowers instead! That way, the bean vines can grow up the sunflower stalks for support. And in return, the beans supply much-needed nitrogen to help your sunflowers grow up big and strong.

GREAT IDEA!

Would you believe that an old tire rim makes a great holder for your garden hose?

Just mount the rim on the wall or a post right by the water spigot, paint it so that it won't rust, and hang up your hose. You'll never have to fight with a snarled-up hose again!

Whitefly Wipeout Tonic

If you catch whitefly problems early, you can often dash their hopes for a happy summer by spraying your plants with anything soapy—including a good washdown with 2 tablespoons of baby shampoo or dishwashing liquid per gallon of water. Be sure to thoroughly cover the undersides of leaves, because that's where the babies are found. In more serious situations, hit 'em hard with my Whitefly Wipeout Tonic.

INSTRUCTIONS: Mix these ingredients in a bowl, and spray the mixture over any plants that are troubled by whiteflies. You'll get the best results by applying it first thing in the morning, before the dew dries and the whiteflies become airborne.

INGREDIENTS:

1 cup of sour milk (let it stand out for two days)
2 tbsp. of flour
1 qt. of warm water

◆ WOODY-SEED STARTER TONIC

Having trouble getting seeds with woody coats, like those of beets and parsnips, off to a good start? Then mix 1 cup of vinegar with 2 tablespoons of dishwashing liquid and 2 cups of warm water. Soak the seeds in this mix for 24 hours, sow them outdoors, and then cover them with a strip of burlap. This creates a nice warm environment that lets moisture in and encourages sprouting. Once the seeds have sprouted, remove the burlap to avoid growing leggy seedlings.

ASK JERRY

Q *There are so many different kinds of fertilizers on the market. Which should I use on my strawberry beds?*

A You can use any dry plant food, as long as you mix in ½ cup of sugar per 5 pounds of food. Broadcast this mixture over the area, then water well.

Wild Mustard Tea

No cabbage moth worth her spots will lay eggs in your vegetable garden if you spray your plants with this tea. It works like a charm for repelling cabbage loopers and potato beetles, too!

INSTRUCTIONS: Steep these ingredients in a bowl for 10 minutes. Let the elixir cool, then strain out the solids. Pour the liquid into a hand-held sprayer, and spray the plants thoroughly. Repeat after each rain to keep the repellent action fresh.

INGREDIENTS:

4 whole cloves
1 handful of wild mustard leaves
1 clove of garlic
1 cup of boiling water

◆ BEETLE BEATER

To control cucumber beetles, mix ½ cup of wood ashes with ½ cup of hydrated lime in 2 gallons of warm water. Spray this mix on both the upper and the lower sides of the leaves.

◆ LEAVE IT TO THE LEAVES

Are your veggies lookin' a little frazzled by midsummer? Foliar feeding—spraying liquid fertilizer or tonic right on their leaves—gives them a snack they can sink their leaves into right away. Simply fill a hose-end sprayer with compost tea or diluted fish emulsion, and spray away!

GRANDMA PUTT'S POINTERS ☞ Tired of running back and forth from the garden to the garage every time you need something? Try this trick from Grandma Putt: Get yourself an old mailbox, paint it up fancy, and fill it with those small things you use all the time, like hand tools, gloves, and twine. Put it next to your garden, so that it's always right at hand. You can even mount a whirligig on top of the box and let it do double duty as a scarecrow!

Wild Weed Wipeout Tonic

When you've got weeds that won't take no for an answer, knock 'em flat on their backs with this powerful potion.

INSTRUCTIONS: Mix these ingredients in a bucket, then pour the tonic into a hand-held sprayer. Drench each weed to the point of run-off, taking care not to get any spray on the surrounding plants. For stubborn weeds, use apple cider vinegar instead of white vinegar.

INGREDIENTS:

1 tbsp. of gin
1 tbsp. of white vinegar
1 tbsp. of baby shampoo
1 qt. of warm water

◆ TRY A TRIPLE THREAT

Plant clover in the pathways between rows and beds in your vegetable garden. Weeds won't have room to grow, and the clover flowers will attract beneficial insects. Mow it now and then, and use the clippings as a nutrient-rich mulch!

◆ TURN UP THE HEAT

A hot, windy day is the very best time for weeding. Why? Because weeds don't care for that kind of weather any more than most folks do. So when you hoe 'em out, they'll go belly-up in a hurry!

◆ TIMING IS EVERYTHING

Perennial weeds, like dock and dandelion, depend on the food that's stored down in their roots. This stash is at its lowest just before the plants flower. So go after 'em when they're just about to burst into bloom!

TERRIFIC TIME⌛SAVERS

Not sure how to tell the weed seedlings from your veggies? Try planting fast-growing radishes around each bed or row. That way, you'll know exactly where your seedlings should come up. Anything else that raises its head outside the border will be a candidate for elimination by the Weed Patrol!

CHAPTER 8

HAPPY HOUSEPLANTS

MOST FOLKS I KNOW have at least a few houseplants hanging around (literally!), or taking up windowsill space. Our potted pals purify the air we breathe, add color and interest to any room, and just make a house feel more like a home. I can't imagine living without them!

Whether you tend to just a few or have every room filled with pots and planters, there's no big secret to keeping houseplants healthy and happy. Just keep their pots clean, give 'em fresh potting soil every so often, keep 'em well fed and watered, and take care of any pest problems as soon as you spot them. To make this TLC a breeze, I've come up with a bevy of top-notch tonics that'll keep all your houseplants in peak condition!

AROUND the YEAR

Not sure what your houseplants need? Just follow these simple steps to keep all of your flowering and foliage favorites looking lush and lovely all year-round.

 **Spring**

◆ **Step 1:** If your indoor beauties are getting a little too big for their britches, spring is the right time to move them up to a bigger pot. While you're at it, use my Houseplant Repotting Mix (see **page 323**) to give them lots of good stuff to grow on:

1 lb. of potting soil
1 lb. of professional potting mix
¼ cup of Epsom salts
¼ cup of bonemeal
1 tbsp. of instant tea granules

Mix these ingredients in a bucket, and use the mixture to fill in around the root mass when you repot your houseplants. DON'T pack it in, though—you don't want to suffocate the roots!

◆ **Step 2:** Plants enjoy a vacation as much as people do, so move 'em outdoors as soon as the weather's dependably warm. While they are out there, give 'em a regular shot of my All-Season Green-Up Tonic (see **page 315**):

1 can of beer
1 cup of ammonia
¼ cup of dishwashing liquid
¼ cup of liquid lawn food
¼ cup of molasses or clear corn syrup

Mix these ingredients in a large bucket, pour into a 20 gallon hose-end sprayer, and spray everything in sight—not just your houseplants, but also your flowers, trees, shrubs, lawn, and

GRANDMA PUTT'S POINTERS ☞ Don't get pricked when it comes time to transplant your cactus! Do what Grandma Putt did, and protect your fingers by using an old pair of kitchen tongs to lift and move your prickly plant safely.

even vegetables. Apply this tonic every three weeks while your houseplants are outdoors, and they're sure to come through the hot summer months with flying colors!

Summer

◆ **Step 3:** When houseplants spend the summer outdoors, they're possible prey for the same problems that bother your other yard and garden plants. My All-Season Clean-Up Tonic (see **page 314**) is the one tonic that you ABSOLUTELY need to use religiously throughout the growing season to keep your plants free of pests and diseases:

1 cup of baby shampoo
1 cup of antiseptic mouthwash
1 cup of tobacco tea*

Mix these ingredients in a 20 gallon hose-end sprayer, and give everything in your yard—including the houseplants that are spending their summer vacation outside—a good shower in the early evening every two weeks throughout the growing season. You'll have the healthiest houseplants in town—GUARANTEED!

*To make tobacco tea, place half a handful of chewing tobacco in an old nylon stocking and soak it in a gallon of hot water until the mixture is dark brown.

Fall

◆ **Step 4:** If you've moved your houseplants outdoors for the summer, it's time to think about bringing them back inside for the winter. To make sure they're clean and pest-free, treat them with my Safe-and-Sound Pest Spray (see **page 331**):

⅓ cup of cooking oil
1 tsp. of baking soda
1 cup of water

Mix the oil and baking soda in a small bowl. Then combine 2 teaspoons of this mixture with 1 cup of water in a hand-held sprayer, and fire away.

◆ **Step 5:** Just like people, plants can get bored if they eat the same old thing day in and day out. So alternate the kinds of plant foods you offer your houseplants. I use my Balanced Houseplant Food (see **page 316**) as the basis for a regular feeding program:

1 tbsp. of instant tea granules
1 tsp. of 15-30-15 plant food
½ tsp. of ammonia
½ tsp. of dishwashing liquid
1 gal. of warm water

Mix these ingredients in a 1-gallon plastic milk jug, and use the mix at full strength when you water your houseplants. Be sure to label it! Alternate this with my other feeding tonics—my Foliage Plant Food (see **page 319**) and my Natural Houseplant Food (see **page 328**).

❄ *Winter*

◆ Step 6: Indoor plants are exposed to all sorts of household pollutants, and grimy leaves can keep 'em from growing their best. My Indoor Clean-Up Tonic (see **page 325**) unblocks leaf pores and gets plants squeaky clean and growin' strong:

1 tbsp. of dishwashing liquid
1 tbsp. of antiseptic mouthwash
1 tsp. of ammonia
1 tsp. of instant tea granules
1 qt. of warm water

Mix these ingredients in a bucket, and pour into a hand-held sprayer. Liberally mist-spray your houseplants, and wipe off any excess with a clean, dry cloth. Your plants will really enjoy this refreshing shower!

◆ Step 7: Flowering plants make great holiday gifts! If you're lucky enough to be on the receiving end, keep your new acquisitions chipper for the rest of the winter by feeding them my Holiday Houseplant Tonic (see **page 321**):

$\frac{1}{4}$ cup of beer
$\frac{1}{2}$ tbsp. of unflavored gelatin
$\frac{1}{2}$ tbsp. of fish emulsion
$\frac{1}{2}$ tbsp. of vitamin B_1 plant starter
$\frac{1}{2}$ tbsp. of ammonia
$\frac{1}{2}$ tbsp. of instant tea granules
1 gal. of water

Mix these ingredients together in a watering can, and use the solution every time you water your holiday plants to help keep them lush and lovely.

GREAT ✳ IDEA!

Are your houseplants looking less than lively?

They might be getting too much food all at once. Instead of feeding and watering them separately, add 10 percent of the recommended dose of your regular plant food to 1 gallon of water each time you give them a drink, and mix in this kicker: 1 vitamin B_1 tablet (dissolved in hot water), $\frac{1}{2}$ tablespoon of unflavored gelatin, 1 ounce of hydrogen peroxide, and 1 capful of whiskey.

All-Purpose Houseplant Tonic

Whether you grow one houseplant or a bunch, it can be a hassle to remember to water them AND fuss with fertilizers, too. Here's a terrific tonic that'll save you loads of time—it waters and feeds in one easy step!

INSTRUCTIONS: Mix these ingredients in a bucket or watering can. Use this liquid instead of plain water on your houseplants, and you won't believe how quickly they will grow big and strong.

INGREDIENTS:

2 tbsp. of whiskey
1 tbsp. of hydrogen peroxide
1 tbsp. of fish emulsion
¼ tsp. of instant tea granules
½ tsp. of unflavored gelatin
½ tsp. of dishwashing liquid
½ tsp. of ammonia
½ tsp. of corn syrup
1 gal. of warm water

◆ LET 'EM ROCK!

Place your smaller houseplants on top of your radio, CD player, or stereo system every once in a while, and treat them to a concert. Whether you're playing country, rock, pop, classical, or jazz, the vibrations will keep their circulation moving—and besides, they just love music!

GRANDMA PUTT'S POINTERS ☞ My Grandma Putt used to perform acupuncture on her houseplants, and boy did they ever enjoy it! How's that work? Well, watering reduces the spaces between the soil particles in pots, driving air out of the soil and suffocating the roots. You can give them quick relief by taking a large, long nail and gently working it down into the soil. Two or three holes are fine for a small pot; larger pots will need more. Then plan on repotting the plant in fresh, fluffy soil in the near future for a longer-lasting fix.

All-Season Clean-Up Tonic

This is the one tonic that you ABSOLUTELY need to use religiously throughout the growing season. The shampoo cleans the plants and helps the other ingredients stick better; the mouthwash kills bad bacteria and discourages insects; and the tobacco tea contains nicotine, which does a double whammy on those pesky pests.

INSTRUCTIONS: Mix these ingredients in a 20 gallon hose-end sprayer, and give everything in your yard—including the houseplants that are spending the summer outside—a good shower in the early evening every two weeks throughout the growing season. You'll have the healthiest houseplants in town—GUARANTEED!

> ### INGREDIENTS:
> 1 cup of baby shampoo
> 1 cup of antiseptic mouthwash
> 1 cup of tobacco tea*

To make tobacco tea, place half a handful of chewing tobacco in an old nylon stocking and soak it in a gallon of hot water until the mixture is dark brown.

◆ PLAN AHEAD

If your houseplants have spent the summer outdoors, there's a good chance they've picked up a few unwanted hangers-on. Give nasty bugs the brush-off by placing a mothball on the soil of each pot about one month before you bring your plants back inside for the winter.

ASK JERRY

Q *What's the best way to keep the shine on my houseplant leaves? Is it okay to use soapy water?*

A Not just soapy water—add a bit of beer! Stir ½ teaspoon of baby shampoo and ½ teaspoon of beer into a quart of warm water, then gently wash down the leaves.

All-Season Green-Up Tonic

If your houseplants are looking a bit peaked during their summer vacation outdoors, give them a taste of this sweet snack. It's rich in nutrients and packed with energizers, too—just what your plants need to green up in a jiffy!

INSTRUCTIONS: Mix these ingredients in a large bucket, pour into a 20 gallon hose-end sprayer, and spray everything in sight—not just your houseplants, but also your flowers, trees, shrubs, lawn, and even vegetables. Apply this tonic every three weeks while your houseplants are outdoors, and they'll come through the hot summer months with flying colors!

INGREDIENTS:

1 can of beer
1 cup of ammonia
$1/2$ cup of dishwashing liquid
$1/2$ cup of liquid lawn food
$1/2$ cup of molasses or clear corn syrup

◆ BEAT THE HEAT WITH PEAT

Here's a great way to help your houseplants keep their cool when they're outdoors for the summer: Place one potted plant, pot and all, inside of another, larger pot, and fill the space between the pots with peat moss. This will help keep the roots moist and cool, even during the dog days of August!

GREAT IDEA!

Did your houseplants spend their summer vacation outdoors?

Then give them a nice tea bath before bringing them back indoors. Steep a tea bag in a quart of warm water, then add 3 teaspoons of dishwashing liquid. Pour into a hand-held sprayer and mist-spray each plant thoroughly until the solution runs off. The tea's tannic acid helps the plants manufacture more sugar and starch, while the soap opens up leaf pores, enabling the plants to absorb nutrients better.

Balanced Houseplant Food

Just like people, plants can get bored if they eat the same old thing day in and day out. So it's a good idea to alternate the kinds of plant foods you offer your houseplants. I like this basic formula for regular feeding, but I recommend alternating it with a few of my other feeding tonics—like my Foliage Plant Food (see **page 319**) and my Natural Houseplant Food (see **page 328**) —for fantastic results.

INGREDIENTS:

1 tbsp. of instant tea granules
1 tsp. of 15-30-15 plant food
$\frac{1}{2}$ tsp. of ammonia
$\frac{1}{2}$ tsp. of dishwashing liquid
1 gal. of warm water

INSTRUCTIONS: Mix these ingredients in a 1-gallon plastic milk jug, and use the mix at full strength whenever you water your houseplants. Just be sure to label it!

◆ USE THE NEWS

Going on vacation and don't want to bother searching for a plant sitter? This trick will save the day: Line the bottom of your bathtub with newspapers, and soak them thoroughly with water. Set the plants on top of the wet papers, and they'll stay moist and happy for at least two weeks.

TERRIFIC TIME⌧SAVERS

If you don't have the patience to go through your house every few days, sticking your finger into the soil of your houseplants to see if they need watering, I've got the answer for you—in a word, pinecones! Yep, these are Mother Nature's own moisture meters. Just stick a fresh pinecone about two "petals" deep into the soil of each of your potted plants. The petals of the cone open when the plant is dry and close when it's wet, so there's no more wondering when it's time to water!

Flourishing Fern Tonic

When your indoor ferns are ailing, give 'em what your grandma gave you: a dose of castor oil. Here's how to do it the easy way—with my Flourishing Fern Tonic.

INSTRUCTIONS: Mix these ingredients in a bucket, and give each of your ferns 1 cup of the solution. They'll turn green and fresh again almost overnight!

INGREDIENTS:

1 tbsp. of castor oil
1 tbsp. of baby shampoo
1 qt. of warm water

◆ STAIN THE GRAIN

Did you know that plain old food coloring makes a great stain for wooden planters or any unfinished wood? (White pine works best.) Mix 1 part food coloring with 5 or 6 parts water. Saturate the wood surface, wait about five minutes, and wipe with a soft cloth. Let dry overnight, then wipe again to reveal your pretty new planter!

◆ SAY GOOD-BYE, FLIES!

If whiteflies are winging their way around your houseplants, whip up this simple solution: 2 tablespoons of baby shampoo in 1 gallon of water. Pour into a hand-held sprayer and mist-spray your plants liberally. Be sure to pay special attention to the undersides of leaves, where the little buggers hide out.

GRANDMA PUTT'S POINTERS ☞

When you need to pour a houseplant tonic from a bucket into a sprayer, and you can't find a funnel, don't panic—and don't spill the stuff all over the floor! Try this great old-time trick from Grandma Putt: Lay a sheet of wax paper over a sheet of newspaper and roll it all up to form a cone, with the wax paper on the inside. Put the tip of the cone into the sprayer bottle, and pour away!

Flowering Houseplant Soil Formula

Making loads of beautiful blooms takes lots of energy, so it's worth giving your flowering houseplants a little extra TLC to keep 'em fit and well-fed. Besides using one of my regular feeding tonics, treat 'em to a taste of this special soil-boosting mix every eight weeks, and they'll reward you with flowers galore.

INGREDIENTS:
6 parts cottonseed meal
4 parts bonemeal
4 parts wood ashes
1 part Epsom salts

INSTRUCTIONS: Mix these ingredients in a bucket. Apply at a rate of 1 teaspoon for every 6 inches of pot diameter, working the mixture well into the soil with an old fork. Your houseplants will be blooming like gangbusters before you know it!

◆ LET THERE BE LIGHT

If your flowering cacti aren't flowering, they may not be getting enough light. Put them outside for the summer, gradually exposing them to more and more sunlight over a week or two before leaving them out there full-time. This will activate the buds, which will blossom in a spectacular show next spring!

◆ A QUICK TRICK

When potting up your houseplants, cut a piece of coffee filter to put over the drainage holes. That'll keep the soil from leaking out, and the plants' roots will have plenty of room to grow.

If it's feeding time for your houseplants and you're fresh out of fertilizer, just give them a drink of beer instead. Don't worry, they won't get tipsy—they'll perk right up! It's one of the best all-purpose fertilizers a plant could ask for.

Foliage Plant Food

Here's a dependable feeding formula that'll do a fantastic job keeping ferns, spider plants, and many other foliage plants looking their leafy-green best.

INSTRUCTIONS: Mix these ingredients in a bucket, then add 1 cup of the mix to each gallon of water used to feed your plants.

For flowering houseplants, use vodka instead of bourbon.

INGREDIENTS:

$\frac{1}{2}$ tbsp. of ammonia
$\frac{1}{2}$ tbsp. of bourbon*
$\frac{1}{2}$ tbsp. of hydrogen peroxide
$\frac{1}{4}$ tsp. of instant tea granules
1 vitamin tablet with iron
1 gal. of warm water

◆ IT'S THE PITS

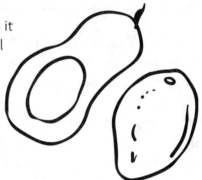

Don't throw away that avocado pit! You can turn it into a handsome houseplant in no time. Just peel off the brown covering, and stick three toothpicks into the middle of the seed so that you can suspend it, flat end down, over a jar of water. (The bottom of the pit should just touch the water.) Place the glass in a dark, warm area. As the water evaporates, add more to keep the bottom of the pit wet.

Once a green stem and leaves appear, plant the seed in a container filled with potting soil, and keep it in a sunny location. When warm weather comes, move it outdoors for the summer. The ample sun and heat will make your avocado plant grow by leaps and bounds—and youll be the envy of the neighborhood!

TERRIFIC TIME⌛SAVERS

Let Mother Nature lend you a helping hand with your houseplants whenever she can. When rain is on the way, set your plants outside to get a good shower and a thorough soil drenching, too.

Healthy Houseplant Tonic

To keep your houseplants in the picture of good health, feed them with this elixir. Besides providing a balanced supply of nutrients, it'll help discourage pesky pests, too!

INSTRUCTIONS: Mix these ingredients in a 1-gallon plastic milk jug. Then use 3 tablespoons per gallon of water every other time you water your houseplants to give them a super nutrient boost. And make sure you label the container!

INGREDIENTS:

1 can of apple juice
1 can of beer
1 can of regular cola (not diet)
1 cup of lemon-scented dishwashing liquid
1 cup of lemon-scented ammonia
$\frac{1}{2}$ cup of fish emulsion

◆ TAP WATER'S NOT THE TOPS

Everyone knows that plants don't have teeth—so why are you watering them with fluoridated tap water? Fluoride causes the tips of houseplants to turn yellow, while other chemicals in your drinking water make the potting soil crust over, slowing plant growth. So use only filtered water for all your houseplants, and they'll stay a lot healthier and happier.

GRANDMA PUTT'S POINTERS ☞

Every winter, Grandma Putt's windows were packed with all kinds of houseplants. But before she'd set in the plants, she always lined the sills with aluminum foil, shiny side up. It reflected light onto the plants and kept them growin' strong all winter long. To increase light levels even more, she'd cover a panel of cardboard with foil, then hang it from the curtain rod to reflect winter light onto the backs of the houseplants, too.

Holiday Houseplant Tonic

Nothing makes a nicer gift than a pretty potted plant! To keep holiday houseplants chipper long after the holidays are gone, feed 'em with this power-packed potion.

INSTRUCTIONS: Mix these ingredients together in a watering can, and use the solution every time you water your holiday plants to help keep them lush and lovely.

INGREDIENTS:

$^1/_4$ cup of beer
$^1/_2$ tbsp. of unflavored gelatin
$^1/_2$ tbsp. of fish emulsion
$^1/_2$ tbsp. of vitamin B_1 plant starter
$^1/_2$ tbsp. of ammonia
$^1/_2$ tbsp. of instant tea granules
1 gal. of water

◆ DON'T GET FOILED

If you're lucky enough to receive a beautiful potted plant as a holiday gift, keep in mind that the colorful foil wrapping that covers the pot is just for display. It can actually be harmful if left on for long, so remove it after several days to prevent problems. In the meantime, poke your finger through the foil on the bottom of the pot; otherwise, excess water will have no way to drain out, and your plant will drown!

ASK JERRY

Q *How often should I water the potted plant I received as a gift during the holidays?*

A Most potted gift plants are as easy to water as common houseplants—water them well when the soil feels dry to the touch, then don't water again until the soil feels dry. The exceptions are mums, cinerarias, and hydrangeas, all of which require a daily drink. Quench their thirst by filling a bucket about half full of tepid water and submerging the entire pot in the water. Let it sit for a few minutes, then remove and drain before returning the plant to its window seat.

Houseplant Colorizer Tonic

Spotted or striped, patterned or plain, houseplants come in practically every color of the rainbow. Here's a simple formula that will keep all of 'em at their most vibrant best all through the year.

INSTRUCTIONS: Mix these ingredients in a bucket, and let the mixture steep for about 10 minutes. Fish out the tea bag, pour the liquid into a hand-held sprayer, and mist-spray your plants' foliage every week or so.

INGREDIENTS:

1 twice-used tea bag
1 tsp. of antiseptic mouthwash
1 tsp. of baby shampoo
1 tsp. of ammonia
1 qt. of water

◆ A REFRESHER COURSE

If you've been properly watering your houseplants and they're still too moist, the drainage holes in the pots might be clogged. Remove the plants and clean their pots thoroughly, then repot them with fresh potting soil. You should notice a big improvement in the drainage—and in the health and happiness of your houseplants!

GREAT IDEA!

Do you need to work with a prickly houseplant like a cactus?

Before you put your gloves on, wrap a piece of heavy tape around each of your fingers. That way, even if the stickers penetrate the gloves, they won't jab your skin. Duct tape, fabric tape, or electrical tape will give you the surest protection, but several layers of transparent tape will do the job in a pinch.

Houseplant Repotting Mix

If your indoor beauties are getting a little too big for their britches, then it's time to move them up and out. To help them settle into their new homes without missing a beat, blend up a batch of my Houseplant Repotting Mix.

INSTRUCTIONS: Mix these ingredients in a bucket, and use the mixture to fill in around the root mass when you repot your houseplants. DON'T pack it in, though—you don't want to suffocate the roots!

INGREDIENTS:

1 lb. of potting soil
1 lb. of professional potting mix
¼ cup of Epsom salts
¼ cup of bonemeal
1 tbsp. of instant tea granules

◆ DON'T BUG ME

What's the best indoor insect repellent for houseplants? Moth crystals! Simply sprinkle the crystals directly onto the soil surface in all your indoor pots, and soon they'll be bug-free. Just be sure to keep these plants out of reach of children and pets.

◆ CANDY IS DANDY

...but liquor is quicker, especially for rejuvenating potted plants that are growing in tired soil! Simply mix a can of beer or a shot of bourbon, scotch, vodka, or gin with a gallon of room-temperature water. Add 1 ounce of dishwashing liquid, and let it sit for half a day or so. Then add your favorite plant food, and water your potted plants with this boozy treat. They will...*hiccup*...thank you!

TERRIFIC TIME⌧SAVERS

To cut down on houseplant watering chores, place three used tea bags in the bottom of the pot before filling it with soil. The tea bags will not only help retain moisture, but will also add much-needed nutrients to the soil as they decompose.

Houseplant Treat Tonic

This simple solution was one of Grandma Putt's favorite formulas for giving her houseplants a special treat. I've found that it's fantastic for potted trees, too!

INSTRUCTIONS: Mix these ingredients in a bucket, and pour into a hand-held sprayer. Mist-spray your plants lightly every week or so to keep them in tip-top shape.

INGREDIENTS:
$1/4$ cup of brewed tea
1 tbsp. of dishwashing liquid
1 tbsp. of Epsom salts
1 qt. of warm water

◆ SUPER SOAPY SOAKER

To help your houseplants make the most of the food you provide, add 2 tablespoons of dishwashing liquid per gallon of water, and water them with this mixture before feeding time. The soap allows the fertilizer to penetrate the soil and plant roots more easily. (If the ends of the leaves suddenly turn brown, this pre-feeding trick may have worked *too* well—eliminate the fertilizer for a while and only use the soap solution.)

◆ TRY THIS!

To make sure that your Christmas cactus blooms in December, put 2 tablespoons of castor oil around the roots in October. It really works!

Don't spend a bundle on a fancy water filter to give your houseplants a pure drink! You can make a simple filter right at home by washing out a quart milk carton and using a nail to poke several holes in the bottom. Fill the carton halfway with agricultural charcoal. Place the carton over a large bowl or bucket and run your tap water through the carton to filter out harmful salts. *Voilà*—free filtered water!

Indoor Clean-Up Tonic

Houseplants are exposed to all sorts of indoor pollutants that can block leaf pores and make it hard for the plants to grow. Here's a terrific tonic that'll turn all of your indoor plants into clean, green, growing machines!

INSTRUCTIONS: Mix these ingredients in a bucket, and pour into a hand-held sprayer. Liberally mist-spray your houseplants, and wipe off any excess with a clean, dry cloth. Your plants will really enjoy this refreshing shower!

INGREDIENTS:

1 tbsp. of dishwashing liquid
1 tbsp. of antiseptic mouthwash
1 tsp. of ammonia
1 tsp. of instant tea granules
1 qt. of warm water

◆ KILL THE CHILL

If you have indoor plants that you keep on windowsills, it's a good idea to move them on winter nights to protect them from the cold. If they're simply too large or difficult to move, try this: Slip a section of newspaper between them and the window for extra insulation.

◆ MAKE YOUR OWN PEBBLE BEACH

Need to raise the humidity around a single, special houseplant? Set it on a shallow saucer or pie tin filled with small pebbles, then add enough water to almost reach the top of the pebbles. Add more water every few days to replace the water that evaporates.

GRANDMA PUTT'S POINTERS ☞

How many times have you given your hanging plants a drink, only to have the water rain down on your head (or your carpet)? Well, say good-bye to drippy plants with this great trick from Grandma Putt: ice! Simply place a few cubes on the soil of each hanging plant. The cubes will slowly melt and be absorbed right into the soil—with no muss, no fuss, and no leaks!

Keep-'Em-Clean Tonic

Sometimes, the insides of pots develop a slimy film from algae or a white residue of salt leaching out from the soil. Before reusing those pots, wash 'em in this solution to remove the harmful buildup.

INSTRUCTIONS: Mix these ingredients in a large plastic bucket, let the pots soak for 15 minutes or so, then scrub them clean with one of those dishwashing scrubber pads. Rinse well, and your old pots will look as good as new!

INGREDIENTS:

2 tbsp. of dishwashing liquid
1 tbsp. of instant tea granules
3 tsp. of bleach
3 tsp. of hydrogen peroxide
3 tsp. of antiseptic
    mouthwash
1 qt. of warm water

◆ FLEE, PESTS!

Don't throw out Fido's or Fluffy's old flea collars! Cut them up, and place them on the soil of your houseplants to get rid of pests. Just remember to keep these plants out of reach of children and pets.

◆ PENCIL 'EM IN

Bugs won't want to call the soil of your houseplants home after this trick: Sprinkle the shavings from your pencil sharpener onto the soil, or place a 3-inch slice of cedar pencil into the soil for every 3 inches of pot diameter (so a 6-inch pot would need two slices, for example).

TERRIFIC TIME⌛SAVERS

Need a quick and easy way to get rid of lime and hard-water deposits on flowerpots, water spigots, or anything else, indoors or out? Dissolve ½ cup of borax in 1 cup of warm water, then stir in ½ cup of white vinegar. Sponge this mixture onto the lime deposits, let it sit for 10 minutes or so (longer for really stubborn spots), and wipe clean. It's that easy!

Magical Mealybug Mix

Are mealybugs literally sucking the life out of your houseplants? These cottony-looking little critters like to congregate along stems, sucking out plant sap and causing weak, off-color growth. But you don't have to put up with these pesky pests—just zap 'em with this Magical Mealybug Mix!

INSTRUCTIONS: Mix these ingredients in a hand-held sprayer, and mist-spray infested plants thoroughly. Repeat the treatment, if needed, to make sure these bad boys bite the dust for good!

INGREDIENTS:
1 ½ cups of brewed black tea
1 tsp. of baking soda
1 tsp. of dishwashing liquid
1 ½ cups of warm water

◆ **ANOTHER OPTION**

Here's an even simpler mixture that can make mealybugs a thing of the past: Mix 2 tablespoons each of corn oil and dishwashing liquid in 1 gallon of water in a bucket. Pour into a hand-held sprayer, and apply thoroughly to any plants that are infested with mealybugs.

◆ **WHAT'S AT STAKE?**

Keep a leggy houseplant on the up-and-up by using a pencil as a stake. Insert the pencil into the soil next to the plant, and tie the plant to the pencil with a small strip cut from old pantyhose.

ASK JERRY

Q *My spider plant has dried-out, discolored leaf tips. What's wrong with it?*

A Drying leaf tips usually indicate a lack of humidity. To tidy up the plant, just snip the tips off. Then move it to a more humid location, like a steam-filled bathroom.

Natural Houseplant Food

Here's a good, all-around feeding formula that works great for all kinds of flowering and foliage favorites. It'll make even the most finicky houseplant stand up and say "Yum, yum!"

INSTRUCTIONS: Mix these ingredients together in a bucket or watering can, then use the mixture to feed and water your houseplants. They'll eat it up!

INGREDIENTS:
1 tbsp. of fish emulsion
4 tsp. of instant tea granules
½ tsp. of dishwashing liquid
1 gal. of warm water

◆ MIGHTY VITAMINS

Perk up winter-weary houseplants by poking a children's vitamin or a One-a-Day® multivitamin into each pot. This will supply some nourishment they miss from the summer sunshine. Go ahead—the neighbors aren't watching!

◆ WARM THOUGHTS

Use extra care if you need to transport your houseplants when the air temperature is below 50°F. Warm up your car and park it as close to the door as you can to keep them from being outdoors for too long. For extra protection, cover the plants with newspaper before taking them outside. You don't want these pampered plants to catch a cold!

GREAT IDEA!

This secret's all wet—you can actually make water "wetter"!

How? By adding 5 teaspoons of dishwashing liquid to each quart of water you use to water your houseplants. The soap breaks through the static barrier caused by warm, dry air, so your plants can absorb water better.

Perfect Herb Soil Mix

Did you know that herbs can do double duty around your home? Many of them—including basil, bay, mint, parsley, rosemary, and sage—make great outdoor container plants during the warmer months. Then it's a snap to bring them indoors for winter color and flavor, too! This super soil blend will keep potted herbs happy and healthy all year-round.

INGREDIENTS:

1 part sand
1 part clay loam
1 part compost
1 part topsoil
Epsom salts
Dried coffee grounds
Eggshells

INSTRUCTIONS: Mix the sand, clay loam, compost, and topsoil in a bucket. Per bushel of this soil mixture, add a pinch of Epsom salts, a handful of dried coffee grounds, and some eggshells, dried and crushed into a powder. Your herbs will adore this nutritious mix!

◆ SOAK CLAY FOR A DAY

If you plan to use clay pots for your houseplants, soak the pots in a mild soapy-water solution for a day or so before using them. If you don't do this, the dry pots will draw all of the moisture out of your potting soil, and you might as well be planting in the Sahara Desert!

For the price of two packs of seed, you can enjoy fresh-picked salad fixin's even in the dead of winter! Plant radish seeds ¼ inch deep and 1 inch apart in a 9- by 12-inch cake pan. Scatter leaf lettuce seeds on the surface of the soil in another cake pan, and cover with ⅛ inch of soil. Set the pans in a sunny windowsill, and keep the soil damp. The plants will be ready for your salad bowl in just 8 to 10 weeks.

Potted Plant Booster Shot

Even the most pampered houseplants appreciate a little extra TLC now and then. Give it to them with this power-packed feeding formula.

INSTRUCTIONS: Mix these ingredients in a bucket or watering can, and use the mixture to feed your potted plants every time you water. They'll grow like gangbusters—GUARANTEED!

INGREDIENTS:

1 vitamin B_1 tablet dissolved in
   1 cup of hot water
2 tbsp. of hydrogen peroxide
2 tbsp. of whiskey
$^1/_2$ tbsp. of unflavored gelatin
1 gal. of water

◆ LET DARKNESS FALL

I don't know why folks seem to think that plants want light 24 hours a day, but I'll let you in on a little secret—plants only grow when they get the proper amount of sleep in the dark. If they stay up too long, they'll wilt just like you will, and their leaves will also get burned spots.

◆ BAG 'EM!

Indoor air can be mighty dry in winter, and that's really tough on houseplants. To give them a bit of a boost, place a plastic bag or plastic sheeting loosely over the plants at night. Just be sure to remove the plastic every morning before the bright sunlight causes excessive moisture to build up on the plants.

TERRIFIC TIME⌧SAVERS

If you tend to forget about watering your houseplants, why not let the plants get their own water when they need it? Look for automatic watering pots, which have a wick that hangs down into a reservoir of water. The wick brings water up to the soil, keeping it evenly moist. This watering method work wonders with many plants, especially African violets, and gets you off the hook!

Safe-and-Sound Pest Spray

When you're using a pest control spray inside your home, you want to make sure that it's harmless to people and pets. Well, look no further—they don't come any safer than this. (That is, unless you're an aphid or other houseplant pest!)

INSTRUCTIONS: Mix the oil and baking soda in a small bowl. Then combine 2 teaspoons of this mixture with 1 cup of water in a hand-held sprayer, and fire away when ready to send houseplant pests packin'.

> **INGREDIENTS:**
> ⅓ cup of cooking oil
> 1 tsp. of baking soda
> 1 cup of water

◆ Tea, Please

Houseplants need lots of humidity around their leaves for good growth. So in the winter, when the heat is on and the air is dry, mist-spray leafy plants at least every other day in the early morning. Use weak tea water: Soak a used tea bag and 1 teaspoon of dishwashing liquid in a gallon of warm water until the mix is light brown. Follow this schedule in summer as well if your home dries out because of air-conditioning.

◆ Spray Away!

Here's another super-safe (and super-simple) spray that controls a wide range of pests—and feeds your plants at the same time, too! Mix 1 tablespoon each of dishwashing liquid and seaweed extract with 1 quart of lukewarm water in a hand-held sprayer. Then liberally spray your houseplants once a month.

GREAT IDEA!

The most "nutritious" water for your houseplants sure is fishy!

When you change the water in your fishbowl or freshwater aquarium, save the old stuff and feed it to your potted plants. The fish have already added the best natural fertilizer that money can buy!

Super Citrus Potting Soil

Citrus trees will grow well indoors in large tubs provided they have good, rich soil—like my Super Citrus Potting Soil—to sink their hungry roots into.

INSTRUCTIONS: Mix these ingredients in a bucket, then sift the mixture through a half-inch screen to get rid of any large lumps before using it to pot up lemon, orange, or grapefruit trees. You won't believe the results!

INGREDIENTS:
2 parts garden loam
1 part sand
1 part leaf mold
1 part cow manure
1 tbsp. of bonemeal
1 qt. of professional potting mix

◆ SCRUB-A-DUB

Never let dirty, moldy, or salt-crusted pots lie around, because that's just asking for trouble. I use a little soap and bleach in water and a scouring pad on clay pots, or one of those sponges that are soft on one side and rough on the other for scrubbing my plastic, metal, glass, and ceramic containers.

◆ TURN, TURN, TURN

If your houseplants tend to look lopsided all of the time, you need to take them for a spin! Move the pots at least half a turn each day so the plants get the same light exposure all over. That should keep them standing straight and tall.

ASK JERRY

Q *The large, lower leaves of my African violet keep breaking or rotting off. What's going on?*

A You'd break or rot off, too, if your arms rubbed against a rough old pot edge for long enough! To fix the problem, take an old wax candle, and rub it like the dickens along the edge of your pot to give it a nice, smooth coat.

Transplant Treat Tonic

When you transplant your house-plants into new pots, ease the painful transition by feeding them this terrific treat. They'll settle into their new digs in no time at all!

INSTRUCTIONS: Mix these ingredients in a bucket or large watering can. Douse your newly potted plants thoroughly to help them feel right at home.

INGREDIENTS:

2 tbsp. of whiskey
1 tbsp. of unflavored
    gelatin
1 tbsp. of baby shampoo
2 tsp. of instant tea
    granules
$\frac{1}{2}$ tbsp. of fish emulsion
2 gal. of water

◆ MOVE IT, DON'T LOSE IT!

Have you had bad luck when transplanting your houseplants—in other words, do they die shortly after they've made the move? If so, it's because they've gone into shock. To transplant without trauma, first water your plant 24 hours beforehand. Then soak the new clay pot overnight before transplanting into it, and use already-moistened, fresh potting soil to fill in around the roots. Give your plant a light snack by feeding it with my Transplant Treat Tonic (above), or with plant food at 25 percent of the recommended rate. If you do this, your newly potted plant should thrive in its new home.

GRANDMA PUTT'S POINTERS ☞ After repotting her cacti, Grandma Putt always had me use a large-toothed comb to remove any particles of soil that got caught in the cacti spines. It sure beat pickin' the stuff off by hand and suffering the prickly consequences!

Winter Wash

Being cooped up inside all winter long will get anyone down, including your houseplants. So give all of your winter-weary friends a good misting with this formula to keep them looking moist and refreshed.

INSTRUCTIONS: Mix these ingredients in a hand-held sprayer. Mist-spray your plants twice a week to keep the leaves clean and provide a little nutrient boost, too!

> **INGREDIENTS:**
>
> 3 tsp. of baby shampoo
> 3 tsp. of ammonia
> 1 tsp. of antiseptic mouthwash
> 1 qt. of room-temperature water

◆ SEEING RED

To enjoy your poinsettia for another season, stop watering it after Christmas and store it in a cool, dry place when the leaves fall off. In spring, water it again and cut the stems back to 6 inches tall. From early October until blooming starts, place the plant in a dark closet for 12 hours each night, say from 8:00 P.M. to 8:00 A.M. Keep the plant in a sunny window for the other 12 hours a day, and it should be in full color again in time for the holidays!

◆ SHOWER POWER

A great way to water several indoor plants all at once is to put them in the shower. Just don't scald them—keep the temperature at a tepid 70°F or so. Once they've had a good soaking, dry off the foliage before putting them back in their sunny homes.

TERRIFIC TIME⌛SAVERS

Going away for a few days? Water your plants well, then put a plastic dry-cleaning bag over a wire coat hanger, and hang it up somewhere to make a tent for them. This will help retain soil moisture for up to two weeks, so you won't have to worry about your little darlings while you're gone.

Winter Wonder Drug

To keep indoor herbs, veggies, and citrus trees happy and healthy all winter long, douse them with this terrific tonic every now and again.

INSTRUCTIONS: Mix these ingredients in a hand-held sprayer, and mist-spray your plants every two to three weeks. It'll feed 'em AND help fight pests in one easy step!

> **INGREDIENTS:**
> 1 tbsp. of liquid kelp
> ⅛ tsp. of dishwashing liquid
> 1 gal. of water

◆ THE OLD BRUSH-OFF

Are your African violets, gloxinias, and other hairy-leaved plants looking a little dusty? Give them a gentle going-over with a soft baby's hair-brush. Never, ever wash them off with water!

◆ CUTTING REMARKS

Want to make more of your favorite houseplants? Some—such as African violets, gloxinias, rex begonias, and peperomia—root in a flash from leaf cuttings. Simply cut off the mature leaves with 2 or 3 inches of leafstalk, and insert them into the rooting medium until the leaf stands upright. (Make sure you insert the leaf stems far enough into the soil that the leaf blades are touching the soil.) An added benefit of leaf cuttings? Sometimes you get two or more new plants from a single leaf!

ASK JERRY

Q *The first year I had my amaryllis bulb, it had flowers, but last year, it only made leaves. Help!*

A I plant my amaryllis in pots, and sink them into the ground for the summer. Come fall, I cut the foliage back to 3 inches; set the plants in a cool, dry area; and keep them damp, not wet. Try this method with your bulb—it should do the trick!

TONICS FOR THE GARDENER

WELL, IF YOU'VE READ THIS FAR, you know that throughout this book, I've shared hundreds of tonics to help your plants grow strong and healthy—and I'm not done yet! Here's a special collection of tonics just for YOU—terrific remedies for sore muscles, solutions for smoother skin, and excellent elixirs to keep pesky pests away while you're enjoying the great outdoors. Along with these top-notch tonics, you'll find a bounty of handy hints for getting rid of grass stains, beating the flu bug, and a whole lot more!

Let's not forget how important it is to keep our critters happy, too. If you enjoy attracting all kinds of beautiful birds to your yard, you'll love my very best recipes for tasty bird treats; they're GUARANTEED to bring our fine feathered friends flocking to your feeders. And for Fido, I've got a surefire cure for skunk stink, a fragrant flea repellent, and other tricks any dog (and dog owner) will love!

Aching Muscle Magic

Did you spend way too much time digging, raking, or weeding your garden today? Then ease your sore, aching muscles with this minty mix.

INGREDIENTS:

1 tbsp. of petroleum jelly
6 drops of peppermint oil
Warm water

INSTRUCTIONS: Mix the petroleum jelly and oil in a small bowl, then set the bowl in a larger bowl of very warm water. While the mixture is warming, soak a towel in warm tap water, wring it out, and drape it over your sore spots. After three minutes or so, remove the towel, and rub the warmed oil-and-jelly mixture into your skin for deep relief.

◆ FIGHT MUD WITH A SPUD

Got some mud on your cotton or synthetic clothing? Rub the spots with a slice of raw potato, then toss the clothes in the wash. That dirt will come right out!

◆ MAGIC MARIGOLD SALVE

To relieve the pain of sore, burning feet after a long, hard day in the garden, use my Magic Marigold Salve. For fast, soothing relief, mix 1 cup of marigold petals with ½ cup of petroleum jelly in the top half of a double boiler, then keep over low heat for about 30 minutes. Strain the mixture through cheesecloth until it's clear, and store in a jar. Give your tired dogs a good rub with this salve at bedtime, and put on a pair of soft socks to prevent the grease from staining your sheets.

GREAT IDEA!

Here's a nifty use for ice cube trays.

Use 'em to freeze your favorite skin lotion (homemade or store-bought). That way, you'll always have cool, soothing relief on hand for sunburn, chapped skin, or insect bites.

Arthritis Tea

Aching hands can quickly turn your time in the garden from a pleasure into a pain. Now, this clover tea won't cure your arthritis, but if you start the day with a cup of this steaming brew, it will go a long way toward easing some of those aches and pains.

INSTRUCTIONS: Mix the clover blossoms and alfalfa leaves in a cup, pour in the boiling water, and let the mixture steep for five minutes. Strain out the herbs and add a teaspoon of honey if you want to sweeten it up a bit. Then sip your way to easier movement.

INGREDIENTS:

1 tsp. of dried red clover blossoms, crushed

1 tsp. of dried alfalfa leaves, crushed

1 tsp. of honey (optional)

1 cup of boiling water

◆ CUKES TO THE RESCUE

Want to soothe and revitalize your skin at the same time? Purée ¼ of a small cucumber (peeled and seeded), strain it, and pour its juice into a bowl. Mix in 2 tablespoons of honey, add 1 tablespoon of milk, and stir. Using cotton pads, apply the mixture to your face and neck. Wait 20 minutes, then rinse. It's that easy!

◆ RUB OUT GRASS STAINS

Got grass stains on your clothes or white sneakers? Rub molasses into the spots, let the garments sit overnight, then wash them with mild laundry soap (not detergent). The stains will vanish like magic!

TERRIFIC TIME⧗SAVERS

Save your back with this terrific tool tip: Lightly spritz your shovel with nonstick cooking spray before each use. It'll make the heavy job go a whole lot easier!

Baker's Best Bird Treats

This is a fun summertime project to keep bored kids occupied, and your fine feathered friends will appreciate their special treats!

INSTRUCTIONS: Bring the water to a boil, and add the oats. Turn down the heat and let simmer for a minute. Remove from the heat, and stir in the remaining ingredients in the order listed. When the mixture is cool enough to handle without sticking to your hands, mold it into round cakes that are about the size of tennis balls. Set aside any cakes that you plan to use immediately. Put the rest on a waxed-paper-lined cookie sheet, and put them in the freezer for future use.

INGREDIENTS:

1 1/2 cups of water

1 cup of dry oats

1 1/2 cups of creamy peanut butter

1 cup of Cream of Wheat®

1 cup of hominy grits or cornmeal

3/4 cup of lard or bacon grease, melted

1/2 cup of raisins or dried currants

2 handfuls of birdseed

◆ NOW, THIS TAKES GRIT!

Here's another simple treat that birds just go wild over: Mix cornmeal and birdseed with room-temperature bacon grease until the mixture is doughy. Then add a tablespoon or so of sand or crushed eggshells for grit. Shape the dough into a ball, put it in a mesh onion bag, and hang it from a tree branch.

GRANDMA PUTT'S POINTERS ☞

What bird can resist a tempting shish kebab made with suet, whole peanuts, orange halves, doughnuts, apple halves, and dates? Not many, according to my Grandma Putt! So thread a heavy cord through the morsels, and hang the shish kebab from a tree or post to give your resident winged wonders an exotic treat.

Bird Brain Granola

Here's a tasty treat that's GUARANTEED to keep your fine feathered friends coming back for more.

INSTRUCTIONS: Mix the oil and honey, then heat gently just until they blend together. Mix the remaining ingredients in a large bowl, add the warm honey and oil, and stir to combine. Press the mix into a shallow baking pan, and bake at 375°F for 10 minutes. Let cool, then crumble and serve to the birds.

INGREDIENTS:

1 cup of corn oil
1 cup of honey
2 cups of chopped nuts
2 cups of millet
2 cups of raisins
2 cups of hulled sunflower seeds
2 cups of crumbled dog biscuits
1 cup of wheat germ

◆ BIRDSEED BOOSTER

This mix can't be beat for attracting all kinds of birds from far and wide! Start with a good general birdseed mix and measure out 5 parts. Add to that 1½ parts millet or commercial finch food, 1 part black oil sunflower seeds, 1 part cracked corn, ½ part shelled raw peanuts, a little thistle seed (for any visiting finches), and ½ part clean sand or ground oyster shells.

◆ PUP-SICLES

Birds aren't the only critters to appreciate homemade goodies. For hot-weather dog treats, blend up a few batches of these pup-sicles! Add ½ cup each of finely chopped vegetables and plain yogurt to 1 quart of beef or chicken bouillon, and pour the mixture into ice cube trays. Then tuck them into the freezer until treat time rolls around.

MAKING CENTS

Have a teething puppy in the house? No need to buy fancy chew toys at the pet store; simply give him a crunchy raw carrot to gnaw on. It'll soothe his gums—*and* save your slippers!

Bug-Be-Gone Spray

Here's a bug-repellent spray for people that's a whole lot safer—and CHEAPER—than those store-bought ones!

INSTRUCTIONS: Mix these ingredients in a hand-held sprayer. Shake well, then spray lightly on your clothing, arms, and legs, being careful to avoid your eyes or open cuts. Reapply every hour or so. Keep the bottle sealed up when you're not using it, and you'll have a dynamite bug repellent that'll last for up to two years!

INGREDIENTS:

1 tsp. of citronella essential oil
1 tsp. of pennyroyal essential oil
1 tsp. of lavender essential oil
1 tsp. of rose geranium essential oil
1 cup of isopropyl (rubbing) alcohol
1 cup of water

◆ Aw, Shoo!

Here's another super-simple insect-repellent potion: Mix 2 drops of eucalyptus oil into 2 cups of pennyroyal tea, then pour into a small spray bottle. Apply it to any exposed skin whenever you go outside. It'll keep those pesky bugs away like a charm!

◆ Don't Dump the Pump

If you use hair spray that comes in a pump bottle rather than an aerosol can, hang on to those bottles! Washed and rinsed, they're perfect for handling all kinds of homemade tonics, like my Bug-Be-Gone Spray (above).

GRANDMA PUTT'S POINTERS ☞ Grandma Putt knew just how to bring relief to a bug bite, sting, or poison ivy rash. Here is one of her favorite remedies: Make a paste out of witch hazel (or rubbing alcohol) and baking soda, apply it to the area, and leave it on for 10 minutes. Then rinse. Reapply every few hours until the itch and swelling are gone.

Bug Off, Bugs! Spray

Does the faint BZZZ, BZZZING of mosquitoes hovering around your window screens drive you buggy? Here comes one of my favorite herbs to the rescue! First, wash the screens with a mild soap. Then spray on this easy bee balm brew.

INSTRUCTIONS: Bring the water to a boil in a saucepan. Crumble the dried bee balm and place in a 1-quart glass jar with a lid. Pour the boiling water over the herbs in the jar, bringing the water level to about an inch from the top. Put the lid on the jar and let the potion steep for about 15 minutes. Then strain out the herbs, pour the liquid into a hand-held sprayer, and spray your screens from the inside out.

INGREDIENTS:

2 cups of dried bee balm flowers and leaves

3 cups of water

◆ BUG-FREE WINDOW GLASS

Here's another way to keep mosquitoes, flies, and other winged warriors from staging a "we-want-in" convention at your windows. Simply mix ¼ cup of vinegar, 3 cups of water, and 8 tablespoons of essential oil of bay in a spray bottle. Tighten the nozzle and shake well, then use the liquid to clean your windowpanes. They'll be sparkling clean *and* bug-free, too!

GREAT IDEA!

Every gardener's first-aid kit should include a bar of soap.

Why? Well, if you rub a wet bar of soap directly on a mosquito bite, the itch will vanish quickly, and the swelling will soon disappear, too! The same trick works to draw a bee's stinger out of your skin; rub the soap over it, and the buzzer's business end should slide right out.

Energizing Elixir

If Grandma Putt could walk through a supermarket today and see the price tags on those fancy "sports drinks," she'd have a fit! Back in her day, when folks took a break from working in the hot sun, they'd sit under a shady tree and revive themselves with this restorative elixir.

INSTRUCTIONS: Mix these ingredients in a big jug. Then pour yourself a nice, tall glass, settle down in the shade, sit back and relax!

INGREDIENTS:

2 ½ cups of sugar
1 cup of dark molasses
½ cup of vinegar (either white or cider)
2 tsp. of ground ginger
1 gal. of water

◆ COOL-AID FOR SUNBURN

Need fast relief from sunburn? Try any of these tricks:

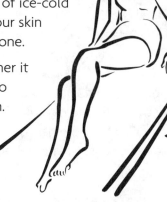

◆ Mix 1 to 2 teaspoons of salt in a glass of ice-cold milk, and sponge the solution onto your skin once or twice a day until the pain is gone.

◆ Reach for cold, plain yogurt, and slather it onto your skin. It works like a charm to lower the heat and take away the pain.

◆ Soak cotton pads in cold, strong brewed black tea. Apply them to your skin every 10 to 15 minutes until the pain subsides.

MAKING CENTS

After a busy day of lawn mowing, weeding, and other yard and garden chores, your aching feet will appreciate this homemade nighttime treat: Mix ¼ cup of coarsely ground almonds, ¼ cup of dry oats, 3 tablespoons of cocoa butter, and 2 tablespoons of honey. Massage into your skin, pull on cotton socks, and leave on overnight. In the morning, rinse your feet clean with cool water.

Herb Garden Potpourri

Why spend a bundle for fancy, store-bought air fresheners, when you can make your own from ingredients right in your garden? For a potpourri that smells good enough to eat, give this magical mix a try.

INSTRUCTIONS: Mix these ingredients in a large bowl with your hands (they'll smell great afterward). Put the mixed potpourri in closed glass jars for storage, or sew into fabric sachets and use them to freshen up closets and drawers.

INGREDIENTS:

2 cups of thyme shoots

1 cup of dried rosemary leaves

1 cup of dried mint leaves

$\frac{1}{4}$ cup of dried lavender flowers

$\frac{1}{4}$ cup of whole cloves

2 tbsp. of powdered orrisroot

◆ HERBAL RENEWAL

Is your face feeling a little rough after spending time outdoors? Make a fabulous herbal facial steam bath by pouring 1 quart of boiling water over 1 cup of herbs in a large bowl. (A mixture of peppermint, sage, and linden flowers is especially nice.) Hold your head approximately 4 inches above the bowl, and cover it and the bowl with a towel to retain the steam. Remain over the bowl for up to 10 minutes. This will cleanse your pores, and soften and moisturize your skin.

GRANDMA PUTT'S POINTERS ☞

Here's one of Grandma Putt's favorite herbal secrets—a natural moth repellent made from equal parts dried sage, rosemary, and thyme leaves crumbled together in a mixing bowl. She'd place half a handful of the mixture in a loosely woven cotton bag, then sew the bag shut. Hung in closets or laid in drawers among our clothes, these scented sachets kept the pesky little critters away.

Moss-Grow Tonic

There's nothing like a little moss to make a new garden look like it's been around forever. Here's an easy recipe for making moss grow between stepping stones in a path, along a stone wall, or on the sides of a planter.

INGREDIENTS:
½ qt. of buttermilk
1 tsp. of corn syrup
1 cup of moss

INSTRUCTIONS: Mix these ingredients in a blender, then dab the mixture onto the ground or the sides of the planter. Once the moss is growing, keep it in good health by "watering" it with plain buttermilk every few weeks or so.

◆ TAKE A POWDER

After you've emptied a baby powder container, wash it out, and turn it into a mini sprinkling can. It's perfect for giving seedlings a gentle shower, and it's just the ticket for tiny tots who want to help water the garden.

◆ MOSS SLURRY

Here's another formula for getting moss to grow on stones, walls, or containers: Mix ½ can of beer, ½ teaspoon of sugar, and 1 cup of moss in a blender on low speed. Evenly paint the mixture wherever you want moss to grow, and you'll have an instant antique!

◆ BAKING SODA SCRUB

Has your outdoor lawn and patio furniture seen better days? Scrub it with a solution of 1 gallon of warm water and 2 cups of baking soda to bring back its good looks.

ASK JERRY

Q *I put my leather gardening gloves away when they were wet, and now they're as stiff as a board! Is there any way to save them?*

A There sure is—just rub a little vegetable oil into them. They'll be as soft as new in no time at all!

Rose Hips Tonic

When your rose blooms are done and have turned to pretty orange fruits (called hips), use 'em to brew up a batch of my vitamin-rich Rose Hips Tonic.

INSTRUCTIONS: Steep the rose hips in the boiling water for 20 minutes, then strain out the solids. Drink this tonic as is (sweeten as desired), or add it to your favorite tea. It's great for colds (it's loaded with vitamin C), and it can help shorten your recovery period.

INGREDIENTS:

2 tbsp. of rose hips
2 cups of boiling water

◆ FLEE, FLU!

Try this old-time garden remedy when a cold or the flu gets you down: Peel and chop a whole bulb of garlic, cover with 1 tablespoon of honey, and bake until the juice oozes from it. Take 1 teaspoon of the liquid per hour until your symptoms vanish.

◆ GET FRUITY

Here's a great-smelling, fruit-filled masque that'll do wonders to nourish and moisten your skin after spending the day in the sun and wind. Purée three or four ripe, medium-sized strawberries in a blender or food processor. In a bowl, mix the purée with 1 tablespoon each of evaporated milk and honey to form a thick paste. (If it's too runny, mix in a teaspoon or so of cornstarch.) Apply the mixture to your face and neck, leave it on for 10 minutes, then rinse and pat dry.

Want to put blond highlights in your hair—without the beauty salon price tag? Stir 3 tablespoons of chopped rhubarb into 3 cups of hot water. Simmer for 10 minutes, strain, and cool. Use the solution as a rinse after each shampoo.

Skunk-Away Pet Bath

P.U.! There's nothin' worse than getting up close and personal with man's best friend when he's had a run-in with a stinky skunk. Fortunately, you can rely on this super de-skunking solution to get Rover back in the clover!

INSTRUCTIONS: Mix these ingredients in a bowl, and apply to your dog's coat (but don't get it on his head or near his eyes or ears). Rub the mixture in, then wash it out. After this deodorizing rubdown, your best friend should smell fresh and clean.

INGREDIENTS:

2 cups of hydrogen peroxide
$1/4 - 1/2$ cup of baking soda
1 tbsp. of mild dishwashing liquid

◆ SKUNK ODOR-OUT SOLUTION

Pets aren't the only victims when skunks let loose—the stinky scent can linger for a long time on outdoor furniture, paving, and other hard surfaces. So when a skunk comes a-callin' and leaves some fragrant evidence behind, mix 1 cup of bleach or vinegar and 1 tablespoon of dishwashing liquid with $2\frac{1}{2}$ gallons of warm water. Thoroughly saturate walls, stairs, or anything else your skunk has left his mark on. (Caution: Use this tonic only on nonliving things—*not* pets or humans.)

GRANDMA PUTT'S POINTERS ☞ Anytime I gave Grandma Putt's dog, Charley, a bath, Grandma would prepare a rosemary rinse first. She'd add 1 cup of rosemary (fresh or dried) to 1 quart of boiling water, cover it, let it cool, and strain out the herb. After I washed Charley, we'd pour the rosemary tea on him, work it in well, and then let it dry. The rosemary took care of the rest, repelling fleas, bugs, and anything else Charley came in contact with!

Soothing Sunburn Bath

Did you spend a little too much time out in the garden without your sunscreen? This foaming bath is the perfect soother for sunburned skin—or for anytime you just want to treat yourself to something special!

INSTRUCTIONS: Mix these ingredients in a bowl, then pour into a bottle with a tight stopper. At bath time, shake the bottle, then pour $\frac{1}{4}$ cup or so under the faucet as you run the water. Aaaaah, sweet relief!

INGREDIENTS:

1 cup of vegetable oil
$\frac{1}{2}$ cup of honey
$\frac{1}{2}$ cup of liquid hand soap
1 tbsp. of pure vanilla extract (not artificial)

◆ SWEET FLAG BATH

Soak away your cares after a weekend's worth of yard work with this super-soothing bath made from sweet flag (*Acorus calamus*). This good-looking, moisture-loving perennial produces handsome clumps of iris-like leaves, but it's not the leaves you use in this relaxing elixir—it's the roots. Put $\frac{1}{2}$ pound of chopped sweet flag roots and 8 pints of water in a large stockpot, and bring to a boil. Simmer for 30 minutes, then strain out the root pieces. Add the remaining liquid to your bath water, and you'll feel the day's tensions fade away.

GREAT IDEA!

If you get a splinter while you're out working in your garden, use this trick to get it out.

Tape a slice of raw potato onto the affected site, or if the sliver is in your finger or toe, hollow out a space in the potato flesh that's just the right size, and slip the digit into the spud. (Hold it in place with a sock.) Leave it there overnight, and you'll be able to easily pluck the splinter out in the morning.

Super-Simple Lavender Soap

Get your hands squeaky clean after a day of gardening with this sweet-smelling—and easy-to-make—lavender soap.

INSTRUCTIONS: Put the soap and boiling water into a bowl, then set the bowl over a pot of hot water. Stir until the mixture is smooth, then remove the bowl from the hot water, and stir in the powdered lavender flowers and lavender oil. Store in a glass or plastic container, and use as needed to get grimy hands as clean as a whistle!

INGREDIENTS:

10 tbsp. of Castile soap, finely grated

8 tbsp. of boiling water

2 tbsp. of dried lavender flowers, crushed into a powder

4 drops of lavender oil (available at craft stores)

◆ VIOLETS ARE VONDERFUL

If you like the sweet, old-time scent of violets, you'll *love* this fantastic face cleanser! Simply put ¼ cup each of evaporated milk and whole milk, and 2 tablespoons of sweet violets (fresh or dried), in the top half of a double boiler, and simmer for about 30 minutes. (Don't let the milk boil!) Turn off the heat, let the mixture sit for about two hours, then strain it into a bottle. Keep it in the refrigerator. To use the cleanser, pat it onto your face with a cotton ball, massage gently with your fingers, rinse with cool water, and pat dry.

ASK JERRY

Q *I hate to wear gloves when I garden, so my nails get pretty grubby. Any tips for getting off the grime?*

A You bet! Clean them up with a lemon scrub! Cut a fresh, juicy lemon in half, and dig your fingers into the flesh. Keep them there for one minute, then rinse them clean.

INDEX

D

Daffodils, 207, 210, 211

Dahlias, 203, 204, 208

Damping-Off Prevention
Tonic, 126

Dandelions, 45, 53

Daylilies, 199, 229

Daylily Transplant Tonic, 127

Dead Bug Brew, 175

Deadheading, 110, 174

Deer, 72, 138, 204

Deer-Buster Eggnog Tonic, 72

Deicers, for walkways, 54

Diatomaceous earth, 302

Digging, 112, 225

Disease control. See also
    specific diseases
        for bulbs, 199
        for flowers, 103, 108,
            120, 135, 140
        for herbs, 291
        for lawns, 6, 7, 9, 12
        for roses, 172
        for trees and shrubs,
            63
        for vegetables, 255,
            264, 291

Dishwashing liquid
        in aeration tonic, 11
        in animal pest control
            tonics, 24, 25, 37,
            64, 105, 128, 204,
            205, 210, 224
        in bulb fertilizer tonic,
            198
        in clean-up tonics, 325,
            326
        in compost activator
            tonics, 27, 71
        in deicing tonic, 54
        in disease control

tonics, 9, 103, 126,
    172, 248, 249, 291
in flower fertilizer
    tonics, 107, 109,
    121
in grass clipping dis-
    solver tonic, 28
in herb fertilizer
    tonics, 266, 267
in houseplant fertilizer
    tonics, 313, 315,
    316, 320, 324, 328,
    335
for insect pest control,
    331
in insect pest control
    tonics, 14, 15, 46,
    86, 91, 131, 155,
    168, 175, 178, 182,
    207, 227, 231, 275,
    301, 327
in lawn fertilizer
    tonics, 6, 8, 34, 39
in lawn repair tonic, 31
in mulching tonic, 159
in planting tonics, 67,
    112, 115, 127, 139,
    146, 148, 189, 202,
    296
properties of, xii–xiii
in rose fertilizer
    tonics, 167, 186,
    192
for rose health, 179
in seed-starter tonics,
    147, 152, 289, 306
in skunk odor
    remover tonic, 347
in soil-building tonics,
    237, 294
for thatch control, 50
in tree and shrub
    fertilizer tonics, 66,

73, 82, 85, 87, 93
in tree wound
    sterilizer, 95
in vegetable fertilizer
    tonics, 247, 260,
    305
in vine and ground-
    cover fertilizer
    tonics, 218, 229
in weed control
    tonics, 53, 160, 222,
    253

Division
        bulbs, 197, 198, 199
        groundcovers, 223,
            236
        perennials, 127, 139,
            148

Dog-Be-Gone Tonic, 128

Dog food, 96, 141, 152, 233,
    340

Doggy Damage Repair
    Tonic, 18

Dogs, 18, 24, 246, 347

Dog treats, 340

Double-Punch Garlic Tea,
    176

Downy mildew, 249

Drainage, 12, 14

Drought, 19–20, 247

Drought Buster Brew, 4, 19

Drought Recovery Tonic, 20

Dry ice, for pest control, 25

Drying techniques, 123, 182,
    267, 295

Dusters, homemade, 254

E

Earthworm castings, 239,
    258, 277

G

H

I

for houseplants, 314,
320, 323, 326, 331
for lawns, 7, 42, 46
mulch and, 159, 226
for roses, 174, 175,
176, 178, 180, 182,
187, 191
for trees and shrubs,
63, 65, 76, 83, 86
vacuum cleaners for,
219
for vegetables, 243,
265, 271, 275, 276,
280, 282–283, 286,
305
for vines and
groundcovers, 226,
230, 232
Insect repellents, 341, 342
Iris, 139
Iris borers, 139
Iris Energizer Tonic, 139
Iron, 177
Iron sulfate, 77

J

Japanese beetles, 165, 174
Jell-O®, 268
Jerry's Lime Rickey, 274
Just Desserts Tonic, 214, 229

K

Keep-'Em-Clean Tonic, 326
Kelp, 75, 204, 236, 335
Kick-in-the-Grass Tonic, 31
Kitchen scraps, 136, 287
Kneeling pads, 233

Knock-'Em-Dead Insect
Tonic, 275
Kool-Aid®, 291

L

Lacewings, 10, 184
Ladders, as herb gardens,
270
Lady beetles, 10, 63
Lamb's ears, 239
Lamp shades, for frost protection, 260
Last Supper Tonic, 32
Laundry soap, 21, 23, 92
Lavender, 134, 271, 341, 344,
349
Lawn Freshener Tonic, 33
Lawn mowers. See Lawns,
mowing
Lawns, 1–55. See also specific
pests or diseases
aerating, 6, 11, 45
animal pest control
for, 24–25, 37
Around the Year guide
for, 2–5
dethatching, 15, 46, 50
disease control for, 6,
7, 9, 12
drought protection
for, 19–20
fertilizing, 6, 8, 20, 23,
26, 32, 34, 45, 47, 52
heat stress in, 48
insect pest control for,
7, 42, 46
mowing, 9, 28, 30–31,
41, 48, 49, 89
overseeding, 22, 47
pollutants or gas on, 40

removing, 40
repairing, 18, 31, 39,
41, 44, 51
from seed, 29, 35
trimming, 52
watering, 20, 33, 39
weed-and-feed
products for, 35
weed control for, 6, 8,
16, 38, 41, 53
Lawn Snack Tonic, 3, 5, 34
Lawn Starter Tonic, 35
Lawn sweepers, 32
Layering, 231
Leaf-cutter bees, 186
Leafhoppers, 30, 132
Leaf mold, 263, 332
Leaves
as fertilizer, 135
raking, 32
in tonics, 252, 259
Lemons, for hand washing,
349
Lethal Leaf-Eater Spray, 230
Lethal Weapon Tonic, 276
Lettuce, 254, 258, 282, 329
Light, for houseplants, 318,
320, 330, 332
Lilies, 199, 206
Lime
in clean-up tonic, 40
in disease control
tonic, 249
in fertilizer tonics, 45,
77, 221
in insect pest control
tonics, 274, 307
in planting tonics, 149,
153, 270
soil testing and, 47
Limestone, 143

M

Magical Mealybug Mix, 327
Magical Mildew Control, 140
Magical Mildew Remover, 36
Magic Marigold Salve, 337
Mailboxes, for garden
    storage, 307
Manure
        as fertilizer, 260
        in fertilizer tonics, 26,
            113, 221, 259
        as mulch, 167
        in planting tonic, 183
        in potting soil mixes,
            158, 332
        in seedling tonic, 156
Marigolds, 232, 282, 337
Marvelous Melon Soil Mix,
    277
Matches, as fertilizer, 285
Mealybugs, 327
Melons, 277, 283, 290, 303
Mice, 96, 105, 259, 278
Mighty-Mite Rhubarb Spray,
    231
Mighty Mouse Control, 278
Mildew Relief Tonic, 179
Milk
        in facial tonics, 346, 349
        in garden tonics, 135,
            171, 223, 268, 276,
            299, 306
        for sunburn, 343
Milk jugs, recycling, 277
Milky spore, 42
Millet, 340
Milorganite®, 239
Mineral oil, 272
Mint, 270, 305, 344
Miracle Mum Booster, 141
Mite-Free Fruit Tree Mix, 279

Mites, 231, 279
Molasses
        in bulb fertilizer tonic,
            198
        in disease control
            tonic, 135
        in flower fertilizer
            tonics, 107, 129, 161
        in houseplant fertilizer
            tonic, 315
        in insect pest control
            tonic, 145
        in lawn fertilizer tonic,
            8
        properties of, xiv
        in rose fertilizer
            tonics, 167
        in sports drink tonic,
            343
        as stain remover, 338
        in tree and shrub
            fertilizer tonics, 66,
            74, 87
        in vegetable fertilizer
            tonic, 247
        in vine and ground-
            cover fertilizer
            tonic, 218
Mole Chaser Tonic, 3, 37
Moles, 37, 218
Mosquitoes, 14, 342
Moss, 36, 38, 78
Moss Buster Brew, 38
Moss-Grow Tonic, 345
Mothballs or flakes, 24, 25,
    37, 94, 314, 323
Moth repellent, 344
Mouthwash
        in clean-up tonics, 7,
            22, 42, 188, 325,
            326, 334
        in disease control
            tonics, 9, 12, 21, 199

    in fertilizer tonics, 47,
        267, 322
    in insect pest control
        tonics, 17, 46, 76,
        83, 131, 199
    in lawn repair tonic, 31
    in mulching tonics,
        142, 159
    properties of, xii
    in soil-building tonics,
        237, 294
    in tree wound
        sterilizer, 95
    in weed control tonic,
        38
Mouthwatering Melon Mix,
    277
Movable beds, 152
Mud stains, 337
Mugwort, 134
Mulch
        animal pests and, 64,
            105
        applying, 142, 159
        carpeting as, 246
        coffee as, xii
        grass clippings as, 5, 27
        for grass seed, 29
        insect pests and, 159,
            226
        for roses, 167
        snow as, 140
        watering and, 225
        for weed control, 180
Mulch Moisturizer Tonic,
    100, 142
Murphy's Oil Soap®
        in animal pest control
            tonics, 105, 278, 295
        in clean-up tonics, 42,
            188
        in disease control
            tonics, 119, 140

S